Dictionary Of Computer Terms
Third Edition

Michael Covington, Ph.D.
Artificial Intelligence Programs
The University of Georgia

Douglas Downing, Ph.D.
School of Business and Economics
Seattle Pacific University

BARRON'S

All inquiries should be addressed to:
Barron's Educational Series, Inc.
250 Wireless Boulevard
Hauppauge, New York 11788

Library of Congress Catalog Card No. 91-21529

International Standard Book No. 0-8120-4824-5

Library of Congress Cataloging-in-Publication Data

Covington, Michael A.
Dictionary of computer terms / Michael Covington, Douglas Downing.
—3rd ed.
p.   cm.
ISBN 0-8120-4824-5
1. Computers—Dictionaries.   I. Downing, Douglas.   II. Title.
QA76.15.C68   1992
004'.03—dc20

                                                        91-21529
                                                        CIP

PRINTED IN THE UNITED STATES OF AMERICA

2345   977   987654321

CONTENTS

ACKNOWLEDGMENTS

We thank Melody Covington for information about typography and computer graphics. We thank Trudy Gaynor for information about the Macintosh and Mark Yoshimi for information on DB2.

ABOUT THE AUTHORS

Michael Covington is a research scientist and teacher in natural language processing and artificial intelligence at the University of Georgia. He is a contributing editor for *PC Techniques* magazine and was a first prize winner in the 1989–90 IBM Supercomputing competition. He is the author of *Study Keys to Computer Science*, *Prolog Programming in Depth* (with Donald Nute and Andre Vellino), *Astrophotography for the Amateur*, *Syntactic Theory in the High Middle Ages*, and numerous articles in computer magazines. He holds the Ph.D. degree in linguistics from Yale University.

Douglas Downing teaches economics at Seattle Pacific University. He is the author of several books in Barron's Easy Way series including *Computer Programing in BASIC*, *Computer Programming in Pascal* (with Mark Yoshimi), *Algebra*, *Trigonometry*, *Calculus*, and *Statistics* (with Jeff Clark). He is also the author of *Business Statistics* and *Quantitative Methods* (both with Jeff Clark for the Barron's Business Review series), *Computers and Business Tasks*, and *Dictionary of Mathematics Terms*, all published by Barron's Educational Series, Inc. He holds the Ph.D. degree in economics from Yale University.

PREFACE TO THE THIRD EDITION

This book is intended to help you understand what computers are, what they do, and how they do it. The entries cover a wide range of topics, including hardware, software, programming concepts and languages, operating systems, electronics, logic circuits, history of computers, and specific models of personal computers. The lists of terms by categories at the front of the book will help you find entries that relate to a particular topic.

Thousands of software packages are now available that allow computers to perform a wide variety of tasks, and new packages are constantly being introduced. We discuss some popular software packages (for example, we show how to set up a simple spreadsheet using the program Lotus 1-2-3). We also describe some of the general tasks that software packages perform and explain much of the terminology that appears in software advertisements. However, it would be impossible to include a listing for every worthwhile item of software or hardware. Instead, we have chosen to concentrate on those items that, in our judgment, have become especially common or were unusually innovative.

This book will also help you if you are interested in writing your own programs. We provide articles on nearly all of the programming languages in widespread use today, with several sample programs. In addition, we include ready-to-run programs illustrating several important algorithms (selection sort, Quicksort, etc.) and quick-reference tables of information often used in programming (ASCII characters, hexadecimal numbers, Epson printer control codes).

We also include descriptions of the electronic components and logic circuits of which computers are made. For example, we describe how a transistor works and illustrate how a machine made with transistors can perform arithmetic calculations. You do not need to know much about how computers work in order to use one, but a knowledge of their inner workings can make them less mysterious and help you appreciate their capabilities.

The field of computers changes very rapidly, making this new edition of the book necessary. For example, desktop publishing systems have become widespread in recent years, so many new terms have been added in this area. Microcomputer hardware has rapidly improved, with much larger memories, faster processors, and improved graphics becoming available. Many entries have been added to reflect these improvements.

Windows 3.0 became a big seller after being introduced in 1990, so information is included about that. Computer hardware continues to advance rapidly; newer machines often have more memory and faster CPU's than do the machines of a couple of years earlier. If you are considering buying a new computer, this book can help you understand the terms and acronyms used in descriptions of machines.

Michael Covington
August 1991   *Douglas Downing*

LOGIC SYMBOLS

In formulas:

$-x$, $\neg x$, $\sim x$, $\bar{x}$	not x
$x \,\&\, y$, $x \wedge y$, $x \cdot y$	x and y
$x \vee y$, $x + y$	x or y
$x \oplus y$	x or y, but not both
$x \rightarrow y$, $x \supset y$	x implies y
$x \leftrightarrow y$, $x \equiv y$	x is equivalent to y

In circuit diagrams:

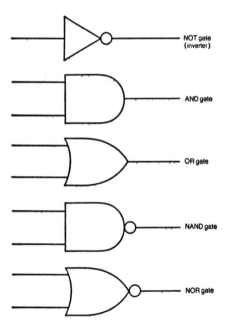

FLOWCHART SYMBOLS

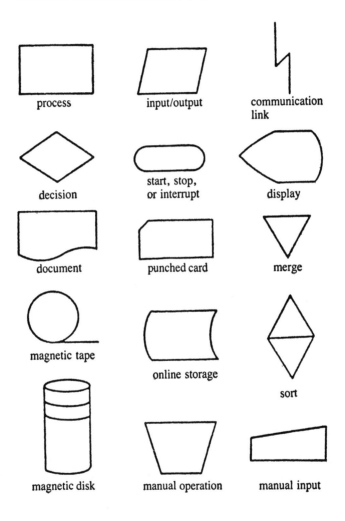

process

input/output

communication link

decision

start, stop, or interrupt

display

document

punched card

merge

magnetic tape

online storage

sort

magnetic disk

manual operation

manual input

READER'S GUIDE TO SELECTED TERMS
BY CATEGORY

Communication

ADM3A	EIA-232D	packet radio
ARCNET	electronic data interchange	packet switching
ARPAnet	electronic mail	parity
asynchronous	EMAIL	Prodigy
bandwidth	end user	RBBS
baud	Ethernet	RS-232
BBS	FAX	RS-422
Bell 103A	FCC	RS-423A
Bell 202	fiber optics	serial
Bell 212A	file server	server
BITNET	framing error	SMTP
BPS	FTP	start bit
call waiting	full duplex	stop bit
CB simulator	half duplex	SYSOP
CCITT	handshaking	TBBS
checksum	Hayes compatibility	TCP/IP
Class A	Internet	telex
Class B	ISDN	telnet
cluster	Kermit	token ring
CompuServe	LAN	topology
current loop	local area network	USENET
data bits	modem	V series
data communication	modem eliminator	wide area network
data rate	Netware	X OFF, X-ON
DCE	network	XMODEM
DECNET	newsgroup	YMODEM
download	null modem	ZMODEM
DTE	packet	

Desktop Publishing

ascender	Courier	elite
bitstream	cut	em dash
block move	dash	en dash
camera ready	descender	fixed pitch
clip art	desktop publishing	floating illustration
column move	document	flush left

Electronics

Firms

Digital Equipment Corp.
Epson
Hewlett-Packard
IBM

Intel
Lotus Development
Microsoft
Novell Netware
Racal-Vadic

Radio Shack
Sun Microsystems
Texas Instruments

Graphics

ANSI graphics
antialiasing
bit-mapped graphics
bitmap
BMP
CAD
CEG
CGA
Corel Draw
dithering
draw program
EGA
fat bits
fractal
frame grabber

GIF
graphics
graphics card
grid
grid system
Hercules graphics card
MacDraw
Mandelbrot set
mapping software
MCGA
megapixel
object-oriented graphics
paint program
palette
pixel

plane
presentation graphics
ray tracing
resolution
spline
sprite
super VGA
three-dimensional
  graphics
TIFF
vector graphics
VGA
video modes
  (IBM PC)
XGA

Hardware

ADC
analog monitor
analog-to-digital
  converter
bank switching
board
bubble memory
buffer
bus mouse
cache
cartridge
CD-ROM
Centronics interface
coaxial cable
composite video

coprocessor
CRT
daisywheel printer
digital computer
dipswitch
direct-connect modem
disk
disk drive
diskette
dot matrix printer
DRAM
drum
EEPROM
electrostatic printer
EPROM

ESDI
file protect ring
fixed disk
floppy disk
full height drive
gas plasma display
half height drive
hard card
hard disk
hardware
IDE
ink jet printer
interlacing
jacket
joystick

laser printer
light pen
line printer
liquid crystal display
mainframe computer
matrix printer
memory chips
Micro Channel
microcontroller
MIDI
minicomputer
modem
monitor
monochrome
  monitor
mouse
notebook
numeric keypad
OCR
optical character
  reader

parallel port
plotter
port
print spooler
printer
PROM
punched card
RAM
RAM disk
raster
RGB monitor
RGBI monitor
RLL
ROM
RS-232
scanner
SCSI
sector
serial port
SIMM
slot

snow
ST-506
supercomputer
tape
tape drive
terminal
terminal-node
  controller
thermal printer
trackball
tractor feed
TTL monochrome
  monitor
vector processor
video adaptor
VT-100
VT-101, VT-102,
  VT-220, VT-320
workstation
WORM
Z80

Logic Gates and Computer Design

absolute address
accumulator
AND gate
assembler
assembly language
binary addition
binary multiplication
binary subtraction
bit
Boolean algebra
bus
byte
CISC

complement
computer design
CPU
decoder
EISA
flip-flop
full adder
gate
half adder
inverter
ISA
logic gate
machine language

NAND gate
NOR gate
NOT gate
offset
OR gate
PCX
register
RISC
segment
shift register
SPARC

Machines

Amiga
AT

Commodore
Compaq

Cray
IBM 3270

IBM 7171
IBM PC, PS/1,
    and PS/2
IBM RS/6000
LaserJet

Laserwriter
Macintosh
Proprinter
Sparcstation
Sun workstations

System 7
VAX
XT

Mathematics

ABS	e	logarithm
angle	EXP	natural logarithm
arcsin	exponent	numerical integration
arctan	exponential function	octal
argument	exponential notation	pi
base	factorial	precision
binary numbers	fixed point number	radian measure
common logarithm	floating point number	radix
COS	hexadecimal	real number
decimal number	integer	rounding error
degree measure	LN	SIN
double precision	LOG	TAN

Operating Systems and Operating Systems Concepts

autoexec. bat	filter	root directory
BAT file	JCL	subdirectory
BIOS	MS-DOS	SunOS
CMS	multiple virtual	System V
COM file	mode	TSO
CP/M	MVS	TYPE
DIR	operating system	ULTRIX
directory	OS/2	UNIX
DOS	OS/360	VAX/VMS
EDLIN	OS-9	virtual 8086 mode
EXE file	path	virtual machine
expanded memory	presentation manager	VM/CMS
extended memory	protected mode	VM/SP
extension	real mode	X Windows

Programming Concepts

algorithm	array	assignment statement
archive	artificial intelligence	backtracking

benchmark
binary coded decimal
binary search
boolean variable
branch
bubble sort
bug
CAD
CALL
CAM
character string
circularity
comment
common user access
compile time error
concatenation
conditional branch
constant
context sensitive
  help
CUA
data structures
data types
debug
declare
decryption
default
default logic
defeasible logic
delimiter
dimension
documentation
dyadic operation
efficiency
encryption
END
error trapping
event driven
  programming
expert system
expression
file

flat file database
flowchart
FOR
full text search
function
fuzzy logic
global variable
hashing
help
heuristic
hierarchical
hypertext
identifier
IF
incremental compiler
indexed file
inference engine
information hiding
inheritance
input
insertion sort
instance variables
internal rate of return
interpreter
interrupt
interrupt service routine
iteration
keyword
knowledge base
limits of computer
  power
linked list
list
literal
local variable
logic programming
loop
macro assembler
make
management information
  systems
memory resident

menu
merge sort
message sending
metalanguage
method
mnemonic
module
monadic
  operation
Monte Carlo
multiple inheritance
multiprocessing
multiprogramming
multitasking
natural language
  processing
nest
neural network
node
object-oriented
  programming
outline
parallel processing
parameter
parsing
pointer
polymorphism
precedence
present value
primitive
procedure
program
programming
project
query language
queue
Quicksort
radix sort
record
recursion
regular expression
relational database

SELECTED TERMS

reserved word
run length encoding
run time error
selection sort
Shell sort
side effect
simulation
software interrupt
sort
stack

string
string operations
structured programming
subroutine
symbolic algebra
syntax
timesharing
top-down programming
transparent
trapping

traveling salesman
  problem
tree
Turing machine
user-friendly
user interface
variable
virtual storage
WHILE
window

Languages

Ada
ALGOL
ANSI C
APL
AWK
Backus-Naur form
BASIC
BASICA
C
C++
COBOL
compiler

FORTH
FORTRAN
GW-BASIC
high-level language
LISP
LOGO
Modula-2
Pascal
PILOT
PL/I
programming language
Prolog

Quick C
Quick Pascal
QuickBASIC
REXX
RPG
Smalltalk
SNOBOL
Turbo C++
Turbo Pascal
Turbo Prolog
Visual Basic
WATFIV

Software

accounting software
ARC
AutoCAD
Corel Draw
database
database
  management
DB2
dBase IV
desk accessory
Excel

Hypercard
Lotus 1-2-3
mapping software
Microsoft Word
Norton Utilities
PageMaker
PC-Globe
pop-up utility
Prodigy
project manager
spreadsheet

statistics program
three-dimensional
  spreadsheet
TSR
Ventura
VisiCalc
Windows, Microsoft
Word Perfect
word processing
WordStar

Windows and the Macintosh

activate
active window
alert box
button
cascaded windows
check box
click
clipboard
command button
DDE
desk accessory
desktop
dialog box
double click
drag
draw program
drop-down menu
finder

folder
graphical user
  interface
GUI
hierarchical file
  system
hourglass icon
Hypercard
icon
list box
Macintosh
maximize
menu bar
message box
MiniFinder
minimize
Motorola 68000
mouse

option button
overlaid windows
pop-up menu
presentation manager
press
pull-down menu
radio button
ResEdit
resource
restore
scroll bar
send to back
text box
tiled windows
title bar
watch icon
window
Windows, Microsoft

LIST OF TABLES

LIST OF PROGRAMS

a

A4 German (DIN) standard A4 denotes a paper size that is 210 x 297 mm, about 8 1/4 x 11 3/4 inches. This is the standard size of typing paper in Europe. Sizes A3, A2 and A1 are larger. American typing paper is 8 1/2 x 11 inches.

ABS The function ABS(X) in BASIC and other programming languages calculates the absolute value of X. If X is positive, then ABS(X) = X; if X is negative, then ABS(X) = –X. For example, ABS(37) = 37; ABS(–37) = 37; ABS(–2.5) = 2.5; ABS(1985) = 1985. Then absolute value of zero is zero. The absolute value of any other number is positive.

ABSOLUTE ADDRESS (1) An absolute address refers to a fixed location in the computer's memory. (See **computer design.**) (2) In a spreadsheet program, an absolute address is a cell address that refers to a fixed location that will not change when a formula is copied to another location. In Lotus 1-2-3, absolute addresses are indicated by placing a dollar sign before the column and row indicator. For example, if the formula 2*$D$7 is entered into a cell, then $D$7 is an absolute address. If this formula is copied to another cell, the $D$7 will not change. For contrast, see **relative address.** (See **segment; offset.**)

ACCESS TIME The access time of a memory device is the amount of time required from the instant that the computer asks for data until those data are transferred to the computer. For example, the access time of a disk drive can be about 20 milliseconds, and the access time of a memory chip is typically 10^{-7} second.

ACCOUNTING SOFTWARE An accounting software package is a computer program designed to computerize the accounting process for a business. A complete system should include modules for the following functions: entering transactions data; posting that data to accounts at the appropriate times; presenting year-end reports, including balance sheets and income statements; and maintaining records of accounts receivable and accounts payable. Because of the importance of the data included in the system, a program should have a security mechanism, such as requiring the use of passwords, in order to prevent unauthorized users from altering the data. A system also should

1

keep a record of transactions that have been entered (called an *audit trail*) so it is possible to trace how the figures that appear on the reports were derived. An example of an accounting program that has become widely used for small businesses is DAC Easy accounting, produced by DAC Software.

ACCUMULATOR The accumulator is the register where a computer stores the results of an arithmetic operation. For example, the assembly language command ADD 7 could mean to add the contents of memory address 7 to the number in the accumulator, and then store the result in the accumulator. (See **computer design; assembly language**.)

ACOUSTIC COUPLER An acoustic coupler is a type of modem that couples to the telephone line by means of a microphone and speaker arrangement into which the telephone handset is placed, as opposed to a direct-connect modem, which is wired to the telephone line. (See **modem**.)

ACRONYM An acronym is a word or name that is formed by joining the first letters (or first few letters) of a series of words. For example, NASA stands for National Aeronautics and Space Administration, and BASIC stands for Beginner's All-Purpose Symbolic Instruction Code.

ACTIVATE To activate a window is to make it the active window. This is done by moving the mouse pointer into it and clicking one button. (See **window**.)

To activate a piece of software is to start it by clicking on its name or icon. (See **click; icon**.)

ACTIVE WINDOW On the Macintosh or in Microsoft Windows or similar software environments, the active window is the window currently in use. (See **window**.)

ADA The programming language Ada was developed in the late 1970s for the U.S. Department of Defense. It is named for Augusta Ada Byron, Countess of Lovelace, who worked with Babbage's mechanical calculator in the nineteenth century.

Ada is based on Pascal, with some influence from PL/I and ALGOL 68. Comments begin with two hyphens and continue to the end of the line. Every statement ends with a semicolon even if it is embedded within another statement (such as an *if-then* or *loop-end loop* structure); in this respect Ada is like PL/I and C and unlike Pascal.

Like Pascal, Ada allows the creation of data types by specifying ranges or sets of possible values. For example:

type COLOR is (RED, GREEN, BLUE);

Ada subprograms can be compiled separately and linked together before execution; if only part of a program is changed, it is not necessary to recompile the whole program. This is an old FORTRAN feature that is missing from ALGOL 60 and Pascal. In the sample program, the *with* and *use* statements specify that this program uses a library of precompiled subroutines called I_O_PACKAGE.

Much of the original motivation for designing Ada was the need for a better language for real-time programming, that is, programming computers to control automatic or semiautomatic equipment. Toward this end, Ada allows the programmer to create multiple tasks that run concurrently (see **timesharing**), to pass signals from one task to another, and to introduce controlled time delays.

The Department of Defense has prepared an Ada compiler validation package that verifies that Ada has been implemented correctly on any given computer. Ada compilers that pass this test can be expected to be more reliable than compilers for other languages.

Here is a sample program written in Ada:

```
with I_O_PACKAGE;
procedure FACTORIAL is
   use I_O_PACKAGE;
   -- This program reads a number and
   -- computes its factorial.
   NUM, FACT, COUNT: INTEGER;
begin
   GET(NUM);
   FACT := 1;
   for COUNT in 2..NUM loop
      FACT := FACT * COUNT;
   end loop;
   PUT("The factorial of ");
   PUT(NUM);
   PUT(" is ");
   PUT(FACT);
end;
```

ADAPTIVE SYSTEM An adaptive system is a system that is able to learn from what has happened in the past.

ADC See **analog-to-digital converter.**

ADDRESS Each location in computer memory is identified by an address, which allows the computer to find the location of a specific data item (or instruction).

ADM3A The Lear Siegler ADM3A computer terminal was popular in the early 1980s. Like most terminals, it transmits and receives ASCII characters asynchronously through an RS-232 serial port. It is not VT-100 compatible (see **VT-100**), but it has its own simpler set of codes for controlling the screen.

ADOBE Adobe Systems, Inc. (Palo Alto, California), is a software company that produces the PostScript command language for laser printers. (See **PostScript**.)

ALDUS Aldus is a software company located in Seattle, Washington, that produces products such as PageMaker, one of the pioneer programs for page layout and desktop publishing.

ALERT BOX See **message box.**

ALGOL ALGOL (for <u>Algo</u>rithmic <u>L</u>anguage) is the name of two programming languages that had a strong impact on programming language design. The first of these, ALGOL 60, was designed by an international committee led by Peter Naur of the University of Copenhagen; the official description of it was published in final form in 1963.

Figure 1 shows a sample ALGOL 60 program. The words **begin** and **end** function like brackets to group statements together; a basic rule of the language is that, anywhere a statement can occur, a group of statements bracketed by **begin** and **end** can be substituted. This means that, whereas BASIC and FORTRAN programs are simply numbered lists of instructions, ALGOL programs consist of blocks of statements, grouped together to form larger blocks.

Note that in the example the *for* and *while* keywords together define a single loop with two termination conditions; in Pascal, a *for-while* combination creates a loop within a loop.

ALGOL 60 was the first language to have its syntax described in Backus-Naur form (See **Backus-Naur form**); it was also the first to allow subprograms to call themselves (see

```
begin
  comment
            Sieve of Eratosthenes -- sample
            ALGOL 60 program by Michael A. Covington.
            Prints the prime numbers from 1 to 1000 ;

  integer procedure next(last,limit,prime);
      value limit;
      integer last, limit;
      boolean array prime;
      begin
          integer i;
          boolean found;
          found := false;
          for last := last + 1
              while not found and last <= limit do
                  if prime [last] then found := true;
          if found then
              begin
                  last := last - 1;
                  for i := last step last until limit do
                      prime [i] := false;
                  next := last
              end
          else next := 0

      end;

  boolean array numbs [1:1000];
  integer latest, i;
  for i := 1 step 1 until 1000 do
      numbs [i] := true;
  latest := 1;
  for latest := next (latest,1000,numbs)
      while latest > 0 do
          output(61,`7ZD',latest)
end
```

FIGURE 1 Sample ALGOL 60 Program. It is written in the form in which ALGOL programs are usually published (using **boldface** type for basic symbols, and *italic* for user-assigned names).

ALGORITHM 6

recursion). The programming languages JOVIAL, Pascal, and Modula-2, among others, are direct outgrowths of ALGOL 60.

The standard syntax of ALGOL 60 describes how programs are to be presented in published papers, but not how they are to be typed into a computer. In published papers, ALGOL keywords (called *basic symbols*) are printed in boldface type to distinguish them from variable names; on most computers, they are flanked by quotation marks or asterisks.

ALGOL 68 is quite different from ALGOL 60; it includes many new features and has a reputation for being powerful but difficult to learn. ALGOL 68 programs are easy to recognize because the ends of blocks of statements are marked by spelling keywords backward (*do. . .od, if. . .fi, case. . .esac*). The language allows a wide variety of data types, including combinations (called *united modes or unions*) that can take on values of more than one type; for example, if X is declared as the union of types *int* and *char*, then 2, 4, 32767, X, and '&' are among its possible values. In addition, data items can be declared as references (*ref*), which means that they refer to the location at which an item is stored rather than the value of the item itself.

An important principle of ALGOL 68 is *orthogonality*, which means that all meaningful combinations of features are allowed. (In geometry, two things are *orthogonal* if they meet at right angles; the use of the term in ALGOL 68 comes from the square tables in which combinations of orthogonal features can be listed.)

Discontent with the complexity of ALGOL 68 led Niklaus Wirth to design first ALGOL W and then Pascal (see **Pascal**), which has almost completely replaced ALGOL in practical use today.

ALGORITHM An algorithm is a sequence of instructions that tell how to solve a particular problem. An algorithm must be specified exactly, so there can be no doubt about what to do next, and it must have a finite number of steps. A computer program is an algorithm written in a language that a computer can understand, but the same algorithm could be written in several different languages. An algorithm can also be a set of instructions for a person to follow.

A set of instructions is not an algorithm if it does not have a definite stopping place, or if the instructions are too vague to be followed clearly. The stopping place may be at variable points in the general procedure, but something in the procedure must determine precisely where the stopping place is for a particular case.

If you study the game of tic-tac-toe long enough, you will be able to develop an algorithm that tells you how to play an unbeatable game. However, some problems are so complicated that there is no algorithm to solve them. (See **heuristic; limits of computer power.**)

ALPHA TEST Alpha testing is the first stage of testing of a new software product, carried out by the manufacturer's own staff. By way of contrast, see **beta test.**

ALPHANUMERIC CHARACTER The characters that a computer can print or display are classified as alphabetic, numeric, special, and control. *Alphabetic* characters are the letters A to Z; *numeric* characters are the digits 0 to 9. *Special* characters are the other printable characters, that is, punctuation marks and other symbols. *Control* characters are codes that represent actions such as backspacing, starting a new line, or going to the top of the next page.

Alphanumeric characters are all the characters that are either alphabetic or numeric, that is, all the letters and digits.

On large IBM computers, the characters @, #, and $ count as alphabetic, and hence as alphanumeric. They are called *national* characters because they print differently on computers designed for use in different countries.

ALT KEY The Alt key on the IBM PC and PS/2 is used like a shift key; that is, you hold it down while pressing another key. For example, to type Alt-P, type P while holding down Alt.

The Alt key gives the other key a new meaning, which depends on the software being used. For example, in Word Perfect and Lotus 1-2-3, the Alt key is used in combination with various letters to call up macros (see **macro**).

Keys pressed while holding down Alt do not have ASCII codes (see **ASCII**). Instead, each such key is read by the computer as two bytes. The first byte is zero, and the second byte serves to identify the key.

AMIGA The Amiga is a computer produced by Commodore especially suitable for graphics and sound generation. It is based on the Motorola 68000 microprocessor, and it contains three additional custom processors to improve its capabilities for sound generation and graphics, including animation. The Amiga provides the option of a menu-driven interface involving icons, or an interface where the user types commands.

The Amiga can be programmed in Microsoft Amiga BASIC, which is a version of BASIC that contains special commands for accomplishing tasks such as creating windows in different areas of the screen; displaying color pictures; drawing shapes on the screen and filling them in; and creating animation with images that move around the screen. The Amiga can also be used to generate sounds of specified frequences—in other words, it can create music. (See **MIDI**.)

AMPERE An ampere (or amp, for short) is the unit for measuring electric current. A current of 1 ampere means that 6.25×10^{18} electrons are flowing by a point each second. A group of 6.25×10^{18} electrons has a charge of 1 coulomb, so 1 ampere = 1 coulomb per second.

ANALOG COMPUTER An analog computer is a computer in which information is stored in a form that can vary smoothly between certain limits rather than having discrete values. (By way of contrast, see **digital computer**.) A slide rule is an example of an analog computer, because it represents numbers as distances along a scale.

All modern, programmable computers are digital. Analog computer circuits are used in certain kinds of automatic machinery, such as automotive cruise controls and guided missiles. Also, a fundamental analog computer circuit called the operational amplifier is used extensively in audio, radio, and TV equipment.

ANALOG MONITOR An analog monitor is one that displays an unlimited range of brightnesses for each primary color, from fully on to fully off. As a result, a vast range of colors can be displayed. By contrast, with an ordinary RGB monitor, each of the primary colors (red, green, and blue) is either on or off. (See **RGB monitor**.)

ANALOG-TO-DIGITAL CONVERTER An analog-to-digital converter is a device that changes data from analog to digital form, making it possible to feed them into a computer. For example, the temperature in a room may be measured by a device that represents it as a continuously varying voltage. An analog-to-digital converter transforms this voltage into a set of signals representing decimal or binary digits.

"ANALYTICAL ENGINE" See **computers, history of.**

FIGURE 2

AND GATE An AND gate (Figure 2) is a logic gate that produces an output of 1 only when all of its inputs are 1. The operation of a two-input AND gate is completely described by the following table:

Input 1	Input 2	Output
0	0	0
0	1	0
1	0	0
1	1	1

One simple way to make an AND gate is to use two switches connected in series (Figure 3). There will be an output voltage only if both switches are on (closed). Exactly the same principle can be used to make an AND gate with two transistors connected in series; each transistor acts as a switch.

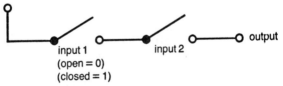

FIGURE 3

Figure 4 shows how this works. In this circuit, logic level 0 is represented by 0 volts, and logic level 1 is represented by 5 volts. Each transistor conducts if its input is positive. However, the positive voltage cannot reach the output unless both transistors are conducting. (The resistors limit current flow to keep the transistors from overheating.)

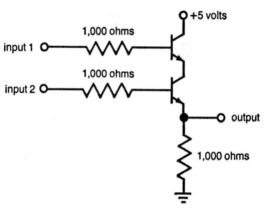

FIGURE 4

AND gates are used in computer arithmetic. (See **binary addition.**) In addition, AND gates with more than two inputs are used to recognize signals coming in simultaneously on several wires, such as memory addresses. (See **decoder.**)

ANGLE The size of an angle can be measured by the number of degrees it contains. One complete rotation measures 360 degrees (written as 360°). A square corner (called a *right angle*) measures 90°. Angles can also be measured in radians. A complete rotation measures 2π radians, and a right angle measures $\pi/2$ radians.

ANONYMOUS FTP See **FTP.**

ANSI The abbreviation ANSI stands for Ａmerican Ｎational Ｓtandards Ｉnstitute. There are official ANSI standards in almost all industries, and quite a few of them have to do with computers. In computer programming, ANSI most often refers to one of the following:

1. ANSI standard versions of FORTRAN, COBOL, or other programming languages. ANSI standard languages are de-

signed to make it possible to run the same program on any computer without worrying about variations in the details of the language. Typically, a particular manufacturer's version of FORTRAN or COBOL will include all of the features defined in the ANSI standard, plus additional features devised by the manufacturer. To be easily transportable from one computer to another, a program should not use any features that are not in the ANSI standard.

2. ANSI standard escape sequences for controlling the screen of a computer terminal or microcomputer. An escape sequence is a series of character codes which, when sent to the screen, causes the screen to do something other than simply display the characters to which the codes correspond. The ANSI escape sequences all begin with the ASCII Escape character (code 27). (See **ANSI screen control.**)

The advantage of using escape sequences for screen control is that any program can control the screen, even if it is written in a language that has no statements for screen control. All the program need do is send a special sequence of characters to the screen exactly as if the characters were to be displayed.

ANSI C The American National Standards Institute (ANSI) issued a standard for the C programming language in 1989. Unlike the older language, ANSI C includes a "void" declaration for functions that do not return values, as well as additional error checking features and other extensions. (See **C.**)

ANSI CHARACTER SET The ANSI character set is an extended set of characters used in Microsoft Windows and OS/2, and shown in Table 1. It includes all the ASCII characters plus many others. (See **ASCII; Windows; IBM PC.**)

To type any ANSI character in Microsoft Windows, hold down the Alt key while typing 0 followed by the character code number on the numeric keypad. For example, to type é, hold down Alt and type 0233.

ANSI GRAPHICS On BBSes, the use of ANSI terminal control codes in combination with the IBM PC special character set is sometimes called ANSI graphics. Strictly speaking, the term is inappropriate, because the computer is not in graphics mode and the special characters are not covered by an ANSI standard.

TABLE 1 ANSI Character Set used in Microsoft Windows

```
0-127 Same as ASCII
145 '
```

146 '	176 °	192 À	208 Ð	224 à	240 ð
161 ¡	177 ±	193 Á	209 Ñ	225 á	241 ñ
162 ¢	178 ²	194 Â	210 Ò	226 â	242 ò
163 £	179 ³	195 Ã	211 Ó	227 ã	243 ó
164 ¤	180 ´	196 Ä	212 Ô	228 ä	244 ô
165 ¥	181 µ	197 Å	213 Õ	229 å	245 õ
166 ¦	182 ¶	198 Æ	214 Ö	230 æ	246 ö
167 §	183 ·	199 Ç	215 ×	231 ç	247 ÷
168 ¨	184 ¸	200 È	216 Ø	232 è	248 ø
169 ©	185 ¹	201 É	217 Ù	233 é	249 ù
170 ª	186 º	202 Ê	218 Ú	234 ê	250 ú
171 «	187 »	203 Ë	219 Û	235 ë	251 û
172 ¬	188 ¼	204 Ì	220 Ü	236 ì	252 ü
173 -	189 ½	205 Í	221 Ý	237 í	253 ý
174 ®	190 ¾	206 Î	222 Þ	238 î	254 þ
175 ¯	191 ¿	207 Ï	223 ß	239 ï	255 ÿ

ANSI SCREEN CONTROL An ANSI standard specifies a set of sequences of characters (escape sequences) which, when sent to the screen of a computer, make it perform actions such as clearing the screen.

Some computers obey these codes at all times. These include all DEC VT-100-compatible terminals.

The IBM PC obeys ANSI screen control codes only if the CONFIG.SYS file contains a line of the form

```
DEVICE = ANSI.SYS
```

and the codes are sent to the screen using DOS services rather than BIOS services. (On the IBM PC, ANSI control codes can also be used to redefine keys; see the DOS Technical Reference Manual for details.)

Table 2 show some commonly used ANSI control code sequences.

All ANSI control sequences begin with Esc (code 27) followed by "["; many of them contain numbers that specify how far the cursor is to be moved or where it is to be placed. For example,

```
Esc [ 1 5 C
```

moves the cursor 15 spaces to the right, and

```
Esc [ 3 C
```

moves it only 3 spaces to the right.

TABLE 2 Commonly Used ANSI Screen Control Sequences

Characters sent	Effect
Esc [1 2 ; 3 5 H	Move cursor to row 12, column 35
Esc [1 2 ; 3 5 f	Same as above
Esc [4 A	Move cursor up 4 lines
Esc [3 B	Move cursor down 3 lines
Esc [6 C	Move cursor 6 columns to the right
Esc [7 D	Move cursor 7 columns to the left
Esc [s	Save current cursor position
Esc [u	Return cursor to where it was when you did Esc [s
Esc [2 J	Clear whole screen and home cursor
Esc [K	Erase from cursor position to end of line
Esc [0 m	Select normal type (white on black)
Esc [1 m	Select bold (bright white) type
Esc [4 m	Select underlined type (on VT-100 or IBM Monochrome Display; blue on other IBM displays). (Other numbers, all the way up to 47, alter the foreground and/or background color on IBM color displays.)
Esc [6 n	Place a cursor position report in the keyboard buffer. (For example, if the cursor is on row 3, column 4, then *Esc [3 ; 4 R* will appear in the keyboard buffer as if the user had typed it.)

ANTIALIASING Ordinarily, vertical and horizontal lines appear straight when drawn on computer screens, but lines in other directions have a stairstep appearance because the line is drawn by turning on pixels that are arranged in a square grid. Antialiasing is a way of smoothing out this stairstep effect. The line is thought of as cutting a swath across the grid of pixels, and pixels that are only partly covered by the line are only partly illuminated. This doubles the apparent resolution of the screen.

APL APL is an interactive programming language that is well suited for handling complex operations on arrays. APL (<u>A</u> Programming <u>L</u>anguage) uses several Greek letters and some other special symbols, so this language requires a specially designed terminal. Some features of APL are as follows:

1. A function, or program, is defined by the symbol ∇, as in ∇ FN1. To execute the function, just type FN1. The return key signifies the end of a statement. The APL system automatically keeps track of the statement numbers in a function.

2. Arithmetic operations are symbolized by the following: + addition, − subtraction, × multiplication, ÷ division, and * exponentiation. All operations are executed from right to left (if no parentheses are present). An assignment statement is written in the form

    X ← expression

    such as

    X ← 4 × 20

3. The statement X ← □ in a function causes the computer to type a question mark, ?, and then wait for the user to type in a value for X. To display the value of X, either manually or as part of a function, just type X.

4. A regular branch statement is written as → S1, where S1 is the label of the statement where you want to go. A conditional branch is written as → (I < N)/S1, which will cause a jump to S1 if the condition in the parentheses (in this case 1 < N) is true.

5. APL has many facilities for handling arrays. For example, the expression X ← (3,3) ρ 5 causes X to become the 3 × 3 array

```
5 5 5
5 5 5
5 5 5
```

Subscripts of arrays are written with brackets, such as X[1;2]. The expression ⍉X calculates the transpose of X, and the expression A + . × B calculates the matrix product *AB*. One of the advantages of APL is that this language makes it very easy to change the size of arrays in the middle of a program.

6. Some other features of APL are:

+ /X calculates the sum of all the elements in a vector X.

× /X calculates the product of all the elements in a vector X.

ιN is a vector of all the integers from 1 to N.

2 φ X is the vector formed by rotating all the elements of X two places to the left.

Figure 5 is a program written in APL. (Note that it is possible to write a complete APL program that is only one line long.)

```
    ∇ CHECK PRIME N
[1] ((1-K)/'PRIME'),(K←(∨/(⌊Q)=Q←N÷1+ι⌈(N*0.5)))/'NOT PRIME'
[2] ⍝ THIS PROGRAM CHECKS WHETHER N IS PRIME.
    ∇
```

FIGURE 5

Here are two examples of the use of this program. The user types the lines that are indented.

    CHECKPRIME 3
PRIME
    CHECKPRIME 45
NOT PRIME

APPLE Apple is one of the largest personal computer manufacturers. The Apple II, introduced in 1977, was one of the earliest popular microcomputers. A wide range of software was written for the Apple II and its followers. More recent Apple products include the Macintosh (introduced in 1984), which contains innovations in graphics, word processing, and ease of use. The company, located in Cupertino, California, was founded by Steve Jobs and Steve Wozniak, who began work in a garage.

APPLICATION PROGRAM An application program is one that performs useful work not related to the computer itself. Examples of application programs include a word processor, a spreadsheet, an accounting system, or an engineering program. By way of contrast, see **utilities** and **operating system**.

APPLICATIONS PROGRAMMER An applications programmer is a person who writes programs that use the computer as a tool to solve particular applied problems. By way of contrast, see **systems programmer**.

ARC ARC is a popular data-compression program published by System Enhancement Associates. Two shareware programs written by Phil Katz, PKARC and PKXARC, do the same work and use the same file format. ARC originated on the IBM PC, but versions have been developed for UNIX and for the Amiga.

ARC takes one or more files, compresses them, and combines them into an "archive" file (with a name ending in .ARC), which ARC can later decompress. ARC is often used for files that are to be transmitted by telephone because the compressed file takes less time to transmit; also, a group of files is easily kept together by storing them in a single archive.

See also **data compression; ZIP; StuffIt**.

ARCHIVAL STORAGE Archival storage is storage for data that must be kept for a long time but will seldom be used, such as backup copies of working programs. Microcomputers with hard disks often use tape cartridges or floppy disks for archival storage. Magnetic tape is usually the cheapest form of archival storage, but the tapes should be copied every 2 or 3 years if their contents are still needed, since tapes can become demagnetized with age.

ARCHIVE (1) An archive is a filing system for information designed to be kept for a long time.

(2) An archive file, or ARC file, is a file containing compressed information from other files. The original files can be reconstructed from it. (See **ARC**.)

(3) In MS-DOS (PC-DOS) and other operating systems, every file has an archive bit that says whether or not it has been backed up by copying to another disk or tape. The ATTRIB command can be used to examine or change archive bits. It is possible to back up only the files that have not already been backed up.

ARCNET ARCNET is a type of local-area network that works like a token-ring network except that the connections between computers need not be in the shape of a ring. A special message, the *token*, is passed from computer to computer and only the computer holding the token is allowed to transmit. ARCNET usually uses Ethernet hardware. See **token ring; local area network; Ethernet.**

ARCSIN The arcsin function is the inverse of the sine function. If $y = \sin A$, then $A = \arcsin y$. (See **SIN**.) If you are using a programming language that does not have the arcsin function, then the value of the arcsin can be found by using this formula involving the arctan function:

$$\arcsin y = \arctan\left(\frac{y}{\sqrt{1-y^2}}\right)$$

ARCTAN The arctan function is the inverse of the tangent function. If $y = \tan A$, then $A = \arctan y$. (See **TAN**.)

ARGUMENT The arguments of a function or subprogram are the value or values given to it by the main program. For example, in BASIC the SQR function finds the square root of a number. In the expression SQR(25), which asks for the square root of 25, the argument is the number 25. See also **parameter.**

ARPANET The ARPAnet is a computer network originally developed for the U.S. Defense Advanced Research Projects Agency (ARPA, now known as DARPA) to link research institutions. It included the TCP/IP protocols and has now developed into the Internet. See **Internet; wide area network; TCP/IP.**

ARRAY An array is a collection of data that is given one name. An array is arranged so that each item in the array can be located when needed. An array is made up of a group of elements, which may be either numbers or character strings. Each element can be identified by a set of numbers known as subscripts, which indicate the row and column in which the element is located. The dimension of an array is the number of subscripts needed to locate a particular element. For example, it takes two subscripts to identify an element in a two-dimensional array.

　　If seven basketball players scored respectively 18, 10, 16, 20, 11, 7, and 14 in one game, these scores can be stored in a one-dimensional array containing seven elements. If we call the array name SCORE and write the subscripts in parentheses, then:

SCORE(1) = 18, SCORE(2) = 10, SCORE(3) = 16, and so on.

(Each programming language has its own rules for how to name arrays and where to write the subscripts.)

If we need to score four statistics for each player, then we can use a two-dimensional array, where the first subscript indicates the player and the second subscript indicates the statistic.

If we need to store statistics for more than one game, we can use a three-dimensional array, where the first subscript indicates the game number, the second subscript indicates the player number, and third subscript indicates the statistic number.

ARROW KEYS Many computer keyboards have arrow keys that move the cursor up, down, or to the left or right. The effect of these keys depends on the software being used; some pieces of software ignore them or handle them incorrectly. You should be especially cautious about using the arrow keys when communicating with another computer; even if the cursor moves correctly, the other computer may not understand what you are doing.

On the IBM PC and PS/2, the arrow keys do not have ASCII codes. Instead, each of them is read as 2 bytes, a zero byte and a byte that identifies the key.

ARTIFICIAL INTELLIGENCE Artificial intelligence (AI) is the branch of computer science that deals with using computers to simulate human thinking. Artificial intelligence is concerned with building computer programs that can solve problems creatively, rather than simply working through the steps of a solution designed by the programmer.

For an example, consider computer game playing. Some games, such as tic-tac-toe, are so simple that the programmer can specify in advance a procedure that guarantees that the computer will play a perfect game. With a game such as chess, however, no such procedure is known; the computer must use, instead, a *heuristic*, that is, a procedure for discovering and evaluating good moves.

One possible heuristic for chess would be for the computer to identify every possible move from a given position, and then evaluate the moves by calculating, for each one, all the possible ways the game could proceed. Chess is so complicated that this would take an impossibly long time (on the order of millions of years with present-day computers).

A better strategy would be to take shortcuts. Calculating only five or six moves into the future is sufficient to eliminate most of the possible moves as not worth pursuing. The rest can be evaluated on the basis of general principles about board positions. In fact, an ideal heuristic chess-playing machine would be able to modify its own strategy on the basis of experience; like a human chess player, it would realize that its opponent is also following a heuristic and try to predict her behavior.

One of the main problems of AI is how to represent knowledge in the computer in a form such that it can be used rather than merely reproduced. In fact, some workers define AI as the construction of computer programs that utilize a *knowledge base*. A computer that tells you the call number of a library book is not displaying artificial intelligence; it is merely echoing back what was put into it. Artificial intelligence would come into play if the computer used its knowledge base to make generalizations about the library's holdings or construct bibliographies on selected subjects. (See **expert system**.)

Computer vision and robotics are important areas of AI. Although it is easy to take the image from a TV camera and store it in a computer's memory, it is hard to devise ways to make the computer recognize the objects it "sees." Likewise, there are many unsolved problems associated with getting computers to move about in three-dimensional space—to walk, for instance, and to find and grasp objects—even though human beings do these things naturally.

Another unsolved problem is natural language processing—getting computers to understand speech, or at least typewritten input, in a language such as English. In the late 1950s it was expected that computers would soon be programmed to accept natural-language input, translate Russian into English, and the like. But human languages have proved to be more complex than was expected, and progress has been slow. The English-speaking computers of *Star Wars* and *2001* are still some years away. (See **natural language processing**.)

The important philosophical question remains: Do computers really think? Artificial intelligence theorist Alan Turing proposed a criterion that has since become known as the *Turing test:* a computer is thinking if a human being, connected to it by teletype, cannot tell whether he is communicating with a machine or with another person. In response, Terry Rankin has pointed out that it makes little sense to build a machine whose purpose is to deceive human beings. Increasing numbers of AI workers are taking the position that computers are not artificial minds, but merely tools to assist the human mind, and that this is true no matter how closely they can be made to imitate human behavior.

ASC The ASC function in many versions of BASIC calculates the ASCII code number associated with a given character. (See **ASCII.**) For example, ASC("A") is 65 because the ASCII code of the character "A" is 65 (expressed in decimal).

Here is a short Microsoft BASIC program that reads in a string of characters and converts all of the lower-case letters to upper case letters, using the ASC function:

```
10 REM PROGRAM READS IN CHARACTER STRING
11 REM THEN PRINTS OUT THE STRING
12 REM WITH ALL OF THE LOWER CASE LETTERS
13 REM CHANGED TO CAPITAL LETTERS
14 REM NOTE THE USE OF THE MID$, ASC,
15 REM AND CHR$ FUNCTIONS
20 INPUT X$
30 FOR I = 1 TO LEN(X$)
40 C = ASC(MID$(X$,I,1))
50 IF (C>=97) AND (C<=122) THEN C=C-32
60 MID$(X$,I,1) = CHR$(C)
70 NEXT I
80 PRINT X$
90 END
```

ASCENDER An ascender is a part of a printed character that extends upward. For instance, the letter "d" has an ascender and the letter "o" does not. (See **descender; typeface.**)

ASCII ASCII is a standard code for representing characters as binary numbers, used on most microcomputers, computer terminals, and printers. ASCII stands for American Standard Code for Information Interchange. In addition to printable characters,

TABLE 3 ASCII Printable Characters

(decimal, hexadecimal, and character representations)

Dec.	Hex.	Char.	Dec.	Hex.	Char.	Dec.	Hex.	Char.
32	20	space	64	40	@	96	60	`
33	21	!	65	41	A	97	61	a
34	22	"	66	42	B	98	62	b
35	23	#	67	43	C	99	63	c
36	24	$	68	44	D	100	64	d
37	25	%	69	45	E	101	65	e
38	26	&	70	46	F	102	66	f
39	27	'	71	47	G	103	67	g
40	28	(	72	48	H	104	68	h
41	29	)	73	48	I	105	69	i
42	2A	*	74	4A	J	106	6A	j
43	2B	+	75	4B	K	107	6B	k
44	2C	,	76	4C	L	108	6C	l
45	2D	–	77	4D	M	109	6D	m
46	2E	.	78	4E	N	110	6E	n
47	2F	/	79	4F	O	111	6F	o
48	30	0	80	50	P	112	70	p
49	31	1	81	51	Q	113	71	q
50	32	2	82	52	R	114	72	r
51	33	3	83	53	S	115	73	s
52	34	4	84	54	T	116	74	t
53	35	5	85	55	U	117	75	u
54	36	6	86	56	V	118	76	v
55	37	7	87	57	W	119	77	w
56	38	8	88	58	X	120	78	x
57	39	9	89	59	Y	121	79	y
58	3A	:	90	5A	Z	122	7A	z
59	3B	;	91	5B	[	123	7B	{
60	3C	<	92	5C	\	124	7C	
61	3D	=	93	5D	]	125	7D	}
62	3E	>	94	5E	∧	126	7E	~
63	3F	?	95	5F	—			⌷

TABLE 4 ASCII Control Characters

Numerica Value Decimal	Hex	Code Name	How Typed	Action (on most computers)
0	00	NUL	CTRL @	—
1	01	SOH	CTRL A	—
2	02	STX	CTRL B	—
3	03	ETX	CTRL C	Interrupt program
4	04	EOT	CTRL D	—
5	05	ENQ	CTRL E	—
6	06	ACK	CTRL F	—
7	07	BEL	CTRL G	Sound beeper
8	08	BS	CTRL H	Same as backspace key
9	09	HT	CTRL I	Same as tab key
10	0A	LF	CTRL J	Same as line feed key
11	0B	VT	CTRL K	—
12	0C	FF	CTRL L	Top of page (on printer)
13	0D	CR	CTRL M	Same as return key
14	0E	SO	CTRL N	Change typeface
15	0F	SI	CTRL O	Undo effect of CTRL N
16	10	DLE	CTRL P	—
17	11	DC1, X-ON	CTRL Q	Undo effect of CTRL S
18	12	DC2	CTRL R	—
19	13	DC3. X-OFF	CTRL S	Make computer stop typing
20	14	DC4	CTRL T	—
21	15	NAK	CTRL U	—
22	16	SYN	CTRL V	—
23	17	ETB	CTRL W	—
24	18	CAN	CTRL X	—
25	19	EM	CTRL Y	—
26	1A	SUB	CTRL Z	End of file mark
27	1B	ESC	CTRL [	Same as ESC key
28	1C	FS	CTRL \	—
29	1D	GS	CTRL]	—
30	1E	RS	CTRL ∧	—
31	1F	US	CTRL _	—
127	7F	DEL	DEL key	—

Note: The effects of these control characters vary widely from machine to machine; consult the appropriate manual for details and for instructions on how to type them. Many keyboards do not allow the use of the CTRL key with characters other than letters.

CTRL characters are often referred to by prefixing them with ∧; for example, ∧C indicates CTRL C. This is only a notation; the CTRL key is not at all equivalent to the character ∧.

the ASCII code includes control characters to indicate carriage return, backspace, etc. Table 3 shows a list of ASCII printable characters, and Table 4 lists ASCII control characters. For two popular extensions of ASCII, see **IBM PC** (character set chart) and **ANSI character set**. For an alternative to ASCII, see **EBCDIC**.

ASCII FILE An ASCII file is a text file on a machine that uses the ASCII character set. (See **text file**.) In MS-DOS (PC-DOS) and CP/M, each line ends with Carriage Return and Line Feed (code 13 and 10).

ASSEMBLER (1) An assembler is a program that translates assembly language into machine language. (See **assembly language; machine language; compiler**.) (2) The assembly language itself is sometimes called the assembler. The word is used in this sense mainly with the IBM 360 and 370.

ASSEMBLY LANGUAGE An assembly language is a computer language in which each statement corresponds to one machine language statement. Assembly languages are more cumbersome to use than regular (or high-level) programming languages, but they are much easier to use than pure machine languages, which require that all instructions be written in binary code.

See Page 24 for an example of a simple assembly language for an imaginary computer with only 16 different instructions. This language assumes that the computer has an accumulator register, an index register, and a 1-bit condition register.

Since this language has 16 instructions, it will take a 4-bit register to store the instructions ($2^4 = 16$). (See **computer design**.) Real microprocessors use 8-bit instruction registers.

Here is a BASIC program that will print the sum of the squares of N numbers:

```
10  INPUT N: FOR I = 1 TO N
20  INPUT A,B
30  C = A^2 + B^2 : PRINT A,B,C
40  NEXT I : END
```

Here is an assembly language program to do the same task:

Address	Instruction	Comment
11	READ I	;input the number N and place ;it in the index register
12	READ 2	;read in A
13	READ 3	;read in B
14	LOAD 2	
15	MPY 2	;the accumulator now holds A^2
16	STORE 4	
17	LOAD 3	
18	MPY 3	;the accumulator now holds B^2
19	ADD 4	;the accumulator now holds $A^2 + B^2$
20	STORE 5	
21	PRINT 2	
22	PRINT 3	
23	PRINT 5	
24	ST	
25	CGO 12	;go to 12 if all N numbers have not ;been read yet
26	STOP	

This is only a hypothetical example; the assembly language of an actual computer would have dozens or hundreds of different instructions, and operations such as READ and PRINT would be much more complex than they appear here. Assembly languages generally allow you to use symbolic addresses instead of actual machine addresses. This feature makes them easier to use.

The obvious disadvantages of assembly languages are that the programs are lengthy and hard to read, and that the same assembly language cannot be used on different types of computers. The main advantage is that, in general, assembly language programs run faster and occupy less memory than programs produced by compilation from a high-level language, since with an assembly language the programmer can be sure that nothing unnecessary is present.

Binary Code	Assembly Language Statement	
0000	GO A	The next instruction executed will be the instruction located at the address stored in memory address A.

Binary Code	Assembly Language Statement	
0 0 0 1	CGO A	Same as GO, except that A will be executed next only if the condition register is 1.
0 0 1 0	ST	Subtract 1 from the index register and set the condition register to 0 if the index register is 0 (used for loops).
0 0 1 1	STOP	Stop the machine.
0 1 0 0	ADD A	Add the number stored in memory address A to the number stored in the accumulator, and store the result in the accumulator.
0 1 0 1	SUB A	Subtract the number stored at A from the accumulator.
0 1 1 0	MPY A	Multiply the number stored at A by the accumulator.
0 1 1 1	DIV A	Divide the accumulator by the number stored at A.
1 0 0 0	EQU A	If the number stored in A is equal to the accumulator, set the condition register to 1.
1 0 0 1	GTR A	If the number stored in the accumulator is greater than the number stored in A, set the condition register to 1.
1 0 1 0	AND A	The accumulator will become 1 if both A and the accumulator are 1.
1 0 1 1	NOT	The accumulator will become 1 if it now holds 0, and vice versa.
1 1 0 0	LOAD A	Load the contents of memory location A in the accumulator.
1 1 0 1	STORE A	Load the contents of the accumulator in location A.
1 1 1 0	READ A	Read a number from an input device and store the result in A.
1 1 1 1	PRINT A	Send the contents of A to an output device.

ASSIGNMENT STATEMENT An assignment statement is a computer program statement that calculates the value of an expression and assigns that value to a particular variable name. An example of a BASIC assignment statement is

10 LET C = (A*A + B*B)^(0.5)

This statement will calculate the value of $\sqrt{A^2+B^2}$ and then give that value to the name C.

Another example is

```
20 LET I = I + 1
```

This statement will cause I to take on a value one greater than its old value. (In most BASIC systems the keyword LET is optional.)

ASYNCHRONOUS The term *asynchronous* refers to processes that are not synchronized. For example, most computer terminals use asynchronous data transmission, in which the terminal or the computer is free to transmit any number of characters at any time. (The bits constituting each character are transmitted at a fixed rate, but the pauses between characters can be of any duration.)

Synchronous terminals, by contrast, transmit data in packets of more than one character. This is faster than asynchronous communication because there is no need for a start bit or stop bit on each individual character.

AT AT (advanced technology) refers to the class of IBM PC's originally introduced in 1984 using the 80286 microprocessor and a 16-bit bus. (See **IBM PC**.)

AUTOCAD AutoCAD is a popular CAD program produced by Autodesk Inc. of Sausalito, California. See **CAD**.

AUTOEXEC.BAT In MS-DOS (PC-DOS), AUTOEXEC.BAT is the name of a file that contains commands to be executed whenever the computer boots up. For example, an AUTOEX-EC.BAT file containing the following lines will set the date and time and then check the hard disk for lost clusters:

```
DATE
TIME
CHKDSK C: /F
```

AUTOMATION Automation refers to the use of machines to do work that was once done by people.

AUXILIARY STORAGE Auxiliary storage is a storage device that is under the control of the computer, but not directly a part of it. Disks and tapes are examples of auxiliary storage areas. The computer's own memory is called *internal storage*.

AWK AWK is a programming language for scanning text files and processing lines or strings that match particular patterns. AWK was developed by A. V. Aho, P. J. Weinberger, and B. W. Kernighan, and the name "AWK" is an acronym of their initials.

AWK normally reads the input file one line at a time and parses each line into fields separated by blanks. It assigns the fields to the variables $1, $2, $3, and so on. A program consists of tests to apply to each line and actions to be performed when each test is passed. For example,

```
{ print $1, $3 }
```

is a complete AWK program that prints the first and third fields of every line.

Figure 6 shows a more complete AWK program that reads a file of the form

USA	Georgia	23
USA	Florida	19
Canada	Ontario	5
Canada	Newfoundland	8
USA	California	52

and keeps totals of the numbers in the third column (one total for Canada and one for the U.S.A.). In addition, it prints out fields 2 and 3 of lines that begin with "U.S.A" If the input is the table above, the output is:

```
Program starting...
   Georgia   23
   Florida   19
California   52

USA total  94
Canada total  13
```

The program uses regular expressions to test whether each line begins with U or C. (See **regular expression.**) Then it prints results, using not only the simple *print* statement but also a *printf* statement very similar to that of C. (See **printf.**)

AWK is very versatile; it provides many different ways of reading the input file, as well as standard control structures (*while, do, if*), one-dimensional arrays, and automatic interconversion of numbers and strings. All variables are automatically initialized to 0 or the empty string when the program starts.

```
# Sample program in AWK -- M. Covington 1991

# Code to execute at beginning of program

BEGIN   { printf("Program starting...\n") }

# Code to execute when line begins with U

/^U/    { printf("%10s %5d\n",$2,$3)
          utotal = utotal + $3
        }

# Code to execute when line begins with C

/^C/    { ctotal = ctotal + $3
        }

# Code to execute at end of program

END     { printf("\n")
          print "USA total ", utotal
          print "Canada total ", ctotal
        }
```

FIGURE 6 Sample program in AWK.

AX.25 AX.25 is a standard format used in amateur radio for transmitting data in packets. It is an adaptation of the CCITT X.25
standard. See **packet radio; X.25.**

b

BABBAGE, CHARLES Charles Babbage was a nineteenth century inventor who designed several devices, such as the "analytical engine," that included concepts that were later used in
computers. However, the technology of his day was not capable of building everything he designed.

BACKGROUND To run a program in the background is to have
it continue to run while not visible on the screen (or not occupying much of the screen). This is possible only in multitasking
operating systems. See **multitasking; Windows; OS/2; UNIX.**

BACKLIT A liquid crystal display (as on a laptop computer) requires built-in illumination to be easily read; if the illumination
comes from behind the display panel it is said to be backlit.

BACKSLASH The backslash character is "\" as opposed to the forward slash "/."

BACKTRACKING Backtracking is a problem-solving method applicable to certain kinds of problems. The problem is to be solved by making a series of moves. Backtracking works as follows: First, choose a possible move and make it. Then, proceed from there by choosing a possible move, and so on, until a solution is found. If you reach a place where you have not found a solution but no more moves are possible, back up. That is, undo one or more moves until you get back to an alternative you did not take. Follow that different choice to see if the solution lies in that direction. If not, keep backing up until you find what you're looking for (you may have to try *all* possible moves).

Backtracking is built into the programming language Prolog, which uses it extensively (see **Prolog**). In this article we will discuss how to implement backtracking in a conventional language.

For example, consider this problem: Find three whole numbers $x[1]$, $x[2]$, and $x[3]$, each between 1 and 5, such that their sum is equal to their product. While you might try to solve this problem mathematically, it is easier just to try all the combinations. One way to get all the combinations would be to set up three nested loops, as follows:

```
for x[1]:=1 to 5 do
  for x[2]:=1 to 5 do
    for x[3]:=1 to 5 do
      if x[1]+x[2]+x[3] = x[1]*x[2]*x[3] then
        write (x[1],x[2],x[3],' is a solution');
```

This is possible because you know in advance that the solution will take three moves (choosing one number in each move), so you can set up three loops.

Backtracking occurs in this example because if the innermost loop doesn't find a solution, control returns to the middle loop, which increments $x[2]$ and starts the innermost loop over again. Similarly, the middle loop backtracks to the outer loop if it fails to find a solution. The loop counters keep track of untried alternatives, but it's important to understand that any method of generating alternatives one by one would work just as well.

With some problems, you don't know how many moves a solution will take. In such a case you must use recursion to nest the loops at run time. The following Pascal program solves the problem we've just discussed, but uses recursion so that it is a much more typical illustration of how backtracking is done.

```pascal
program backtrack;
var x: array[1 .. 3] of integer;

procedure choose (n:integer);
    { Chooses a value for x[n] }
var
   i: integer; { Must be local }
begin
   if n=4 then { we have chosen three values }
      begin
         if x[1] + x[2] + x[3] = x [1]* x [2]*x[3]
         then begin
            writeln('Solution found: ',
                 x[1]:3,x[2]:3,x[3]:3);
            halt
              {remove this line to get all solutions}
            end
         else
            writeln(x[1]:3,x[2]:3,x[3]:3,
              ' is not a solution; backtracking. . . ')
      end
   else
   { recurse, trying all possible values for x[n] }
   for i:=1 to 5 do
      begin
         x[n]:=i;
         choose(n+1)
      end
end;
   { Main program }
begin
   choose(1)
end.
```

In Prolog, where backtracking is built in, all you have to do is specify possible values for the integers and specify the condition they must meet. You can solve our example problem by typing the query:

```
?-    member(X1, [1,2,3,4,5]),
      member(X2, [1,2,3,4,5]),
      member(X3, [1,2,3,4,5]),
      Sum is X1+X2+X3,
      Product is X1*X2*X3,
      Sum == Product,
      write([X1,X2,X3]).
```

Each clause in the query specifies a condition that the answer must meet. Whenever the computer encounters a clause whose condition cannot be satisfied, it backs up to an untried alternative in a previous clause and tries again.

BACKUP COPY A backup copy of a program or set of data is another copy of that program or those data that can be referred to if the original is lost. When working with a microcomputer, you should make backup copies of important disks and store them away from the working copies. On large computer systems, tape drives are often used to store backup copies of disk files. See also **archival storage.**

BACKUS-NAUR FORM (BNF) Backus-Naur is a notation used to describe the syntax of languages. BNF was devised by J. Backus and Peter Naur and introduced in the first official description of ALGOL 60 (see **ALGOL**); it is sometimes referred to as *Backus normal form.*

Each BNF statement describes some syntactic unit by giving one or more alternative expansions of it, separated by the symbol "|." For example, the following is a BNF description of the assignment statement in BASIC (we assume that <line number>, <variable name>, and <expression> have already been defined, and that <empty> stands for the absence of any written symbol):

```
<let keyword> ::= LET | <empty>
<assignment statement> ::=
    <line number> <let keyword>
    <variable name> = <expression>
```

The first statement defines <let keyword> as standing for either the word LET or no symbol, in order to indicate that the word LET is optional. The second statement defines <assignment statement> as consisting of a line number, an optional let keyword, a variable name, an equals sign, and an expression.

Many languages contain syntactic rules that cannot be expressed in BNF; for instance, BNF provides no way to say that an integer cannot exceed 32767. Still, BNF descriptions are handy because they are concise and definitive and because parsers can be generated directly from them. (See **parsing**.)

BACKUS NORMAL FORM See **Backus-Naur form (BNF)**.

BANDWIDTH The bandwidth of an electronic system is the range of frequencies that it can transmit. In data-communication systems, high bandwidth allows fast transmission or the transmission of many signals at once. On a monitor screen, high bandwidth provides a sharp image.

BANK SWITCHING Bank switching is the ability to use more than one set of memory chips at different times, while giving them the same addresses. This makes it possible to equip a computer with more memory than it was originally designed for—simply store some data in one set of chips, then switch over and use the other set of chips.

Bank switching is used to give the IBM PC more than 640K of memory (see **expanded memory**). Bank switching is also used on the IBM EGA and other advanced color graphics cards.

BAR CODE A bar code is a pattern of wide and narrow bars, printed on paper or a similar material. A computer reads the bar code by scanning it with a laser beam or with a wand that contains a light source and a photocell.

The most familiar bar code is the Universal Product Code (see Figure 7), used with cash registers in supermarkets, but bar codes have been utilized to encode many kinds of data, including complete programs for some programmable calculators. Circular bar codes are sometimes used on boxes or pieces of luggage that may be scanned from many different directions.

FIGURE 7 An Example of a Bar Code (the Universal Product Code from the first edition of this book).

BASE (1) The base is one of the three parts of a bipolar transistor. (See **transistor**.)

(2) In the exponential function $y = a^x$, a is the base.

(3) The base of a number system is the number of digits used in that system. (See **binary numbers; decimal number; hexidecimal, octal**.)

BASIC BASIC is one of the easiest computer languages to learn, and one of the most popular languages for beginning students and for people with microcomputers. It was designed as an interactive language by John Kemeny and Thomas Kurtz in the 1960s. Since then many different versions of BASIC have been developed for different machines. Many computers are sold with the BASIC language already included. This article deals with the traditional BASIC language. Some newer versions of BASIC have evolved far beyond the original language and look more like Pascal, but they will still accept traditional BASIC programs. Some features of traditional BASIC systems are:

1. Each BASIC statement must be preceded by a line number:

```
10 X = 25.5
20 PRINT X
```

Here 10 and 20 are line numbers. To execute the program, type RUN. To see the program displayed on the screen, type LIST. The command SAVE causes the program to be stored on a disk, and the command LOAD causes the program to be read from the disk into the computer's memory. However, the exact form of these two commands varies with different computers.

2. Some versions of BASIC require that numeric variable names be only one or two characters long. Many current versions, however, allow longer variable names, making it easier to give meaningful names to variables. A dollar sign, $, placed at the end of the variable name indicates that the variable is a character string variable.

3. Arithmetic operations in BASIC are as follows: ^ exponentiation, * multiplication, / division, + addition, and − subtraction. In evaluating arithmetic expressions, operations surrounded by parentheses are done first, then exponentiations, then multiplications and divisions, and finally additions and subtractions. An assignment statement is of the form

   ### LET X = expression

   To execute this statement, the computer will calculate the value of the expression and assign that value to the name X. In most versions of BASIC the word LET is optional.

4. Input-output is handled as follows: The statement INPUT X,Y causes the computer to stop, type a question mark, and then wait for you to type in two values. It will call the first value X and the second value Y.

   The statement READ A will cause the computer to look at the top of the data stack and assign that value to A. A data stack is created with a DATA statement, such as DATA 10, 15, 16.04, 30. The first time the computer hits a READ statement, such as READ A, it will give A the value 10. The next time it encounters a READ statement, such as READ B, it will give B the value 15.

   The PRINT statement is used for output. The statement PRINT X,Y causes the values of X and Y to be displayed on the screen. The statement PRINT "WORD" causes the character string WORD to be printed. When a comma is used between the items in a print statement, the computer will space the items apart by a standard amount. When a semicolon is used in place of the comma, the computer will jam the items together.

   In some versions of BASIC the LPRINT command works exactly the same as PRINT except that the output is directed to a printer instead of to the screen.

5. The GOTO command tells the computer to jump to the indicated statement number. For example, the GOTO 50 will cause the computer to jump to statement 50 and start executing at that point. The word IF is used to indicate conditional actions. For example:

```
100  IF X < 0 THEN PRINT "X IS LESS THAN 0"
```

or

```
110  IF A = 10 THEN GOTO 500
```

Loops can be constructed using FOR and NEXT statements. For example:

```
10    FOR I = 10 TO 20 STEP 2
      statements in middle, such as:
         20  J = SQR(I)
         30  PRINT I, J
100  NEXT I
```

This setup will cause the computer to execute the statements in the middle six times. The first time it will use the value I = 10, then the value I = 12, then I = 14, etc., through I = 20.

6. The sizes of arrays are defined with the DIM statement. For example, DIM A(25) defines A to be a one-dimensional array with 25 elements, and DIM B(6,18) defines B to be a two-dimensional array with 6 rows and 18 columns. Each element in the array can be identified by using subscripts, written in parentheses. For example, B(2,1) is the element of B located in row 2, column 1.

7. Subroutines can be defined in BASIC by using the statement GOSUB. Upon reaching the statement GOSUB 150, the computer will jump to statement 150 and start executing there. When the computer reaches a RETURN statement, it knows it has reached the end of the subroutine, so it will jump back to the statement immediately following the original GOSUB statement.

8. Comments can be inserted in a program by using the keyword REM (short for REMARK) at the beginning of the statement. When the computer comes to a statement such as

```
30    REM THIS REMARK IS HERE TO HELP
30    REM ME UNDERSTAND THIS PROGRAM
```

it will completely ignore it and proceed to the next statement.
BASIC is often the best language if you have a simple program that you would like to type and run quickly. Most BASIC

systems use interpreters, rather than compilers. This means that a program can be run quickly and easily. Just type RUN, and the program starts executing immediately. However, interpreted programs generally run much slower than do compiled programs. Therefore, if you have a long program that needs to be executed often but does not require frequent changes, you probably will prefer a compiled language.

Many BASIC versions provide extensive graphics and sound-generation capabilities. However, the details of these commands vary greatly for different machines.

One disadvantage of BASIC is that it does not provide many of the features necessary for writing structured programs. (See **structured programming**.) Long BASIC programs can become very confusing to human readers. However, some versions partially remedy this deficiency by providing for IF/THEN/ELSE structures and WHILE loops. If you are writing a long BASIC program, you can help to clarify your meaning by breaking the program into subroutines and using a REM statement to clearly label the start of each subroutine.

More recent implementations of BASIC, such as Microsoft's QuickBasic and Visual Basic, and Borland's Turbo Basic, consist of compilers; they also contain other features to enhance the power of the language. Line numbers are not required in those versions.

Here is a sample program written in BASIC.

```
1    REM BASIC PROGRAM TO TEST IF A
5    REM NUMBER IS PRIME
10   INPUT "N:"; N
15   PRINT "----------"
20   S = 1
30   T = 1 + INT(SQR(N))
40   I = 2
50   R = N / I
60   Q = R - INT(R)
65   IF Q = 0 THEN GOTO 120
67   REM IF Q = 0 NUMBER IS NOT PRIME
70   I = I + S
80   S = 2
90   IF I < T THEN GOTO 50
```

```
95     REM IF I < T CHECK THE NEXT NUMBER
100    PRINT N;" IS PRIME"
110    GOTO 150
120    PRINT N;" IS NOT PRIME"
130    PRINT "IT IS DIVISIBLE BY ";I
150    END
```

BASICA In PC-DOS (MS-DOS) on the IBM PC family of computers, the command BASICA calls up an interpreter for a special version of Microsoft BASIC (see **BASIC**). This interpreter uses code stored on a ROM chip inside the computer; it works only on IBM machines. A similar interpreter for clones is called GW-BASIC.

BAT FILE In MS-DOS (PC-DOS), A BAT (batch) file is a file whose name ends with ".BAT," and which contains a list of commands. For instance, if you create a file called THREE-DIR.BAT containing the lines

```
dir a:
dir b:
dir c:
```

then you can type THREEDIR and the three "dir" commands in the file will all be executed in succession.

BATCH PROCESSING In batch processing, the user gives the computer a "batch" of information, referred to as a *job*—for example, a program and its input data on punched cards—and waits for it to be processed as a whole. Batch processing contrasts with *interactive processing*, in which the user communicates with the computer by means of a terminal while his program is running. The crucial difference is that with batch processing the user must put all of the data into the computer before seeing any of the results, while with interactive processing the user can decide how to handle each item on the basis of the results obtained with earlier items.

BAUD A baud is a unit that measures the speed with which information is transferred. The baud rate is the maximum number of state transitions per second; for instance, a system whose shortest pulses are 1/300 second is operating at 300 baud.

On an RS-232 serial link, the baud rate is equal to the data rate in bits per second (bps). With other kinds of communication, the data rate may be considerably faster than the baud rate. For instance, a 2400-baud modem takes 2400-baud (2400-bps) serial data and encodes it into an audio signal whose true baud rate is about 1200, near the maximum rate at which a telephone line can transmit pulses. Each pulse carries more than one bit of information. At the receiving end, another modem transforms the signal back into 2400-baud serial data.

BBS A BBS (Bulletin Board Service) is a computer that allows users to log in from remote terminals, exchange messages, and (usually) download programs. Many BBSs are run by microcomputer hobbyists and can be accessed free of charge by dialing a telephone number.

BCD See **binary-coded decimal**.

BELL 103A Bell 103A is the standard format for transmitting data by telephone at speeds of 300 baud or less.

BELL 202 Bell 202 is a standard format for transmitting data by telephone at a speed of 1200 baud. Bell 202 format is half duplex only and has now largely been replaced by Bell 212A. (See **half duplex**.)

BELL 212A Bell 212A is the standard format for transmitting data by telephone at a speed of 1200 baud.

BENCHMARK A benchmark program is a program used to test the performance of a computer or a piece of software. For example, the speed with which computers do arithmetic is often measured by running a prime-number-finding algorithm called the *Sieve of Eratosthenes* (see **ALGOL**).

Benchmark results are always somewhat untrustworthy because no single program tests all aspects of a computer's operation. A particular benchmark may exaggerate a difference between two machines that is unimportant in practice, or it may conceal an important difference. See also **MIPS**.

BETA TEST Beta testing is the second stage of testing a new software product that is almost ready for market. Beta testing is carried out by volunteers in a wide variety of settings like those in which the finished product will be used. By contrast, see **alpha test**.

BINARY ADDITION The first step in designing a computer that can do arithmetic is to develop a machine that can add two binary numbers. When we add decimal (i.e., regular) numbers, we proceed one digit at a time, starting with the rightmost digit. The table lists the results we would like our adding machine to give for each of the four possible combinations of the input digits:

Input 1	Input 2	Output
0	0	0
0	1	1
1	0	1
1	1	0 (with a carry of 1)

If we add together two zeros, the result is zero. The next two cases are also easy: $1 + 0 = 0 + 1 = 1$. The last case is trickier, since it involves a carry to the next digit to the left. The binary equation

$$1_{binary} + 1_{binary} = 10_{binary}$$

is the same as the decimal equation:

$$1_{decimal} + 1_{decimal} = 2_{decimal}$$

When the two input digits are 1, we must have a sum digit of 0, along with something that reminds us that we need to

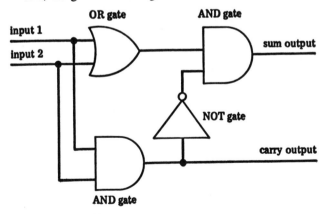

FIGURE 8 Half Adder

carry a 1 to the next digit. A *half adder* (see Figure 8) is a circuit that accomplishes this function. It has two outputs; the sum output and the carry output.

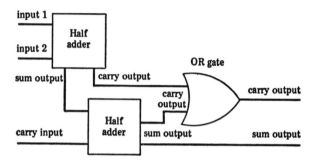

FIGURE 9 Full Adder

A half adder can be constructed with standard logic gates. The carry output is the result of an AND gate. The sum output is the result of an OR gate, with a slight modification that sets the output equal to 0 when both inputs are 1.

The second step in binary addition involves propagating the carries from each digit to the left. A *full adder* (see Figure 9) is constructed to fulfill this function. A full adder consists of two half adders. It requires three inputs: the two digits to be added, plus the carry output from the next digit to the right. The full adder has two outputs: the sum output and the carry output. Figure 10 illustrates the sequence of full adders needed to complete the addition of two 5-bit binary numbers.

Before the addition is carried out, each of the two numbers is stored in a row of *flip-flops* called a *register*. (A flip-flop is a physical device that can flip between one state representing 0 and another state representing 1.) In order for the addition to be carried out, the two registers need to be connected to the computer's addition circuit. It is the job of the computer's boss—the CPU—to determine what numbers are to be added, find those numbers in the memory, load them in the appropriate registers, and then connect the registers to the addition circuit. After the addition has been performed, the resulting sum is usually stored in a register called the *accumulator*.

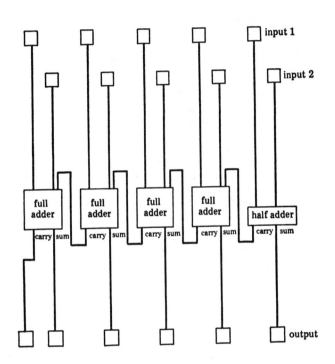

FIGURE 10

BINARY-CODED DECIMAL Binary-coded decimal (BCD) is a way of representing numbers by means of codes for the decimal digits. For example, consider the number 65. In binary, this is 01000001, and that is how most computers represent it. But some computer programs might represent it as the code for 6 followed by the code for 5, i.e., 0110 0101.

The advantage of BCD shows up when a number has a fractional part, such as 0.1. There is no way to convert 0.1 into binary exactly; it would require an infinite number of digits, just like converting 1/3 into decimal (see **rounding error**). But in BCD, 0.1 is represented by the code for 1 immediately after the point, and no accuracy is lost.

BCD arithmetic is considerably slower and takes more memory than binary arithmetic. It is used primarily in financial work and other situations where rounding errors are intolerable. Pocket calculators use BCD.

BINARY FILE A binary file is a file containing bits or bytes in an arbitrary arrangement, which is not readily printable. The term binary file usually denotes any file that is not a text file, such as executable machine language code. Crucially, special software is required to print a binary file or view it on the screen. By contrast, see **text file**.

BINARY MULTIPLICATION Two binary numbers can be multiplied using the same principles that you would use to multiply two decimal numbers. Binary multiplication is even simpler, because there are only two digits.

To find 13×21 in decimal, you proceed like this:

```
        2 1
  ×   1 3
      6 3
    2 1
    2 7 3
```

First, find 3×21. Then find 10×21, and add these two results together to get the final product. Note that the product has more digits than either of the two original numbers.

You can follow the same procedure to multiply two binary numbers:

```
      10101              21
  ×  01101           ×  13
      10101              21        (21 × 2⁰)
      00000               0
      10101              84        (21 × 2²)
      10101             168        (21 × 2³)
  100010001             273        (2⁸ + 2⁴ + 2⁰)
```

To design a multiplication machine, you'll need three registers, plus a binary addition circuit. (See **binary addition**.) The result will be stored in the accumulator (A), which will be 0 at the start of the computation. The multiplier will be stored in a register you can call the multiplier (M), and the multiplicand will be stored in a register called the distributor (D). Both of these registers must be shift registers, meaning that you can shift the numbers they contain one place to the right or to the left when you give the right signal. (See **shift register**.)

First, look at the rightmost digit of the M register. If this bit is 1, then add the contents of the D register to A. If this bit is 0, then don't do anything. Next, shift the M register *right* one place, and shift the D register *left* one place. Now, look at the new rightmost digit of M, and repeat the process. Keep going until you've processed all the digits of M. The procedure is shown in the flowchart in Figure 11.

BINARY NUMBERS Binary (base-2) numbers are written in a positional number system that uses only two digits: 0 and 1. Binary numbers are well suited for use by computers, since many electrical devices have two distinct states: on and off. Writing numbers in binary requires more digits than writing numbers in decimal, so binary numbers are cumbersome for people to use.

Each digit of a binary number represents a power of 2. The rightmost digit is the 1's digit, the next digit to the left is the 2's digit, and so on.

Decimal	Binary
$2^0 = 1$	1
$2^1 = 2$	10
$2^2 = 4$	100
$2^3 = 8$	1000
$2^4 = 16$	10000

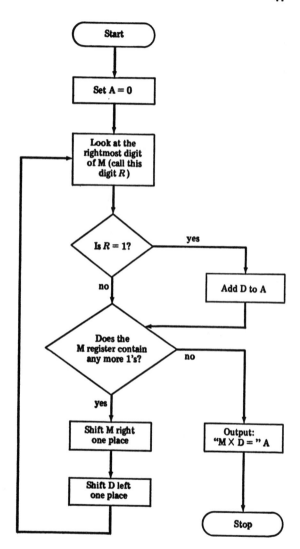

FIGURE 11

45

1. Adams J	6
2. Adams JQ	5
3. Arthur	4
4. Buchanan	5
5. Bush	3
6. Carter	5
7. Cleveland	4
8. Coolidge	5
9. Eisenhower	6
10. Fillmore	2
11. Ford	5
12. Garfield	4
13. Grant	5
14. Harding	6
15. Harrison B	3
16. Harrison W	5
17. Hayes	4
18. Hoover	5
19. Jackson	6
20. Jefferson	1
21. Johnson A	5
22. Johnson L	4
23. Kennedy	5
24. Lincoln	6
25. Madison	3
26. McKinley	5
27. Monroe	4
28. Nixon	5
29. Pierce	6
30. Polk	2
31. Reagan	5
32. Roosevelt F	4
33. Roosevelt T	5
34. Taft	6
35. Taylor	3
36. Truman	5
37. Tyler	4
38. VanBuren	5
39. Washington	6
40. Wilson	7

FIGURE 12

The table shows some numbers written in binary and decimal form.

Decimal	Binary	Decimal	Binary
0	0	11	1 0 1 1
1	1	12	1 1 0 0
2	1 0	13	1 1 0 1
3	1 1	14	1 1 1 0
4	1 0 0	15	1 1 1 1
5	1 0 1	16	1 0 0 0 0
6	1 1 0	17	1 0 0 0 1
7	1 1 1	18	1 0 0 1 0
8	1 0 0 0	19	1 0 0 1 1
9	1 0 0 1	20	1 0 1 0 0
10	1 0 1 0		

BINARY SEARCH A binary search is a method for locating a particular item from a list of items that is in order. Suppose that you need to find the location of a particular word in a list of alphabetized words. To execute a binary search, look first at the word that is at the exact middle of the list. If the word you're looking for comes before the midpoint word, you know that it must be in the first half of the list (if it is in the list at all). Otherwise, it must be in the second half. Once you have determined which half of the list to search, use the same method to determine which quarter, then which eighth, and so on. At most, a binary search will take about N steps if the list contains about 2^N items.

Figure 12 illustrates the number of steps that would be needed to find each name in an alphabetized list of the U.S. presidents. If we look for Jefferson, it only takes one step, since Jefferson happens to be at the middle of the list. In the worst case, the search takes seven steps.

Here is Pascal program that performs a binary search for a list of numbers:

```
PROGRAM binsearch(INPUT,OUTPUT);

VAR n:INTEGER; x:REAL; a:ARRAY[1..500] OF REAL;

PROCEDURE readin;
  VAR i:INTEGER;
```

FIGURE 13

FIGURE 13 Continued

```pascal
BEGIN
  WRITE('How many numbers?'); READLN(n);
  FOR i :=1 TO n DO READLN(a[i])
END;

PROCEDURE binsrch;
  VAR lowbound,upbound,position:INTEGER;
      continue: BOOLEAN;

      PROCEDURE check(j:INTEGER);
      BEGIN
       IF a[j]=x THEN
         BEGIN
           WRITELN('In list at position ',j);
           continue := FALSE
         END
      END;

BEGIN {procedure binsrch}
  lowbound := 1;  upbound := n;
  continue := TRUE;
  WHILE continue DO
    BEGIN
      position := (lowbound+upbound) DIV 2;
      check(position);
      IF continue THEN
        BEGIN
          IF a[position]>x
            THEN upbound := position
            ELSE lowbound := position;
          IF (upbound-lowbound)=1 THEN
            BEGIN
              check(upbound);
              check(lowbound);
              IF continue THEN
                WRITELN('Not in list');
            continue := FALSE
```

FIGURE 13 Continued

```
            END
         END
      END {of WHILE loop}
 END; {of procedure binsrch}

 BEGIN {main program block}
 readln;
 REPEAT
   WRITE('Enter number to search for ');
   READLN(x);
   binsrch;
 UNTIL x=-1; {x=-1 is a signal to stop}
 END.
```

BINARY SUBTRACTION The easiest way to teach a machine how to subtract two binary numbers is to design a circuit so that an addition circuit can be used. A binary adder can be readily constructed with logic gates. (See **binary addition**.)

Suppose that we have a number x, represented as a binary number with k digits. The 2-complement of x (written as $\overline{x}$) is $\overline{x} = 2^k - x$. Then, to find the difference $a - x$, we can write

$$a - x = a + \overline{x} - 2^k.$$

Therefore, to find $a - x$, we have to find $a - \overline{x}$, and then subtract 2^k from that result. This subtraction is very easy, since we ignore the first digit of the result and keep the remaining k digits.

There is a simple way to change a number into its 2-complement. If we consider 3-bit numbers ($k = 3$), then we have

$$x = b_2 2^2 + b_1 2^1 + b_0 2^0$$

where b_0, b_1, and b_2 are the binary digits of x. Then, to find $\overline{x}$:

$$
\begin{aligned}
\overline{x} &= 2^3 - x \\
&= 8 - x \\
&= 1 + 7 - b_2 2^2 - b_1 2^1 - b_0 2^0 \\
&= 1 + 2^2 + 2^1 + 2^0 - b_2 2^2 - b_1 2^1 - b_0 2^0 \\
&= 1 + (1 - b_2)2^2 + (1 - b_1)2^1 + (1 - b_0)2^0
\end{aligned}
$$

Therefore, to find the 2-complement of a binary number all we need to do is reverse each digit (i.e., change all the 0's to 1's and all the 1's to 0's) and then add 1 to the result. For example:

x (decimal)	x (binary)	$\bar{x}$ (binary)	$\bar{x} = 8 - x$ (decimal)
1	0 0 1	1 1 1	7
2	0 1 0	1 1 0	6
3	0 1 1	1 0 1	5
4	1 0 0	1 0 0	4
5	1 0 1	0 1 1	3
6	1 1 0	0 1 0	2
7	1 1 1	0 0 1	1

Now, to subtract $5 - 2$, we have:

$$
\begin{array}{r}
5 \\
+ \quad 2 \\
\hline
11 \\
- \quad 8 \\
\hline
3
\end{array}
\qquad
\begin{array}{r}
1\,0\,1 \\
+ \quad 1\,1\,0 \\
\hline
1\,0\,1\,1 \\
- \quad 1\,0\,0\,0 \\
\hline
0\,1\,1
\end{array}
$$

To subtract $7 - 1$:

$$
\begin{array}{r}
7 \\
+ \quad 1 \\
\hline
14 \\
- \quad 8 \\
\hline
6
\end{array}
\qquad
\begin{array}{r}
1\,1\,1 \\
+ \quad 1\,1\,1 \\
\hline
1\,1\,1\,0 \\
- \quad 1\,0\,0\,0 \\
\hline
1\,1\,0
\end{array}
$$

If we need to find $6 - 6$:

$$
\begin{array}{r}
6 \\
+ \quad 6 \\
\hline
8 \\
- \quad 8 \\
\hline
0
\end{array}
\qquad
\begin{array}{r}
1\,1\,0 \\
+ \quad 0\,1\,0 \\
\hline
1\,0\,0\,0 \\
- \quad 1\,0\,0\,0 \\
\hline
0\,0\,0
\end{array}
$$

This method for handling subtraction suggests a way to represent negative numbers. Suppose that we need to find $6 + (-3)$. We know that this is the same as $6 - 3$. Therefore the negative number -3 can be stored in the machine as $\bar{3}$, which is 1 0 1. There is one slight problem with this plan, though: 1 0 1 is already the binary representation for 5, so it can't also be the representation for -3. We need some way to tell these two numbers apart. To accomplish this, we'll put an extra bit in front of the number to act as the sign bit. In this notation 5 is represented by 0 1 0 1, and –3 is represented by 1 1 0 1. The leftmost bit is the sign bit, with 0 meaning "positive" and 1 meaning "negative."

The table shows how 4 bits can be used to represent the numbers from –8 to 7.

Positive Numbers		Negative Numbers	
Decimal	Binary	Decimal	Binary
0	0 0 0 0		
1	0 0 0 1	– 1	1 1 1 1
2	0 0 1 0	– 2	1 1 1 0
3	0 0 1 1	– 3	1 1 0 1
4	0 1 0 0	– 4	1 1 0 0
5	0 1 0 1	– 5	1 0 1 1
6	0 1 1 0	– 6	1 0 1 0
7	0 1 1 1	– 7	1 0 0 1
		– 8	1 0 0 0

Now, to find $2 - 5$, all we need to do is find $2 + \overline{5}$:

$$
\begin{array}{rr}
2 & 0\,0\,1\,0 \\
+\ \ \overline{5} & +\quad 1\,0\,1\,1 \\
\hline
-3 & 1\,1\,0\,1
\end{array}
$$

BINARY SYNCHRONOUS The IBM Binary Synchronous (BiSync) protocol is a procedure for connecting computer terminals together. Many terminals can share a single link, and a controller determines which terminal can transmit at a particular moment.

BINHEX On the Macintosh, BinHex files provide a way of transmitting binary files through electronic mail services that only accept text files. (See **binary file; text file; electronic mail.**) A BinHex file is an encoded representation of a binary file, but the BinHex file consists only of printable characters arranged in lines of reasonable length. Specifically, the BinHex file consists of one hex digit (0–9, A–F) for each four bits of data in the original file. Thus the BinHex file is about twice as long as the original. See **StuffIt; uuencode; uudecode; binary file; text file.**

BIOS On IBM PC-compatible machines, the BIOS (Basic Input-Output System) is a set of procedures stored on a ROM chip inside the computer. These routines handle all input-output functions, including screen graphics, so that programs do not have to manipulate the hardware directly. This is important because if the hardware is changed—for example, by installing a newer kind of video adapter—the BIOS can be changed to match it, and there is no need to change the application programs.

The BIOS is not re-entrant and is therefore not easily usable by multitasking programs. Windows and OS/2 programs do not call the BIOS; instead, they use procedures provided by the operating system.

BIPOLAR TRANSISTOR A bipolar transistor is formed by sandwiching a thin layer of P- or N-type semiconductors between two regions of the opposite type of semiconductor. (See **transistor**.) The other general type of transistor is the *field-effect transistor*.

BISYNC See **Binary Synchronous**.

BIT *Bit* is a shorthand term for "binary digit." There are only two possible binary digits: 0 and 1. (See **binary numbers**.) Bits are represented in computers by two-state devices, such as flip-flops.

A *byte* is the number of bits (usually 8) that stand for one character. One kilobyte (K) is 1,024 bytes. A computer memory is a collection of physical objects that can represent bits. The size of a computer memory is the number of bits it can represent, usually measured in K's.

One important measure of the capability of a microprocessor is the number of bits that each internal register can contain. For example, the Z80 microprocessor is an 8-bit processor. The Intel 80286 processor found on many popular computers is a 16-bit processor. The Apple Macintosh contains the Motorola 68000 microprocessor, which has 32-bit registers although it can only transfer data 16 bits at a time. The Digital MicroVAX contains a full 32-bit processor. In general, a processor with a greater number of bits per instruction can process data more quickly (although there are other factors to consider that also determine a computer's speed). See also **microprocessor**.

BIT-MAPPED GRAPHICS Bit-mapped graphics offer a method of displaying pictures on a computer. The picture is treated as a large array of pixels (see **pixel**), each of which is stored in a specific memory location. The picture is drawn by specifying the color of each pixel. By contrast, see **vector graphics**. See also **bitmap; draw program; paint program; memory-mapped video.**

BITMAP A bitmap is a graphical image represented as an array of brightness values. For example, if 0 represents white and 1 represents black, then

```
00000000
01111110
01000010
01000010
01111110
00000000
```

is a bitmap of a black rectangle on a white background. Each point for which there is a value is called a *pixel*.

BITNET BITNET is a wide-area network linking university computer centers all over the world. It originated in the northeastern U.S. in the early 1980s. Its most common use is to transmit electronic mail among scholars who are working together. BITNET has gateways to the Internet and USENET.

BITSTREAM A bitstream is a series of bits transferred from one part of a computer system to another. For example, a bitstream can contain the characters in a font (see **soft font**), a bit-mapped image (see **bitmap**), or any other kind of information.

BLOCK When data records are stored on magnetic tape, they are collected together in groups known as blocks. Each block is treated as a unit. Blocks are separated by blank areas called *interblock gaps*.

BLOCK MOVE The operation of moving a section of a file from one place to another within the file is known as a block move. (See **editor**.)

BLOCK PROTECT The block protect command in Word Perfect marks a block of text so that it will not be split across pages. This is useful to prevent a table or formula from being broken up. Other word processors and desktop publishing packages have similar functions.

BMP In Microsoft Windows and OS/2, files with names ending in ".BMP" contain bitmap representations of images. See **bitmap**.

BOARD A printed circuit board is sometimes called a board or a card. Many computers, such as the IBM-PC, contain expansion slots where you can add additional boards to enhance the capability of the machine.

BOLD See **weight**.

BOOLE, GEORGE George Boole was a nineteenth century mathematician who developed principles of mathematical logic that have become known as *Boolean algebra*. These principles are important in the design of computers.

BOOLEAN ALGEBRA Boolean algebra is the study of operations carried out on variables that can have only two values: 1 (true) and 0 (false). Boolean algebra was developed by George Boole in the 1850s; it was useful originally in applications of the theory of logic, and has become of tremendous importance in that area since the development of the computer.

BOOLEAN VARIABLE A Boolean variable in ALGOL or Pascal (equivalent to a logical variable in FORTRAN) is a variable that can have one of two possible values, true or false. Boolean variables are named in honor of George Boole (d. 1864), who was the first to describe logical operations in algebraic notation.

In languages that have them, Boolean variables can be used in place of expressions such as "X is less than Y" and "Y equals Z." For example, in Pascal, the following two programs are equivalent:

```
PROGRAM one(INPUT,OUTPUT);
VAR x,y : INTEGER;
BEGIN
   READ(x,y);
   IF x = y
      THEN WRITELN('values are equal')
END.
PROGRAM two(INPUT,OUTPUT);
VAR x,y : INTEGER; b : BOOLEAN;
BEGIN
   READ(x,y);
```

```
      b := (x = y);
      IF b THEN WRITELN('values are equal')
   END.
```

Boolean variables are useful when the results of a comparison must be saved for some time after the comparison is done. Also, they can be operated on repeatedly to change their values. For example, the following Pascal program reads numbers from the input file, prints them, and reports whether a number over 100 was encountered; the Boolean variable is used somewhat as an integer would be used to keep a running total.

```
PROGRAM booleandemo(INPUT,OUTPUT);
VAR x : INTEGER;
    b : BOOLEAN;
BEGIN
   b := false;
   REPEAT
     READ(x);
     WRITELN(x);
     b := b or (x > 100)
   UNTIL EOF;
   IF b THEN
   WRITELN('There was a number over 100.')
END.
```

BOOT To boot a computer is to start it up. The term *boot* (earlier *bootstrap*) derives from the idea that the computer has to "pull itself up by the bootstraps," that is, load into memory a small program that enables it to load larger programs. Some computers have to be bootstrapped, at least partly, every time a new disk is put into the main drive, so that a directory of the contents of the disk will be present in memory.

The operation of booting a computer that has been completely shut down is known as a *dead start, cold start,* or *cold boot.* A *warm start* or *warm boot* is a restarting operation in which some of the needed programs are already in memory.

BORLAND INTERNATIONAL Borland International, a small but influential manufacturer of microcomputer software, was founded by Philippe Kahn and is headquartered in Scotts Valley, California. Its first products were Turbo Pascal, an extremely popular Pascal compiler released in 1984 (see **Turbo**

Pascal), and Sidekick, a set of IBM PC utilities that are always resident in RAM and can be called up at anytime, even in the middle of another task. Later products include Superkey, which is a utility for redefining the keys on the IBM PC keyboard, compilers for BASIC, C, and other languages, the spreadsheet Quattro, and the database program Paradox.

BPS BPS (bits per second) measures the speed of data transmission. If there are only two signal levels (e.g., 0 and 1), BPS is the same as baud. See **baud.**

BRANCH A GOTO statement in a computer program is called a branch statement because it causes the computer to change its direction and branch to a new section of the program. See also **conditional branch.**

BREAKPOINT A breakpoint is a place in a program where normal execution is interrupted to allow for manual intervention, often as an aid in debugging. For example, in many versions of BASIC the command STOP introduces a breakpoint in the program.

BRING TO FRONT In some graphical editing environments, the Bring to Front puts an object or window "in front," so that it hides other objects or windows that it overlaps. One way to hide part of an object in programs like MacDraw is to create a white object with invisible borders, then put it in front of what you want to hide.

See also **overlaid windows; Send to Back.**

BROWNOUT A brownout is an extended period of insufficient power line voltage. It can damage computer equipment. (See **power line protection.**)

BSD The BSD version of the UNIX operating system was developed at the University of California at Berkeley (UCB). See **UNIX; SunOS; System V.** BSD UNIX introduced the "vi" full-screen editor and a number of other enhancements. SunOS and System V are combinations of BSD UNIX with the original AT&T UNIX.

BUBBLE MEMORY See **magnetic bubble memory.**

BUBBLE SORT The bubble-sort method is a way of arranging items in order (see **sort**). The method works like this. First, examine the first two numbers in the list. If they are in order, leave them alone; if not, interchange them. Do the same with the second and third numbers, then with the third and fourth numbers, until you have reached the last two numbers. At this point you are guaranteed that the largest number in the list has "bubbled" up the list so that it is now the last number in the list. Next, repeat the entire procedure for the first $(n-1)$ numbers. After doing this, you will be guaranteed that the second largest number will be in the second to last place. Keep repeating the procedure until eventually all the numbers are in order.

Here is an example of a BASIC program that performs a bubble sort.

```
10 REM BUBBLE SORT PROGRAM
20 INPUT "N:";N
30 FOR I=1 TO N:INPUT A(I):NEXT I
40 FOR I=1 TO N
50   FOR J=1 TO N-I
60     IF A(J)>A(J+1) THEN SWAP A(J),A(J+1)
70   NEXT J
80 NEXT I
90 FOR I=1 TO N:PRINT A(I):NEXT I
100 END
```

FIGURE 14

BUFFER A buffer is a holding area for data. Several different things are called buffers:

(1) Buffers are areas in memory that hold data being sent to a printer or received from an RS-232 port. The idea here is that the printer is much slower than the computer, and it is helpful if the computer can prepare the data all at once, then dole it out slowly from the buffer as needed. Similarly, an RS-232 port needs a buffer because data may come in when the computer is not ready.

(2) An edit buffer is an area in memory that holds a file that is being edited. Some editors allow you to edit more than one file at once, and each file occupies its own buffer.

(3) A disk buffer is an area in memory that holds data being sent to, or received from, a disk. Some operating systems allow you to adjust the size or number of disk buffers to fit the speed of your disk drive.

(4) A keyboard buffer holds signals from keys that have

been pressed but have not yet been accepted by the computer. The IBM PC keyboard buffer holds 16 keystrokes.

BUG A bug is an error in a computer program. Bugs can be either syntax errors, meaning that the rules of the programming language were not followed, or logic errors, meaning that the program does not do what it is supposed to do.

BUNDLED SOFTWARE Bundled software is software that is sold in combination with hardware and cannot be purchased separately.

BUS The bus is the main communication avenue in a computer. It consists of a set of parallel wires to which the CPU, the memory, and all input-output devices are connected.

The bus contains one wire for each bit needed to give the address of a device or a location in memory, plus one wire for each bit of data to be transmitted in a single step (usually 8 bits), and additional wires that indicate what operation is being performed. For example, if the CPU wants to place the value 0 0 0 1 1 0 0 1 into memory location 1 0 1 0 0 0 0 0, it places 0 0 0 1 1 0 0 1 on the data wires, places 1 0 1 0 0 0 0 0 on the address wires, and places 1 (rather than the usual 0) on the "write memory" wire. The memory unit is responsible for recognizing the "write memory" request, decoding the address, and storing the data in the right location.

The bus can transmit data in either direction between any two components of the system. If the computer did not have a bus, it would need separate wires for all possible connections between components. See also **Micro Channel**.

BUS MOUSE See **mouse**.

BUTTON A button is a small circle within a window that represents a choice to be made. The user makes the choice by moving the mouse pointer to the button and clicking. (See **click; window; HyperCard**.)

BYTE A byte is the amount of memory space needed to store one character, which is normally 8 bits. A computer with 8-bit bytes can distinguish $2^8 = 256$ different characters. (See **ASCII** for the code that many computers use to represent characters.) The size of a computer's memory is measured in *kilobytes*, where 1 kilobyte (K) = 1,024 bytes.

C ───

C C is a programming language developed at Bell Laboratories in the 1970s, based on the two earlier languages B (1970) and BCPL (1967). A C compiler is provided as a part of the UNIX operating system (see **UNIX**), and C was used to write most of UNIX itself. In addition, C is becoming popular as an alternative to assembly language for writing highly efficient microcomputer programs.

C is a general-purpose language like Pascal and ALGOL; but, unlike other general-purpose languages, it gives the programmer complete access to the machine's internal (bit-by-bit) representation of all types of data. This makes it convenient to perform tasks that would ordinarily require assembly language, and to perform computations in the most efficient way of which the machine is capable.

In C, thing that are easy for the CPU are easy for the programmer, and vice versa. For example, character string handling is somewhat clumsy because the CPU can only do it through explicit procedure calls. But integer arithmetic is very simple to program because it is simple for the CPU to execute. Most programmers who use C find themselves writing efficient programs simply because the language pushes them to do so.

Figure 15 shows a program written in C. This language encourages structured programming; the three loop constructs are *while, do* (like *repeat* in Pascal), and *for*. The comment delimiters are /* */. A semicolon comes at the end of every statement (unlike Pascal, where semicolons only come between statements).

C allows operations to be mixed with expressions in a unique way. The expression $i++$ means "retrieve the value of i, and then add 1 to i." So if i equals 2, the statement $j = j(i++)*3$ will make j equal 6 (i.e., 2*3) and will make i equal 3 (by adding 1 to it after its value is retrieved).

C allows operations to be mixed with expressions in a unique way. The expression $i++$ means "retrieve the value of i, and then add 1 to i." So if i equals 2, the statement $j = (i++)*3$ will make j equal 6 (i.e., 2*3) and will make i equal 3 (by adding 1 to it after its value is retrieved).

Another noteworthy feature of C is the *#define* statement. The sample program contains the line

```
#define N 256
```

```
/* CHKSUM.C */
/* Sample program in C  -- M. Covington 1991 */
/* Based on a program by McLowery Elrod */

/* Reads a character string from the keyboard */
/* and computes a checksum for it. */

#include <stdio.h>

#define N 256

main()
{
  int i, n;
  char str[N];

  puts("Type a character string:");
  gets(str);
  printf("The checksum is %d\n",chksum(str));
}

chksum(s,n)
char* s;
int n;
{
  unsigned c;
  c = 0;
  while (n-- > 0)  c = c + *s++;
  c = c % 256;
  return(c);
}
```

FIGURE 15

This tells the compiler that wherever *N* occurs by itself in the program, it should be understood as the number 256.

See also **ANSI C; printf.**

C++ The C++ programming language is an object-oriented extension of C developed by Bjarne Stroustrup at Bell Labs in the mid-1980s as a successor to C. (In C and C++, the expression *c*++ means "add 1 to *c*."

Figure 16 shows a program in C++. Comments are introduced by // and object types are declared as *class*. The part of an object that is accessible to the outside world is declared as *public*. For an explanation of what this program does, see **object-oriented programming**, where the equivalent Turbo Pascal code is explained.

```cpp
// SAMPLE.CPP
// Sample C++ program -- M. Covington 1991
// Uses Turbo C++ graphics procedures

#include <graphics.h>

class pnttype {
  public:
    int x, y;
    void draw() { putpixel(x,y,WHITE); }
};

class cirtype: public pnttype {
  public:
    int radius;
    void draw() { circle(x,y,radius); }
};


main()
{
    int driver, mode;
    driver = VGA;
    mode = VGAHI;
    initgraph(&driver,&mode,"d:\tp\bgi");

    pnttype a,b;
    cirtype c;

    a.x = 100;
    a.y = 150;
    a.draw();

    c.x = 200;
    c.y = 250;
    c.radius = 40;
    c.draw();

    closegraph;
}
```

FIGURE 16

In C++, input-output devices are known as *streams*. The statement

```
cout << "The answer is " << i;
```

sends "The answer is" and *i* to the standard output stream. This provides a convenient way to print any kind of data for which a print method is defined.

C++ lets the programmer *overload* operators (give additional meanings to them). For example, + normally stands for integer and floating-point addition. In C++, you can define it to do other things to other kinds of data, such as summing matrices or concatenating strings.

CACHE A cache is a place where data can be stored to avoid having to read the data from a slower device such as a disk. For instance, a disk cache stores copies of frequently used disk sectors in RAM so that they can be read without accessing the disk.

CAD CAD is an acronym for computer-aided design. This process occurs when a computer is used for design work in fields such as engineering or architecture, with the computer's graphics capabilities substituting for work that traditionally would have been done with pencil and paper. In order to do CAD, it is necessary to have a high-resolution monitor and a software package designed for the purpose.

In order to draw a building, for example, it is necessary to enter the plans by using a graphical input device, such as a mouse or light pen. There are several advantages to having the plans in the computer:

1. The computer can automatically calculate dimensions.
2. Changes can be made (for example, adding a new wall).
3. Repetitive structures can be added easily.
4. The image can be enlarged to obtain a closeup view of a particular part, or it can be shrunk to make it possible to obtain an overall view.

If the CAD program has three-dimensional capability, the image can be rotated to view it from many different perspectives. (See **three-dimensional graphics**.)

CALL The CALL statement in FORTRAN, PL/I, and some assembly languages transfers control of execution to a subprogram;

when the subprogram ends, the main program resumes with the statement immediately after the CALL.

Languages such as ALGOL and Pascal perform calls by simply giving the name of the routine to be called. In BASIC subroutines are called with the GOSUB command.

CALL WAITING Call Waiting is a Bell System telephone service that causes your telephone to beep if someone tries to call you while you are already using the telephone. You can then put the previous call on hold and switch to the incoming call.

These beeps disrupt transmission of computer data by telephone. To make a call that will not be interrupted by beeps, dial * 7 0, wait for a dial tone, and then dial the call in the usual way. If you are using a Hayes-compatible auto-dial modem, then you would give the number 555-1212 as "*70W555-1212" or "*70,,555-1212."

CAM CAM stands for computer-aided manufacturing, which refers to the use of a computer in a manufacturing process. For example, a computer could store a 3-dimensional representation of an object, and then control the manufacture of the object. Some of the principles of CAM are the same as with computer-aided design (see **CAD**), and sometimes a system is referred to as CAD/CAM.

CAMERA-READY A piece of artwork or a printed page is camera-ready if it is ready to be photographed and offset printed. The camera will see only black and white, not shades of gray, so the camera-ready copy must be free of smudges, dust, and stray marks. Usually, pale blue marks do not photograph, and all other colors photograph as black.

CARD (1) See **punched card**.

(2) A card is a printed-circuit board, especially one designed to be added to a microcomputer to provide additional functions.

CARTRIDGE A cartridge is a self-contained, removable part of a computer, usually small and contained in a plastic case. For example, laser printers often take toner cartridges (containing toner, i.e., ink) and font cartridges (containing memory chips on which styles of type are recorded). Game machines often accept software in plug-in cartridges. See **font cartridge**.

CASCADED WINDOWS Cascaded windows look like a stack of cards, with all but the top left edge of each card hidden by the one in front of it. When the windows on a screen are cascaded, you can see the title bar of every window. See **title bar**. For contrast, see **tiled windows; overlaid windows**.

CASE (1) CASE is an acronym for computer-aided software engineering; it refers to the use of computers to help with the process of writing software.
(2) The CASE command in Pascal directs a program to execute one particular action in a list of specific actions, depending on the value of a given variable. Here is an example:

```
CASE place OF
   1 : WRITELN ('First place !!!!');
   2 : WRITELN ('Second place');
   3 : WRITELN ('Third place')
END;
```

If the variable "place" has the value 1, then the first WRITELN statement will be executed, and so on.

CATALOG A catalog is a list of the contents of a disk. (See **directory**.)

CB SIMULATOR On CompuServe, the CB Simulator is a mode in which dozens of people at different locations can converse with each other by typing on their computers, much as if they were using CB (citizen's band) radios.

CCITT The CCITT (Comité Consultatif Internationale Télegraphique et Téléphonique) sets international standards for data communication. (See **V series; X.21; X.25**.)

CD-ROM CD-ROM stands for compact disk read-only memory, which refers to the use of compact disks similar to audio compact disks as a computer storage medium. Audio compact disks became increasingly popular in the mid-1980s. In an audio CD, sound is "digitized" by representing it by a series of numbers corresponding to the amplitude of the sound at a particular time. The binary code for these numbers is then etched in the form of small pits on an aluminum disk about 4 ½ inches in diameter that is covered with a transparent plastic coating. In order to play the music, the compact disk is inserted in a player that uses a laser to detect which spots on the disk are reflective. Since there is no physical contact with the aluminum surface, there is less wear. By contrast, a traditional record represents sound in analog form, where the height of the groove corresponds to the amplitude of the sound.

A computer CD uses the same principle to store information. Computer CDs have capacities of several hundred megabytes (10 to 50 times as much information as can be stored on a typical hard disk, or a thousand times as much as can be stored on a typical 5 ¼ inch floppy disk). Computer CDs are "read-only" because the user cannot store information on the disk; they can only be used to retrieve the information that has been stored on them by the supplier. In the future it may be economical for microcomputer users to obtain compact disks that can be both read from and written to. (See **WORM.**)

The information contained in an encyclopedia can be placed on a compact disk. With the appropriate software, you can search through the CD and find information on a specific topic. The CD might contain graphics as well as text. Other examples of information available from CD suppliers include periodicals and journals, financial data, and artwork. (See **multimedia.**)

CEG CEG stands for continuous edge graphics, which means that the apparent resolution of the screen is increased by antialiasing. See **antialiasing**.

CENTRAL PROCESSING UNIT See **CPU**.

CENTRONICS INTERFACE This is a standard format for parallel data transmission to and from microcomputer equipment, especially printers (originally used on Centronics printers).

CERTAINTY FACTOR See **confidence factor**.

CGA The IBM Color/Graphics Adapter (CGA) was for a long time the most popular video card for the IBM PC. Software written for the CGA will usually run on the EGA, VGA, and MCGA. (See **video modes [IBM PC]**.)

The CGA was designed for video games, not office applications. The lettering on the screen is too blurry for extended sessions of word processing or programming. Office workers who need graphics should use the EGA or VGA with a suitable high-resolution monitor.

CHARACTER A character is any symbol that can be stored and processed by a computer. For example, A, 3, : are computer characters. The ASCII coding system is one way of representing characters on a computer. (See **ASCII; ANSI character set; EBCDIC.**)

CHARACTER STRING A character string is a group of characters, such as "JOHN SMITH" or "R2D2". (See **string.**)

CHECK BOX In a dialog box, a check box is a small box that the user can turn "on" or "off" with the mouse. When "on" it displays an X in a square; when "off" the square is blank.

Unlike option buttons, check boxes do not affect each other; any check box can be "on" or "off" independently of all the others. For picture, see **dialog box.**

CHECKSUM When information is transferred from one computer to another, or is stored and then retrieved, it is important to verify that the information has been transmitted correctly. One way to do this would be to transmit all of the information twice; if there were an error, the two copies would almost certainly disagree. However, this is too time-consuming to be practical.

A better approach is to divide the information into small packets, such as lines of text or disk sectors, and compute a checksum for each packet. A checksum is a number that would almost certainly be different if the information were altered. One simple way to compute a checksum is to add up the ASCII codes for all the characters of data (see **ASCII**) and take the result modulo 256. (For a program that does this, see **C**.) Since this method gives only 256 possible checksums, it is quite possible for two different packets to have the same checksum. However, it is very unlikely that a transmission error would change a packet of information into another packet with the same checksum. Hence errors can be detected by transmitting the checksum along with each packet, and then testing whether the checksum matches the data actually received.

Checksums are used in the XMODEM protocol for error-free transmission of data by telephone. (See **XMODEM.**)

CHIP See **integrated circuit.**

CICS Customer Information Control System (CICS) is an extension to the operating system of IBM mainframe computers.

CICS makes it easy to write programs to enable users to enter, retrieve, and update data on their terminal screens. For example, CICS is often used in point-of-sale systems, hotel reservation systems, billing systems, and the like.

CIRCULARITY A problem of circularity arises when a computer cannot finish a task until it has already finished it—in other words, an impossible situation arises. For example, in Lotus 1-2-3, a circularity problem arises if you enter the formula 2*B1 into cell A1 and then enter the formula A1/2 into cell B1. In order to evaluate cell A1, the computer needs to have the value for cell B1; but in order to evaluate cell B1, it needs to evaluate cell A1. Therefore, a circularity warning message will be displayed.

CIRCUMFLEX The circumflex accent is the mark "^" written above a letter (e.g., ê). The ASCII character "^" is sometimes called a circumflex.

CISC CISC stands for complex instruction set computer; it refers to a computer with many different machine language instructions. The IBM PC, Macintosh, IBM 370 mainframe, and VAX are CISC machines. For contrast, see **RISC**.

CLASS In object-oriented programming, a class is an object type. See **object-oriented programming**.

CLASS A See **FCC**.

CLASS B See **FCC**.

CLEAR (1) To clear a flip-flop or a memory location is to set it to zero.

(2) To clear the screen of a CRT means to cause it to go blank. In many versions of BASIC, the command CLS clears the screen.

(3) In some BASIC interpreters and other interactive environments, the CLEAR command either sets all variables to zero, or frees any memory that has been allocated to specific purposes, such as arrays.

CLICK To click a mouse is to press one button very briefly (usually the leftmost button if there is more than one). By contrast, see press. See also **double-click; window**.

CLIENT A client is a computer that receives services from another computer, or (on multitasking operating systems) a process that receives services from another process. The machine or process that is supplying the services is called the *server*. See **server; X server; DDE.**

CLIP ART Clip art is artwork that can be freely reproduced. Many of the pictures in newspaper advertisements come from clip art. Several clip art collections are available on disk for various drawing, painting, and desktop publishing programs.

CLIPBOARD On the Macintosh and in Microsoft Windows, the clipboard is an area to which information can be copied in order to transfer it from one application program to another. For instance, the clipboard can be used to transfer text from a word processor into a drawing program. See **cut; copy; paste.**

CLOCK (1) The clock of a computer is a circuit that generates a series of evenly spaced pulses. All the switching activity in the computer occurs while the clock is sending out a pulse. Between pulses the electronic devices in the computer are allowed to stabilize. A computer with a faster clock rate is able to perform more operations per second. Powerful computers are now capable of performing an operation every 10 to 20 nanoseconds, and a microprocessor can perform an operation in less than 0.5 microsecond. The clock speed of a computer is often given in megahertz (MHz), where 1 MHz = 1,000,000 cycles per second. The fastest mainframe computers have a clock speed of about 50 MHz. The original IBM PC had a clock speed of 4.77 MHz. More recent microcomputers run at speeds of up to 33 to 50 MHz. See **microprocessor.**

(2) A real-time clock is a circuit within a computer that keeps track of the date and time. Some computers have real-time clocks that run even when the computers are turned off.

CLOCK/CALENDAR The original IBM PC and XT keep track of the time and date as long as they are running, but they lose this information as soon as they are shut down. The PC AT and PS/2 have built-in clock/calendars that are run by batteries independent of other power supplies.

Similar clock calendars have been built for the PC and XT. With these cards, it is necessary to run a special program every time the computer boots up. This program reads the battery-operated clock and sets the PC's original clock to match it. A command to run this program is usually placed in the AU-TOEXEC.BAT file.

CLONE A clone is a computer that is an exact imitation of another (e.g., a clone of the IBM PC), or a software product that exactly imitates another. In biology, a clone is an organism that has exactly the same genetic material as another, such as a plant grown from a cutting.

CLOSED (1) A *switch* is closed when it is turned on, that is, when it is set so that current can flow through it.

(2) A *file* is closed when it is not available for data to be read from it or written to it.

CLUSTER A cluster is a group of disk sectors that are treated as a unit. (See **lost cluster**.)

CMOS CMOS (complementary metal-oxide semiconductor) is a type of integrated circuit noted for its extremely low power consumption and its vulnerability to damage from static electricity. CMOS devices are used in digital watches, pocket calculators, microprocessors, and computer memories. See **field-effect transistor**.

CMOS RAM CMOS RAM is a special kind of low-power memory that stores information about the configuration of an IBM PC AT or PS/2. It is operated by a battery so that it does not go blank when the machine is turned off.

CMS CMS (Conversational Monitor System) is an operating system for IBM mainframe computers, usually used in combination with VM/SP (see VM/SP). The resulting combination, known as VM/CMS, gives the user a working environment much like a large, powerful microcomputer that will run software originally designed for other IBM mainframe operating systems (OS, DOS).

Each VM/CMS user has a virtual disk, that is, one large real disk file that simulates the function of a disk drive on which many small files can be stored. VM/CMS file names are of the form XXXXXXXX YYYYYYYY Z, where XXXXXXXX is an identifying name, YYYYYYYY indicates the type of file, and Z indicates which of several virtual disks the file is on (A for the user's own disk, or a letter such as S for a system disk accessible to all users). In addition, there is a virtual printer for sending files to the system printer, and a virtual card punch and card reader, used respectively to send files to, and receive them from, other users.

Some common CMS commands are as follows:
XEDIT XXXXXXXX YYYYYYYY Z
   Edit the file referred to. (Leave the editor by typing FILE in the command line at the top or bottom of the screen.)
FLIST (full-screen terminals only)
LISTFILE (all types of terminals)
   List the files on the user's virtual disk.
QUERY SEARCH
   List the virtual disks that the user has access to.
HELP
   Display information about other commands.

COAXIAL CABLE Coaxial cable consists of a single conductor surrounded by insulation and a conductive shield. The shield prevents the cable from picking up or emitting electrical noise. (By contrast, see **twisted pair**.)

Coaxial cables are rated for their impedance, given in ohms, which indicates how the inductance and capacitance of the cable interact. For instance, RG-58 cable is rated at 52 ohms. This impedance cannot be measured with an ohmmeter.

COBOL COBOL is a programming language for business data processing, developed in the early 1960s by several computer manufacturers and the U.S. Department of Defense. As the sample program (Figure 17) shows, COBOL statements resemble English sentences, and the structure of the program requires that some documentation be included. COBOL programs are long and wordy, but easy to read, making it easy for programmers other than the author to make corrections or changes.

A COBOL program consists of the IDENTIFICATION DIVISION, which gives some mandatory documentation, such as the program name; the ENVIRONMENT DIVISION, which describes the machine environment; the DATA DIVISION, for data structures and input-output formats; and the PROCEDURE DIVISION, for the algorithm.

COBOL was the first programming language to introduce the record data structure (see **data structure**) and to recognize that the data structures used by a program are as important as the algorithm. In the file section of the program, each file is given not only a name, but also a record format specifying how the data on each line are to be arranged. In the sample program of Figure 17, each record of the input file contains a 4-digit number that is read into the variable X-IN, followed by 76 characters that are assigned the dummy name FILLER, indicating that they are to be discarded. Each record of the output file contains a 4-digit number called X-OUT, followed by a 50-character string called VERDICT.

In many COBOL programs, practically all of the variables are declared in this way. Programs that do a substantial amount of computation can also include a working-storage section to declare variables that are not associated with files.

COBOL is oriented toward reading and writing records of fixed length, each of whose components is also of fixed length. It is difficult to write a COBOL program that accepts input items consisting of variable numbers of characters. (Contrast, for example, the INPUT statement in BASIC, which makes no assumptions about the number of characters typed.) Complex numerical calculation is also difficult in COBOL. However, for applications that involve mostly reading and writing files, with small amounts of computation (e.g., rejecting certain records or keeping totals), COBOL programs can be quite efficient.

One important innovation of COBOL is the INCLUDE statement, which tells the compiler to read another file and treat its contents as part of the program. This makes it easy to use the same piece of code in more than one program. The IN-CLUDE statement is often used with complicated record descriptions; the programmer need write the record description of a file only once and then include it in every program that processes the file.

The procedure division of every COBOL program is divided into paragraphs, each of which has a name (START-UP, READ-A-NUMBER, etc., in the example). The PERFORM statement (not used in the sample program) makes it possible to treat any paragraph or group of paragraphs as a subroutine; this facilitates structure programming. *Structured COBOL* is a style of programming in which this technique and others are used to create a modular, easy-to-understand program. (See **structured programming**.)

```
IDENTIFICATION DIVISION.                                              COB00010
                                                                     COB00020
PROGRAM-ID.        PRIME.                                             COB00030
AUTHOR.            M. A. COVINGTON.                                   COB00040
DATE-WRITTEN.      1982 FEBRUARY 15.                                  COB00050
REMARKS.                                                             COB00060
    THIS PROGRAM READS A LIST OF INTEGERS                            COB00070
    (EACH EXPRESSED AS FOUR DIGITS IN THE                            COB00080
    FIRST FOUR COLUMNS OF A CARD IMAGE)                              COB00090
    AND REPORTS ON WHETHER THEY ARE PRIME.                           COB00100
    THIS IS ANSI COBOL.                                             COB00110
                                                                     COB00120
ENVIRONMENT DIVISION.                                                COB00130
                                                                     COB00140
INPUT-OUTPUT SECTION.                                                COB00150
                                                                     COB00160
FILE-CONTROL.                                                        COB00170
    SELECT INFILE  ASSIGN TO UT-S-SYSIN.                             COB00180
    SELECT OUTFILE ASSIGN TO UT-S-SYSPRINT.                          COB00190
                                                                     COB00200
DATA DIVISION.                                                       COB00210
                                                                     COB00220
FILE SECTION.                                                        COB00230
                                                                     COB00240
FD  INFILE.                                                          COB00250
01  INRECORD.                                                        COB00260
    02  X-IN     PICTURE IS 9999.                                    COB00270
    02  FILLER   PICTURE IS X(76).                                   COB00280
                                                                     COB00290
FD  OUTFILE.                                                         COB00300
01  OUTRECORD.                                                       COB00310
    02  X-OUT    PICTURE IS ZZZ9.                                    COB00320
    02  VERDICT  PICTURE IS X(50).                                   COB00330
                                                                     COB00340
WORKING-STORAGE SECTION.                                             COB00350
                                                                     COB00360
77  X            PICTURE IS S9999999, USAGE IS COMPUTATIONAL.        COB00370
77  REM          PICTURE IS S9999999, USAGE IS COMPUTATIONAL.        COB00380
77  QUOT         PICTURE IS S9999999, USAGE IS COMPUTATIONAL.        COB00390
77  HALF         PICTURE IS S9999999, USAGE IS COMPUTATIONAL.        COB00400
77  DIV          PICTURE IS S9999999, USAGE IS COMPUTATIONAL.        COB00410
                                                                     COB00420
                                                                     COB00430
```

FIGURE 17

FIGURE 17 Continued

```
PROCEDURE DIVISION.                                        COB00440
                                                           COB00450
START-UP.                                                  COB00460
    OPEN INPUT INFILE, OUTPUT OUTFILE.                     COB00470
    MOVE SPACES TO VERDICT.                                COB00480
READ-A-NUMBER.                                             COB00490
    READ INFILE, AT END GO TO FINISH.                      COB00500
    MOVE X-IN TO X.                                        COB00510
    IF X GREATER THAN 0 GO TO CHECK-IF-EVEN.               COB00520
    MOVE ' IS NOT A NATURAL NUMBER.' TO VERDICT.           COB00530
    GO TO WRITE-IT.                                        COB00540
CHECK-IF-EVEN.                                             COB00550
    IF X EQUAL TO 1 GO TO VERDICT-IS-YES.                  COB00560
    IF X EQUAL TO 2 GO TO VERDICT-IS-YES.                  COB00570
    DIVIDE X BY 2 GIVING HALF REMAINDER REM.               COB00580
    IF REM EQUAL TO 0 GO TO VERDICT-IS-NO.                 COB00590
    MOVE 1 TO DIV.                                         COB00600
TRY-ANOTHER.                                               COB00610
    ADD 2 TO DIV.                                          COB00620
    DIVIDE X BY DIV GIVING QUOT REMAINDER REM.             COB00630
    IF REM EQUAL TO 0 GO TO VERDICT-IS-NO.                 COB00640
    IF DIV GREATER THAN HALF GO TO VERDICT-IS-YES.         COB00650
    GO TO TRY-ANOTHER.                                     COB00660
VERDICT-IS-YES.                                            COB00670
    MOVE ' IS PRIME.          ' TO VERDICT.                COB00680
    GO TO WRITE-IT.                                        COB00690
VERDICT-IS-NO.                                             COB00700
    MOVE ' IS NOT PRIME.      ' TO VERDICT.                COB00710
WRITE-IT.                                                  COB00720
    MOVE X TO X-OUT.                                       COB00730
    WRITE OUTRECORD.                                       COB00740
    GO TO READ-A-NUMBER.                                   COB00750
FINISH.                                                    COB00760
    CLOSE INFILE, OUTFILE.                                 COB00770
    STOP RUN.                                              COB00780
```

CODING Coding is the process of writing an algorithm or other problem-solving procedure in a computer programming language.

COLD BOOT, COLD START See **boot.**

COLD LINK See **DDE.**

COLLATING SEQUENCE The collating sequence of a computer is the alphabetical order of all characters (including digits, punctuation marks, and other special characters). The collating sequence is important because it is often necessary to sort (alphabetize) data that includes characters other than letters.

> The collating sequence of a computer is the same as the order of the numeric codes for the characters. (See **ASCII; EBCDIC.**)

COLLECTOR The collector is one of the three areas in a bipolar transistor. (See **transistor.**)

COLUMN MOVE The operation of moving material to the left or right within a file (e.g., moving the material in columns 10–20 into columns 5–15 on several consecutive lines in one step) is known as a column move. (See **editor.**)

COM FILE In CP/M and MS-DOS (PC-DOS), a COM file is a file whose name ends with ".COM" and which contains a non-relocatable machine code program. To execute the program, type the name of the file without the final ".COM"; for example, to execute AAAA.COM, type AAAA.

> In MS-DOS, COM files are usually used for small programs and for programs converted from CP/M. EXE files are used for larger programs and for programs that are OS/2 compatible. (See **EXE file.**)

> In VAX/VMS, a COM file contains a list of commands to be executed, like a BAT file in MS-DOS (see **BAT file**).

COMDEX COMDEX (Computer Dealers' Exposition) is a major computer show sponsored by The Interface Group, Inc., and held annually in several locations. New microcomputer products are often introduced at COMDEX.

COMMAND BUTTON In a dialog box, a command button is a small box that can be actuated by pointing to it with the mouse and pressing a mouse button. Doing this causes the computer to execute a particular command. For picture, see **dialog box.**

COMMAND KEY On the Macintosh, the Command key is the key marked with a cloverleaflike symbol. It is used like a shift key to change the meanings of other keys or to perform special functions. For example, you can print a picture of the current screen by holding down Command and Shift and pressing 4. If you press 3 instead, a picture of the current screen will be saved as a MacPaint document.

COMMENT A comment is information in a computer program that is ignored by the computer and is included only for the benefit of human readers. Here is how several computer languages identify comments:

BASIC	REM statements
Fortran	Lines beginning with the letter C in column 1
C.PL/I	Material bracketed by /* */
Pascal	Material bracketed by { } or (* *)
Assembly languages	Material to the right of the statement, often set off by a semicolon.

Comments reflect the fact that programs are written to be read by human beings, not computers—if we could write in the language that best suited the computer, we would not need compilers to translate BASIC, Pascal, and other programming languages into machine code.

Opinions vary as to how comments are best used. Some software engineers hold that a clearly written program needs few comments. This is certainly true in itself, but it is often impossible to write a program so clearly that another programmer—or even the author, months or years later—can tell at a glance how it works. Here are some general rules for using comments effectively, with the first four examples in Pascal:

1. Begin each program, procedure, or function with a comment stating exactly what it is supposed to do. For example:

```
PROCEDURE swap(VAR x,y : INTEGER);
   {Interchange values of x and y.}
VAR t : INTEGER;
BEGIN
   t := x; x:=y; y:=t
END;
```

A comment of this type may run to many lines or even pages.

2. Use comments to answer questions that the reader may have in mind. For example:

```
q := SIN(x/57.29578);
{x is in degrees,
    sine function expects radians.}
```

Here the comment explains the mysterious number 57.29578.

3. Do not state the obvious. This is an example of bad comment usage:

```
x := x + 1; {Add 1 to x.}
```

Here the comment adds no information.

4. Avoid misleading comments; in debugging a program, resist the temptation to believe that the statements do what the comments say they do. Here is an example of a misleading comment:

```
{ Interchange values of x and y. }
t :=x; x:= y; y:=x
```

In spite of the comments, *x* and *y* do not come out interchanged; both end up with the value that *y* had at the beginning.

5. In assembly language, explain step by step what the program is doing. Assembly language is never easy to read, and the reader needs all the help you can give. Again, however, don't state the obvious. The following example is in 8086 assembly language:

```
   MOV CX,5 ;  initialize loop counter
I: INT 10H  ;  perform video interrupt
   LOOP I   ;  decrement CX, repeat if
            ;  nonzero
```

Here the reader of the program may not remember that INT 10H requests video services on the IBM PC, or that the LOOP instruction uses the CX register for its counter. But to explain MOV CX,5 as "put 5 in CX" would be pointless.

COMMODORE Commodore Business Machines, Inc., of West Chester, Pennsylvania, has produced a popular home computer, the Commodore 64, and its successor, the Commodore 128. These computers can be programmed in BASIC and can run numerous educational and game programs. Commodore also produces the Amiga (see **Amiga**).

COMMON LOGARITHM See **logarithm**.

COMMON USER ACCESS See **CUA**.

COMPAQ Compaq Computer Corporation of Houston, Texas, produces a number of IBM PC-compatible computers. The original Compaq was the first portable PC-compatible computer, and Compaq became one of the fastest-growing companies in history as its products developed a reputation for high quality. In 1988 Compaq led a group of other computer companies in the development of an alternative to the Micro Channel bus used in some IBM PS/2 computers. See **EISA**.

COMPATIBLE (1) Two *devices* are compatible if they can work together. For example, a particular brand of printer is compatible with a particular computer to which it can be connected. This type of compatibility might be called *hardware compatibility*.

(2) Two *computers* are said to be compatible if they can run the same programs. See also **PC compatibility**.

COMPILE-TIME ERROR A compile-time error is an error in a computer program that is caught in the process of compiling the program. For example, a compile-time error occurs if the syntax of the language has been violated. For contrast, see **run-time error**.

COMPILER A compiler is a computer program that translates FORTRAN, Pascal, or a similar high-level programming language into machine language. It contrasts with an *interpreter*, which executes high-level-language statements as it reads them. The high-level-language program fed into the compiler is called the *source program*; the generated machine language program is the *object program*.

On mainframe computers, almost all programming languages are compiled; interpreters are uncommon. However, most microcomputers run BASIC by means of an interpreter. The main reason is that a compiler must translate the entire program before executing any of it, a process that can take several minutes, whereas an interpreter can begin executing the program immediately.

On the other hand, compiled programs run 10 to 1,000 times faster than interpreted programs. Moreover, the machine-language program that the compiler produces usually requires no further help from the compiler; you do not need the compiler in order to run it. For this reason, most commercial software packages are distributed as compiled object programs.

Some criteria often used in evaluating the performance of compilers are the following:

1. Reliability. Is the compiler free of bugs? Does it conform to the official standards for the language that it implements?
2. Efficiency of compilation. How much memory and time are needed to compile a given program?
3. Efficiency of product code. How much memory and time are needed to run the object program? (This varies widely from compiler to compiler, even when the same program is compiled on the same computer. Memory requirements are especially variable because some compilers include large subroutine packages in all object programs, whether they are needed or not, while others are more selective.)
4. Optimization. Can the compiler detect unnecessary repetitions and other faults in the source program and rearrange the instructions to make computation more efficient? This feature is normally provided only on the most sophisticated compilers.
5. File size. With microcomputers, it is often important to know whether the entire compiler package will fit on one diskette. Also, object programs should occupy no more disk space than necessary.

COMPLEMENT The 2-complement of a k-digit binary number x is $2^k - x$. (See **binary subtraction**.) The 2-complement of a binary number can be found by reversing each digit and then adding 1 to the result. For example, the 2-complement of 1 1 0 1 0 1 is 0 0 1 0 1 1.

COMPOSITE VIDEO A composite video signal is the kind of video signal used in a TV set. The whole signal is transmitted on one wire. By contrast, an RGB signal has separate wires for red, green, and blue. (See **monitor**.)

COMPUSERVE The CompuServe Consumer Information Service, based in Columbus, Ohio, is accessible by telephone from anywhere in the United States. Users communicate with CompuServe by using computer terminals or microcomputers with modems. (See **modem**.)

CompuServe offers information on a wide range of subjects, including weather forecasts, airline schedules, the stock market, and a medical question-and-answer service. In addition, CompuServe subscribers can send messages to each other, either in private or via many special-interest forums where anyone can read, and respond to, the messages.

Many CompuServe forums (or SIGs, "Special-Interest Groups") deal with computing as a hobby or profession. Members can exchange programs by modem; CompuServe maintains large libraries of programs for this purpose.

COMPUTATIONAL LINGUISTICS Computational linguistics is the use of computers in the study of human language, and the study of how to make computers understand information expressed in human languages. See **natural-language processing; parsing**.

COMPUTER A computer is a machine capable of executing instructions on data. The distinguishing feature of a computer is its ability to store its own instructions. This ability makes it possible for a computer to perform many operations without the need for a person to type in new instructions each time. Modern computers are made of high-speed electronic components that enable the computer to perform thousands of operations each second.

See the list of terms by category at the front of the book for more information about specific aspects of computers.

COMPUTER DESIGN A computer is best understood by viewing it at a series of levels (see Figure 18). At the basic level are the underlying electronic components, such as *transistors* and *integrated circuits*. These components are used to build logic circuits, such as *gates* and *flip-flops*. These logic circuits are used for simple arithmetic operations, such as arranging a circuit that can add two numbers (see **binary addition**). An adding circuit can serve as the basis for designing a computer that can perform complicated arithmetic instructions.

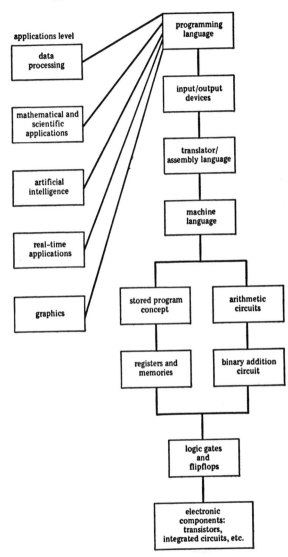

FIGURE 18 Levels of Understanding Computers

A machine language program is a set of instructions written in a binary code. These instructions tell the computer when to transfer data into and out of memory, and what operations to perform upon them. A translator can be added to convert programs written in a programming language such as BASIC into machine language, so that a person using the computer needs to know only the program language, rather than the way the computer itself works. At the application level, a user does not even need to know how to program if a clearly documented, prepackaged program is available for use.

Figure 19 shows a schematic design for a simple computer. It consists of a memory (which can store 128 16-bit words), several registers, and a bus, or connecting wire. Each register, such as the accumulator, is formed by a row of flip-flops. Each flip-flop can be in either state 1 or state 0.

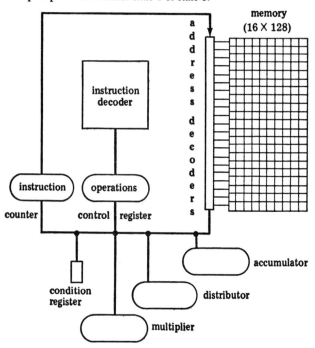

FIGURE 19

The major difference between a computer and a calculator is that a computer can store its own instructions. The instructions, written in machine language binary code, are stored in memory along with the data. (See **assembly language**.) The instruction counter register holds the address of the next instruction to be executed. A computer operates by alternating between two cycles; the fetch cycle and the execute cycle. During the fetch cycle, the computer checks the address stored in the instruction counter register. Then it transfers the contents of that memory address to the operations control register. The operations control register is connected to an instruction decoder circuit that figures out what the binary coded instruction means, and then tells the computer what to do. Then the computer goes into the execute cycle to carry out the instruction.

The simple computer of Figure 19 contains a 1-bit condition register. The value of the condition register will be 1 if some specified condition is true. If the computer faces a conditional branch instruction, it will execute that instruction only if the value of the condition register is 1. This computer also has a distributor register and a multiplier register to help with multiplication. A real computer will have several additional registers. Also, to be very useful a real computer must be connected to input and output devices, such as printers or terminals, so that it can communicate with the outside world.

COMPUTER SECURITY The advent of personal computers has made it easy for important business records or confidential data to be lost, sabotaged, or misused. Computers need protection from the following kinds of hazards:

1. *Machine failure.* Make backups of important files frequently. Every disk drive in the world *will* one day fail, losing all data.
2. *Physical hazards.* Protect the computer from fire, flood, and similar hazards, and store backups at a remote location. Remember, too, that the machine can be stolen.
3. *Operator error.* It is easy to delete information accidentally. This hazard can be minimized with software that retains original files while altered copies are being made.
4. *Computer tampering.* Can someone come in and alter your records without your knowing it? Bear in mind that large numbers of people know how to use popular business software packages. If possible, use software that keeps records

    of changes—recording who made them when—and requires validation (such as a password) to make large changes.

5. *Malicious programming.* Some computer crimes have been perpetrated by programmers who did such things as collect all the money that was lost by rounding interest payments to the nearest penny. A clever bookkeeping system, run by a dishonest programmer, can easily conceal abuse.

6. *Dial-up "break-ins."* This is a hazard only with computers that are physically connected to telephone lines and are programmed to answer incoming calls. Use software that requires user to type passwords and limits their access to the system. The UNIX operating system, designed originally for use in laboratories where no security was needed, is generally thought to be particularly vulnerable. Be aware of the possibility of break-ins through networks of computers.

7. *Easily guessed passwords.* The simplest approach to securing a computer is to require users to type passwords when they sign on. However, some users are sure to choose passwords that are excessively easy to guess, such as the names of their spouses or children. Also, if a user signs on the computer and then leaves the terminal unattended, others can tamper with it without typing the password.

8. *Excessive security measures.* Excessive attempts to build automated security into a computer can easily make the computer so hard to use that productivity is crippled. In the final analysis, all computer security depends on human trustworthiness. Concentrate on securing the people, not the machine. That is, ensure that employees are trustworthy and that strangers have no access to the machine, then give authorized users all the access they need to do their job effectively.

COMPUTERS, HISTORY OF Mechanical computation aids date back many centuries. The abacus, on which information is stored by moving beads along rods, was one of the earliest calculating devices. Blaise Pascal developed an adding machine in 1642 that used toothed wheels to handle carries from one digit to the next. Charles Babbage developed the concept of a stored program computer when he designed the "analytical engine" in 1833. Unfortunately, the mechanical devices of his day could not be made to work reliably, so the "analytical engine" was never completed.

An important data processing device, the punched card, was developed by Herman Hollerith to help the U.S. Census Bureau tabulate the census of 1890. (See **punched card**.) The first electronic digital computer was the ENIAC (<u>E</u>lectronic <u>N</u>umerical <u>I</u>ntegrator and <u>C</u>alculator) which was built for the U.S. Army in 1946, largely because of the need to calculate ballistics tables. The ENIAC was programmed by plugging in cables to connect different units. In 1945 John von Neumann introduced the modern concept of a stored program computer, in which the computer memory can store both programs and data.

Once the concept was established, major improvements were made by developing smaller and more reliable electronic components. The ENIAC was a huge machine made with vacuum tubes. The invention of the transistor in the late 1940s made it possible to build much smaller computers that needed less cooling. Continued improvements in integrated circuits, which were first developed in the late 1950s, made it possible to continue the miniaturization of computers.

An important advance occurred in the mid 1970s when the first microcomputers were built. Previously, all computers had been large and expensive. Microcomputers are small enough and cheap enough that they can be purchased by small businesses and individuals. A microcomputer is built around a microprocessor chip, such as the Z80 or Intel 8088, which contains all of the logic circuits for the computer in a single integrated circuit. After microcomputers became common, innovation continued as new uses were developed for computers in businesses, schools, and homes. New software packages were developed to play games, teach children, perform spreadsheet calculations, and accomplish many other tasks.

CONCATENATION Concatenation is the operation of joining two (or more) character strings together, end to end. For example:

```
"ABC" concatenated with "DEF" equals
   "ABCDEF".
```

See **string operations**.

CONCURRENT PROCESSING Concurrent processing is what happens when 2 computations appear to be carried out at the same time, but in fact a single CPU is rapidly switching its attention back and forth between them. See also **timesharing; multitasking; parallel processing.**

CONDITIONAL BRANCH A conditional branch is a statement that causes a branch (GOTO) instruction to be executed only if a specified condition is true. An example of a conditional branch in BASIC is:

```
60 IF N > 25 GOTO 120
```

First, the computer checks to see whether the condition $N > 25$ is true. If it is, then the computer will jump to statement number 120 and start executing there.

CONFIDENCE FACTOR A confidence factor (certainty factor) is a truth value between 0 and 1, used to describe the reliability of a piece of information whose truth is unclear or uncertain. There are several systems of reasoning that use confidence factors; for one example, see **fuzzy logic.** For contrast, see **default logic.**

CONFIG.SYS In MS-DOS (PC-DOS), the file CONFIG.SYS contains information about the machine configuration, including device drivers, the type of keyboard (if not the standard U.S. model), and the amount of memory to be set aside for disk buffers. CONFIG.SYS is read only when the machine boots up.

CONFIGURE To configure a computer or program is to set it up to be used in a particular way. Many commercial software packages have to be "configured," or installed; this involves setting them up for a particular machine (including video card and printer) and for a particular user's preferences.

CONSTANT A constant is a value that remains unchanged during the execution of a program. Literal expressions, such as 3.5 and "GEORGE WASHINGTON," are constants because they always stand for the same value. In Pascal and some other languages it is possible to define names to represent constants.

CONTEXT-SENSITIVE HELP Many computer programs include a help key that gives you extra information. The help key is context-sensitive if its behavior depends on what you are doing at the time you press it. For example, a context-sensitive help key will give you information about how to edit if you press it while editing, or how to print if you press it while preparing to print.

CONTIGUOUS Two things are contiguous if they are next to each other. For instance, the states of North and South Dakota are contiguous, but Texas and Maine are not.

Most computers can store a disk file in either contiguous or noncontiguous sectors. (See **disk**.) Access is slower if the sectors are not contiguous, since to get from one part of the file to another, the computer must jump from one part of the disk to another.

In general, a copy of a noncontiguous file will be made on contiguous sectors if space is available. See **fragmentation**.

CONTROL DATA CORPORATION Control Data Corporation is a computer manufacturer specializing in very large computers for complicated scientific purposes, such as weather forecasting. The company is headquartered in Minneapolis. (See **CYBER**.)

CONTROL KEY The control (or CTRL or CNTL) key is a special key on the left-hand side of many computer keyboards. When it is pressed in conjunction with another key, it gives the other key a new meaning that depends on the program in use. For example, when you are using WordStar, pressing control-K-D causes the computer to save your document on the disk.

COPROCESSOR A coprocessor is a separate circuit inside a computer that adds additional functions to the CPU (central processing unit) or handles extra work while the CPU is doing something else.

Some computers have **graphics coprocessors** to do some of the computation necessary for displaying images on the screen. As a result, complex pictures can be displayed and changed more quickly than would be possible if the CPU had to do all the computation.

IBM-PC-compatible computers often use a **math coprocessor**, the Intel 8087, 80287, or 80387, to perform floating-point arithmetic. The coprocessor has no effect when the computer is running an ordinary program. However, programs that contain instructions for the math coprocessor can perform arithmetic much more quickly than programs that use the CPU alone.

In general, software that is designed to use the **math coprocessor** will not run at all if the coprocessor is not installed in the machine. However, some programs will sense whether the coprocessor is present and use the CPU alone if the coprocessor is not there.

Similar floating-point coprocessors exist for a variety of other computers, including the VAX.

COPY To copy information is to transfer it from one place to another, leaving the original unchanged. In many editing and drawing programs, "copy" means either of two things:
(1) To copy material from one place to another;
(2) To copy material from the document being edited into a holding area, from which you can then "paste" it elsewhere. (See **cut; paste, clipboard.**)

COPY The COPY command under MS-DOS makes a copy of a disk file. For example, the command

```
COPY PGM.SRC PGMC2.SRC
```

takes the old file (PGM.SRC) and makes a copy of it under the name PGMC2.SRC. Two other examples are as follows:

```
COPY A:*.BAS B:
```

copies all files on drive A whose names end in .BAS onto drive B;

```
COPY A:*.* B:
```

copies all files from drive A onto drive B.

COPY PROTECTION A copy-protected disk cannot be copied by the software normally used to copy disks on a particular computer. Copy protection is usually achieved by changing the size of some of the sectors on the disk. Its purpose is to prevent unauthorized copying of computer programs.

Copy protection has several disadvantages and has become uncommon. Because copy-protected disks use the disk drives in ways other than the way the manufacturer intended, they are often unreadable on later model machines. Further, if there is no way to make a backup disk, the software becomes unusable when the original disk wears out.

There are several commercial programs that enable you to duplicate copy-protected disks or to defeat the copy protection. U.S. copyright law explicitly permits the making of backup disks, whether or not the original disks are copy protected.

COPYRIGHT Copyright law restricts the copying of books, magazines, recordings, computer programs, and other materials, in order to protect the original author's right to ownership of, and compensation for reproduction of, an original work. Most computer programs are protected not only by copyright but also by a software license (see **software license; free software**).

In the U.S., a program is protected by copyright if it contains a notice of the form

Copyright 1992 John Doe

or

© 1992 John Doe

in one or more prominent places. Unlike books and magazines, computer programs need not be registered with the Copyright Office or deposited in the Library of Congress.

U.S. copyright law allows limited copying of books and magazines for private study or classroom use. However, this does not apply to computer programs, which can only be copied with the permission of the copyright owner, or in order to make backup copies that will not be used as long as the original copy is intact.

Copyright protects expressions of ideas, not the ideas themselves. Copyrights do not cover algorithms, mathematical methods, techniques, or the design of machines. The design of a machine can be protected by a patent (see **patent**), but algorithms cannot be protected at all; they are considered to be basic mathematical discoveries free for anyone to use. Copyrights can also protect the visual appearance of a program, comprising such things as menus and icons.

CORE Core storage is the main memory of a computer. The term comes from the doughnut-shaped magnetic cores used as memory devices during the late 1950s and early 1960s.

COREL DRAW Corel Draw is a popular draw program produced by Corel Systems of Ottawa, Ontario. See **draw program**. Corel Draw 2.0 is designed to work with Windows 3.0. In addition to drawing tools, it includes over 4000 clipart images and it has the ability to trace bitmaps and scanned images to import them into the program. There is also a CD-ROM version that contains thousands of additional clipart images.

COS If A is an angle in a right triangle, then the cosine of A (written as cos A) is equal to

$$\cos A = \frac{\text{length of adjacent side}}{\text{length of hypotenuse}}$$

The function COS(A) in BASIC and many other languages calculates the value of cos A. Many computers require that the value for A be expressed in radians. (See **angle**.)

COULOMB A group of 6.25×10^{18} electrons has a charge of 1 coulomb. (See **ampere**.)

COURIER Courier is a typewriterlike typeface often used on laser printers. Unlike other typefaces, Courier has fixed pitch; that is, all characters are the same width. For an illustration, see **typeface**.

CP/M (Control Program for Microcomputers) is an operating system for microcomputers. (See **operating system**.) It is produced by Digital Research of Pacific Grove, California. The original CP/M (now called CP/M-80) is widely employed on computers that use the 8-bit Z80 processor. Other versions, CP/M-86 and CP/M-68, have been developed for the Intel 8086 and Motorola 68000, respectively. However, CP/M is not commonly used on newer microcomputers. (see **MS-DOS**.)

CPU The CPU (central processing unit) is the part of a computer where arithmetic and logical operations are performed and instructions are decoded and executed. The CPU controls the operation of the computer. A microprocessor is an integrated circuit that contains a complete CPU on a single chip.

CRASH A computer is said to crash when a hardware failure or program error causes the computer to become inoperable. A well-designed operating system contains protection against inappropriate input, so that a user's program will not be able to cause a system crash.

CRAY Cray Research, Inc., founded by Seymour Cray, is a manufacturer of supercomputers (see **supercomputer**). Cray's first major product was the Cray-1, introduced in 1977, a vector processor designed for repetitive numeric calculations. See **vector processor**.

CRT CRT stands for cathode ray tube, which is a glass tube with a screen that glows when struck by electrons. An image is formed by constantly scanning the screen with an electron beam. Examples of CRTs include television screens and computer terminals. See also **eyeglasses for computer users.**

CSMA/CD See **Ethernet.**

CTRL See **control key.**

CTRL-ALT-DEL On the IBM PC and PS/2, the computer reboots if you hold down the the the Ctrl and Alt keys simultaneously and press the Del key.

CUA Common User Access (CUA) is a set of guidelines promoted by IBM for standardizing the way that computer programs communicate with the people using them. This will make it easier for people to learn to use new pieces of software.

CUA includes standards for the design of menus and the use of keystrokes. All software manufacturers are encouraged to follow CUA guidelines. See also **SAA; user interface.**

CURRENT A current is a flow of electrons through a conductor. Current is measured in amperes; 1 ampere = 6.25×10^{18} electrons per second.

CURRENT LOOP Older teletypewriters use a high-voltage, constant-current loop instead of an RS-232 serial port to transmit data. (See RS-232.) Do not connect current loop equipment directly to RS-232 equipment; the high voltage may cause damage.

CURSOR The cursor is the symbol on a computer terminal that shows you where on the screen the next character you type will appear. Cursors often appear as blinking dashes or rectangles. Many computers have cursor movement (arrow) keys that allow you to move the cursor vertically or horizontally around the screen. This ability is essential for text-editing purposes such as word processing. If you are working with a computer equipped with a mouse, you can use the mouse to move the cursor quickly around the screen. (See **mouse; pointer; insertion point.**)

CUT To "cut" material is to remove it from the document you are editing and to place it into a holding area. (See **copy; paste.**)

CYBERNETICS Cybernetics is the study of how complex systems are controlled. It includes the comparative study of the operations of computers and of the human nervous system.

CYLINDER See **disk.**

d

DAEMON In some computer systems, a program that runs continuously in the background, or is activated by a particular event, is called a daemon because it is like a magical servant. The word *daemon* is Greek for "spirit" or "soul."

DAISYWHEEL PRINTER A daisywheel printer uses a rotating plastic wheel as a type element. Daisywheel printers were often used with microcomputers in the early 1980s; they print relatively slowly (10 to 55 characters per second), but the quality of print is comparable to that of a good carbon ribbon typewriter.

DASH A dash (—) is a punctuation mark similar to a hyphen, but longer. On a typewriter, a dash is typed as two hyphens. (In Word Perfect, it should be typed as two required hyphens; see **required hyphen.**)

Proportional-pitch type often includes one or more kinds of dashes, such as an em dash, which is as wide as the letter M, or an en dash, which is as wide as the letter N.

DATA Data are factual information. *Data* is the plural of the word *datum*, which means "a single fact." Data processing is the act of using data for making calculations or decisions.

DATA BITS In RS-232 serial communication, either 7 or 8 bits are used for each character. Mainframe computers usually use 7 data bits, and microprocessors usually use 8. (See **RS-232; XMODEM; Kermit.**)

DATA COMMUNICATION Data communication is the transfer of information from one computer to another. In order for communication to take place, several aspects of the communication process must be standardized. The international OSI (Open Systems Interconnection) standard (ISO Standard 7498) defines seven layers at which decisions have to be made:

1. *Physical layer.* What kind of electrical signals are sent from machine to machine? For examples of standards on this level, see **RS-232; modem.**
2. *Link layer.* How do the two machines coordinate the physical sending and receiving of signals? For examples, see **handshaking; packet.**

3. *Network layer.* How does one machine establish a connection with the other? This covers such things as telephone dialing and the routing of packets. For examples, see **Hayes compatibility** (command chart); **packet; X.25.**

4. *Transport layer.* How can the sender be sure the message has been received correctly? For examples, see **XMODEM and Kermit.**

5. *Session layer.* How do the machines identify each other? How do users sign on and identify themselves?

6. *Presentation layer.* What does the information look like when received on the user's machine?

7. *Application layer.* How does the information fit into the system of software that will be used to process it?

The OSI standard does not specify what any of these layers should look like; it merely defines a framework in terms of which future standards can be expressed. In a simple system, some of the layers are handled manually or are trivially simple.

DATA COMPRESSION To compress data is to express data in such a way that they occupy less space. For example, long sequences of repeated characters can be replaced with short codes that mean "The following character is repeated 35 times" or the like. A more thorough form of data compression involves using codes of different lengths for different character sequences so that the most common sequences take up less space.

Most text files can be compressed to about half their normal size. Digitized images can often be compressed to 10 percent of their original size, but machine-language programs often cannot be compressed at all because they contain no recurrent patterns.

See also **ARC; ZIP, StuffIt; PCX.**

DATA RATE See **baud.**

DATA SET (1) A modem is sometimes called a data set. (See **modem.**)

(2) In OS/360 and related IBM operating systems, a data set is a file, referred to under the name by which it is known to the operating system. (The "file name" in such an operating system is the name by which the file is known to a program and is specified by the JCL DD statement, TSO ALLOCATE command, or CMS FILEDEF command.)

DATA STRUCTURES In computer programming, it is often necessary to store large numbers of items in memory in such a manner as to reflect a relationship between them. The three basic ways of doing this are called *data structures*:

An *array* consists of many items of the same type, identified by number. The examination scores of a college class might be represented as an array of numbers. A picture can be represented as a large array of brightness readings, one for each of the thousands of cells into which the picture is divided.

A *record* consists of items of different types, stored together. For example, the teacher's record of an individual student might consist of a name (character data), number of absences (an integer), and a grade average (a floating point number).

Records and arrays can be combined. The teacher's records of the entire class is an array of individual records; each record might contain, among other things, an array of test scores.

A *linked list* is like an array except that the physical memory locations in which the items are stored are not necessarily consecutive; this makes it possible to insert items in the middle of the list without moving other items to make room.

See **array; record; linked list.**

DATA TYPES The type of a data item indicates the range of possible values that the data item might have. Some possible data types include integers, real numbers, Boolean values, or character strings. Some languages, such as Pascal, are very strict about requiring that the type of each variable be declared before it can be used, and an error message occurs if a program attempts to assign an inappropriate value to a variable. Other languages make default assumptions about the types for variables if they are not declared (see **FORTRAN**). The advantage of requiring data types to be declared is that it forces programmers to be more disciplined with their use of variables, and the computer can detect certain types of errors. There also can be disadvantages with a language requiring strict declaration of data types. For example, some operations (such as swapping the values of two variables) are essentially the same for any data type, so it should not be necessary to include separate subroutines for each type. Individual data items can be arranged into various types of structures. (See **data structures.**)

DATABASE A database is a collection of data stored on a computer storage medium, such as a disk, that can be used for more than one purpose. For example, a firm that maintains a database containing information on its employees will be able to use the same data for payroll, personnel, and other purposes. (See **database management.**)

DATABASE MANAGEMENT Database management is the task of storing data in a database and retrieving information from those data. There are three aspects of database management: entering data, modifying or updating data, and presenting output reports. In a well-designed database system the user needs to know only the nature of the information that is available and the type of questions that must be asked, without having to know about the physical arrangement of the data on a storage medium (such as a disk or tape). Many mainframe computers are used by businesses for database management purposes. Several programs are available for microcomputers that perform database functions, such as dBASE IV, and some data management capabilities are provided with integrated programs such as Lotus 1-2-3.

Some examples of database applications including maintaining employee lists and preparing payrolls; maintaining parts order lists and keeping track of inventories; maintaining customer lists and preparing bills for credit customers; and keeping track of the students at a school.

Information in a database system is generally stored in several different files. For example, a business will often have a file of regular customers and a file of employees. Each file consists of a series of records, such as one person or one transaction. Each record consists of several fields, with each field containing an individual data item. For example, in an employee file there would be one record for each employee, and there would be a field containing the person's name, a field for the address, a field for the Social Security number, and so on.

A database management system must make provisions for adding new records (e.g., when an employee is hired); for deleting unneeded records (e.g., when an employee retires); and for modifying existing records. Some fields (such as the Social Security number) will not change; other fields (such as year-to-date pay) must be changed frequently.

When you create a file with a microcomputer database program, you first need to define the structure of the records in that file. You must state how many fields will be in each record, what the label for each field will be, what type of data (numeric or character data) will be stored in the field, and what the width of the field will be. The program will make it as easy as possible for you to enter the data by placing carefully labeled prompts on the screen to tell you where to type each individual field. Each database program has its own commands for adding new records, modifying existing records, or deleting records.

The main purpose of a database management system is to make it possible to obtain meaningful information from the data contained in the database. A database program can respond to brief queries on the screen, or it can present detailed printed reports in a format chosen by the user. Here are some general functions that a database management system should be able to fulfill:

1. Sort the records according to the order indicated by one specific field (e.g., sort in alphabetical order by name, or in numerical order by zip code). You should be able to designate a secondary field along which sorting will occur when there are ties in the primary field. For example, if you are sorting the records by the number of months the customers are overdue in their payments, you probably would like the names of all people 1 month overdue in alphabetical order, then the names of all people 2 months overdue in alphabetical order and so on.

2. Set up selection criteria that allow you to examine only the records that meet a specific condition. For example, you may wish to look only at customers who live in your city, or you may wish to look at all employees whose job title is either "delivery driver" or "warehouse worker."

3. Count the number of records that meet a specific condition. For example, you may wish to count the number of employees who have been with the company for more than 10 years.

4. Perform calculations, such as computing the total amount owed on overdue accounts, or the year-to-date pay for each employee.

5. Connect information from more than one file. For example, a database system might contain an employee file that lists the job classification for each employee. A separate file for each job classification would contain information on wages, fringe benefits, and work schedules that apply to all workers in that classification. (See **relational database**.)

The lists of terms by category in this book were prepared by a microcomputer database program. Information on each entry was stored as a record, with each record containing four fields; the term itself, the category to which it belongs (electronics, programming concepts, etc.), the author, and the current status of the entry (in other words, whether or not the entry was finished). It was then easy to print a list of all the electronics terms, then all of the communications terms, and so on. It was also possible to prepare a tabulation to see how many terms were done by each author. While the book was in progress, it was possible to prepare lists of the terms that remained to be done. Whenever an entry was finished, the status of that entry was changed from "not done" to "done."

DB2 DB2, short for Database2, is IBM's mainframe implementation of a relational database management system. To the DB2 user, data appears to be stored in two dimensional tables. (The user does not need to be aware of the actual internal storage method used.) In order to access these tables, DB2 provides the user with a data manipulation language: Structured Query Language, or SQL for short.

There is an important distinction between base tables and views. One way to think of the two table types is to look at base tables as "real" tables and views as "logical" tables. Associated with base tables are physically stored records which directly represent the table in storage. Views present users with alternate ways of looking at base tables, although the view itself will appear to the user as a simple table. The user may define a view to look at portions of a base table, or to combine portions of several base tables.

In the following example, base tables have been defined for employee and departmental information. Each table is made up of columns and rows (analogous to fields and records). A view has been defined over the two base tables that lists the name and department for each employee.

Base Tables

Employee			Department	
Emp. ID	Emp. Name	Emp. Dept.	Dept. ID	Dept. Name
001	Smith	A	A	Accounting
002	Jones	M	D	Data Processing
003	Thompson	D	M	Marketing

Employee/Department View	
Emp. Name	Dept. Name
Smith	Accounting
Jones	Marketing
Thompson	Data Processing

In addition to manipulating the data in the base tables and views, SQL is used to define the objects and also to control access to the objects.

In DB2, indexes may be defined on the base table. However, the way in which these indexes are used is up to DB2. Specifically, the DB2 optimizer will determine the access path used to get to requested data, and which, if any, indexes will be used.

DBASE IV dBASE IV is a popular database management program produced by Ashton-Tate. It is an improved version of its predecessors: dBASE II, dBASE III, and dBASE III+. dBASE IV provides users with the option of choosing commands by a menu system (which is often easier for new users), or by typing command lines (which can be faster for experienced users). It is also possible to write programs in dBASE IV so that commonly performed operations can be easily repeated.

To start work with dBASE IV, you need to plan the information that you will need and determine what raw data must be stored. Then create a file and determine the structure of the records in the file. A record consists of related fields; for example, one record may contain information about one employee. Each field contains a piece of information, such as a name or Social Security number. You will need to specify the width and type of each field, such as whether it contains numeric or character data or dates. It is also possible to include variable length memos for each record.

Once the data has been entered into the file, you may print or display all of the records in the file, or all records that meet specific criteria. You may save a particular set of criteria on your disk so you do not need to redefine the same criteria each time you wish to use them. You can sort the records in a particular order, for example, alphabetically or by zip code. You may create indexes to make it easier to find specific items. You may perform arithmetic calculations such as updating records with new cumulative totals.

DCE The term DCE (<u>D</u>ata <u>C</u>ommunications <u>E</u>quipment) applies to equipment that uses RS-232 serial communications, with conductor 2 for input and conductor 3 for output. Equipment that uses conductor 3 for input and 2 for output is called DTE (<u>D</u>ata <u>T</u>erminal <u>E</u>quipment). A standard RS-232 cable can link two pieces of equipment only if one of them is DTE and the other is DCE: otherwise, both will try to transmit and receive on the same conductors, and a special cable that interchanges conductors 2 and 3 must be used. Most computer terminals are configured as DTE: most modems, as DCE.

DDE In Microsoft Windows and OS/2, <u>D</u>ynamic <u>D</u>ata <u>E</u>xchange (DDE) is a mechanism by which some programs can exchange data with each other while they are running. For example, through DDE, a cell in a spreadsheet can be connected to data that is being continuously updated by some other program. In this case the spreadsheet is the DDE *client* (the information requester) and the other program is the DDE *server*.

A DDE connection between programs is called a *hot link* if the shared data can be updated continuously by the server, or a *cold link* if the data is updated only when the client requests it.

DEADLOCK See **multitasking**.

DEAD START See **boot**.

DEBUG To debug a program is to remove errors from it. With a complicated program, it often takes longer to correct errors than it did to write the program in the first place.

In MS-DOS (PC-DOS), the DEBUG command allows you to manipulate the contents of memory and modify disk sectors. Considerable knowledge of machine language programming is needed in order to use DEBUG effectively. Symbolic debuggers, which show you the source program as well as the machine code, are generally easier to use. (See **symbolic debugger.**)

DECIMAL NUMBER A decimal number is a number expressed in ordinary base-10 notation, using the digits 0, 1, 2, 3, 4, 5, 6, 7, 8, 9.

DECLARE To declare a variable is to state its attributes. In some programming languages, such as Pascal and C, all variables must be declared. This protects the programmer from accidentally creating another variable by misspelling a variable name. In BASIC and FORTRAN, declaring variables is optional, and declarations are used mainly to create arrays or other variables of special types.

DECNET DECNET is a software product for networking computers made by Digital Equipment Corporation. It is widely used on VAX systems. (See **local-area network; VAX**.)

DECODER A decoder is a circuit that recognizes a particular pattern of bits. Decoders are used in computers in order to recognize instructions and addresses. Figure 20 shows a decoder that recognizes the bit pattern 1011.

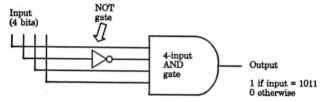

FIGURE 20 Decoder for the Bit Pattern 1011.

DECRYPTION Decryption means decoding—that is, translating information from an unreadable or secret format into a form in which it can be used. (See **encryption**.)

DEDICATED A piece of hardware is said to be dedicated if it performs only one function. For instance, a dedicated phone line is always connected to the same equipment. A dedicated word processor is a computer that performs only word processing.

DEFAULT A default option is an assumption that a computer makes unless it is given specific instructions to the contrary. For example, a word processing program may start out assuming a particular default combination of margins, page length, and so on, which the user can change by issuing specific commands.

FORTRAN makes default assumptions about the type of a variable if that variable is not declared explicitly. Variables whose names begin with I, J, K, L, M, or N are assumed to be integers; variables with other names are assumed to be real numbers.

DEFAULT DIRECTORY In MS-DOS (PC-DOS), OS/2, UNIX, and some other operating systems, the default directory of each disk is the directory in which the operating system looks for files if no directory is specified. The user chooses the dictionary with the command "cd" or "chdir." (See **directory**.)

DEFAULT DRIVE When a microcomputer is operated under MS-DOS, one of the disk drives is designated as the default drive. Any time the computer executes a command that causes it to use a disk file, it will look for that file on the disk in the default drive unless an explicit drive designator was included with the file name. (See **MS-DOS**.)

DEFAULT LOGIC Default logic (defeasible logic) is a formal system of reasoning in which some facts or rules have priority over others. For example, statements about ostriches might have priority over statements about birds, because an ostrich is a specific kind of bird. It is then possible to say without contradiction that birds fly but ostriches don't fly. In classical logic, "birds fly" and "ostriches are birds" together with "ostriches don't fly" is a contradiction.

Default logic is often used in expert systems. See **expert system**. For contrast, see **fuzzy logic; confidence factor**. See also **boolean algebra**.

DEFEASIBLE LOGIC See **default logic**.

DEGREE MEASURE Degree measure is a way of measuring the size of angles in which a complete rotation has a measure of 360 degrees (written as 360°). (See **angle**.)

DELIMITER A delimiter is a symbol that marks the beginning or end of a special part of a program. For instance, { and } are the delimiters for comments in Pascal (see **Pascal**).

DEMIBOLD See **weight**.

DESCENDER A descender is a part of a character that extends below the line. For instance, the letter "p" has a descender; the letter "o" does not. (See **ascender; typeface**.)

DESK ACCESSORY On the Apple Macintosh, desk accessories are programs, such as a calculator, that can be accessed from a menu at any time no matter what other program is running. They correspond to pop-up utilities on other computers.

DESKTOP The opening screen of a window-oriented operating system is called a desktop because it is a blank space on which various objects can be placed. (See **Finder; Macintosh; Presentation Manager; Windows, Microsoft.**)

DESKTOP PUBLISHING Desktop publishing is the use of personal computers to design and print professional-quality typeset documents. (See **typeface.**) A desktop publishing program such as PageMaker or Ventura is much more versatile than a word processor; in addition to typing documents, the user can specify the layout in great detail, use multiple typefaces, insert pictures, and preview the appearance of the printed document on the screen. (See **PageMaker; Ventura; TeX.**)

Since 1990, the distinction between word processing and desktop publishing has become blurred. Most word processors can produce elegantly typeset documents. The difference is that desktop publishing programs put more emphasis on graphic design and give the user somewhat more help with it.

DEVICE DRIVER A device driver is a program that extends the operating system in order to support a specific device, such as a disk or tape drive or a special graphics display. In MS-DOS (PC-DOS), device drivers are usually installed by referring to them in the CONFIG.SYS file (see **CONFIG.SYS.**)

The term *device driver* also refers to programs or configuration files that enable a word processor or other applications program to use a particular device, such as a printer driver in Word Perfect.

DHRYSTONE See **MIPS.**

DIALOG BOX A dialog box is a window that appears in order to collect information from the user. When the user has filled in the necessary information, the dialog box disappears.

Figure 21 shows two kinds of dialog boxes, together with the smaller boxes of which they consist. There is almost always an "OK" button for the user to click after filling in the information. See also command button; option button; list box; text box; check box.

DIGITAL COMPUTER A digital computer represents information in discrete form, as opposed to an *analog computer*, which allows representations to vary along a continuum. For example,

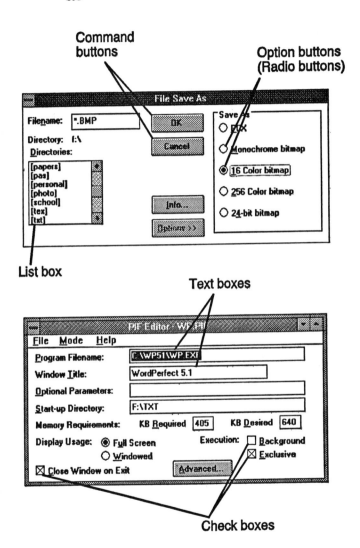

FIGURE 21 Dialog Box

the temperature of a room might be any value between 0° and 100°F. An analog computer could represent this as a continuously varying voltage between 0 and 100 volts. A digital computer, on the other hand, would have to represent it as a decimal or binary number with a specific number of digits (e.g., 68.80 or 68.81).

All modern general-purpose computers are digital. Analog computer circuits are, however, frequently used in industrial control equipment.

A digital computer is more accurate than an analog computer because it only needs to sense the difference between clearly distinguishable states. For example, a slight voltage fluctuation would affect the result in an analog computer, but a slight voltage fluctuation would not affect a digital computer because the computer could still easily distinguish the "0" state from the "1" state of any circuit element. For the same reason, digital music reproduction (i.e., a compact disc) is more accurate than analog reproduction (i.e., a traditional record).

DIGITAL EQUIPMENT CORPORATION Digital Equipment Corporation (DEC) is a large manufacturer of computer equipment, particularly minicomputers. Digital has manufactured several popular minicomputers, including the PDP-8, introduced in 1965, and the PDP-11, introduced in 1970. Digital introduced the first computer in the VAX line of 32-bit minicomputers in 1977. Other products include VT100 computer terminals and DECNET networking software. The company is headquartered in Maynard, Massachusetts.

DIMENSION The number of dimensions of an array is the number of subscripts needed to identify a particular element in the array. A list of objects is a one-dimensional array, while a table is a two-dimensional array.

DIODE A diode is a device that allows electric current to pass in one direction, but not in the other (see Figure 22). A diode is forward biased when the voltage applied to it is the right way for current to flow; otherwise it is reverse biased. The symbol for a diode is a small arrow. Electrons flow in the direction opposite the way that the arrow points.

Diodes are formed by joining two types of doped semiconductors: P type, with a deficiency of free electrons (and an excess of holes), and N type, with a surplus of free electrons. (See

semiconductor.) The place where the two regions are joined is called the junction.

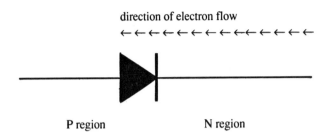

direction of electron flow

P region   N region

FIGURE 22 Diode

If a negative voltage is applied to the N region, the electrons will be driven away from the negative voltage and toward the junction. When a positive voltage is applied to the P region, the holes will be driven away from the positive voltage and toward the junction. At the junction, the electrons from the N region will jump into the holes from the P region, with the result that current can flow across the diode (see Figure 23).

If a positive voltage is applied to the N region, then the free electrons in the N region will be pulled away from the junction. Likewise, a negative voltage applied to the P region will pull all the holes away from the junction. The result is that no current flows across the junction, so the diode does not conduct at all. The only way to make current flow would be to apply a large enough voltage to the P region so that electrons are broken out of their crystal structure. This effect is called *breakdown*, and once it happens most diodes are ruined. Diodes come with ratings that indicate the maximum reverse bias voltage they can withstand before breaking down.

Suppose that the current is turned off. What keeps the extra electrons in the N region from filling up the holes in the P region? If the electrons did that, the N region would acquire a net positive charge, and the P region would acquire a net negative charge. Then all the electrons would be repelled from the P region and attracted back to the N region. Each of the phosphorus atoms in the N region contains 15 protons, while each silicon atom contains 14 protons. If the N region as a whole is to

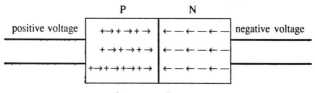

Current can flow.

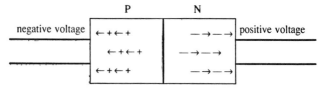

Current cannot flow.

FIGURE 23

remain electrically neutral, it must contain one free electron for every phosphorus atom.

Diodes are used in rectifier circuits and in some logic circuits. Transistors consist of three semiconductor regions separated by two junctions. A special type of diode is the light-emitting diode (or LED), which is used for the display on some clocks. See **transistor; LED.**

DIP SWITCH A DIP switch is a miniature switch or set of switches often used in computer equipment. DIP, or dual-inline package, means that the switch is the same size and shape as an integrated circuit.

DIR The DIR command under CP/M, MS-DOS (PC-DOS), and OS/2 causes a list of all of the files on the current disk to be displayed. DIR stands for "directory." If drive A is the current drive and you want to see the directory of the files on drive B, then type

    DIR B:

To see a directory of all of the files on the current drive that have the file extension BAS, type

    DIR *.BAS

The asterisk acts as a "wild card."

The DIR command is also used in VAX/VMS and some other operating systems. The equivalent commands in TSO and CMS are LISTCAT and LISTFILE, respectively. The equivalent command in UNIX is *ls*.

DIRECT-CONNECT MODEM A direct-connect modem is a modem connected by wires to the telephone line, as opposed to an acoustic coupler (see **acoustic coupler**).

DIRECTORY The directory of a disk is an area where the names and locations of files are stored. On the Macintosh, directories are called *folders*. Each disk has at least one directory (the main, or root, directory), and an operating system has a command that allows the user to see the names of the files on the disk (see **DIR**). Under MS-DOS (PC-DOS) version 2.0 and higher, OS/2, UNIX, VAX/VMS, and many other operating systems, a disk can have more than one directory arranged in a hierarchy (see **hierarchical**).

Subordinate directories are listed in the directory they are contained in as if they were a special type of file. If you are working with a diskette, you will not need to create subordinate directories, since the number of files on the disk is relatively small. However, the number of files on a hard disk rapidly becomes so large that you will have difficulty finding particular files if you have not created subdirectories. For example, you could create a directory called FINANCE to hold all of your financial records, another directory called WORDS to hold word processing files, and so on. Under the WORDS directory you could create further directories: LETTERS for letters to friends, BUSINESS for business correspondence, and so on. If you look at the root directory (assuming you are using MS-DOS), you will see:

```
    Directory of G:\
    FINANCE    <DIR>      8-25-88    3:00p
    WORDS      <DIR>      8-25-88    3:00p
       2 File(s)        636928 bytes free
```

The names of the two subordinate directories are given, but names of the files in those directories are not given. If you now use the CD command to change the directory to WORDS, you will see:

```
        Directory of G:\WORDS
   .              <DIR>      8-25-88    3:00p
   ..             <DIR>      8-25-88    3:00p
   LETTERS        <DIR>      8-25-88    3:00p
   BUSINESS       <DIR>      8-25-88    3:45p
        4 File(s)         636928 bytes free
```

If you now switch to the LETTERS directory, you will see:

```
        Directory of G:\WORDS\LETTERS
   .              <DIR>      8-25-88    3:00p
   ..             <DIR>      8-25-88    3:00p
   FRED1   LET     896       8-25-88    3:49p
   JANE1   LET    1280       8-25-88    3:50p
        4 File(s)         636928 bytes free
```

In this case, FRED1.LET and JANE1.LET are the names of the two files in this directory. (See also **path**.)

DISK A magnetic disk is a computer data storage device. Large computers store information on large disk packs consisting of several disks joined together on one spindle. Microcomputers use removable disks (*diskettes*) or hard disks. A diskette is a round piece of plastic covered with a magnetic coating, such as iron oxide, and encased in a square covering of stiff plastic. A *hard disk* (fixed disk) is permanently mounted in the computer and cannot be removed. The part of the computer that reads and writes the disk is known as the *disk drive*.

The iron oxide on the disk consists of microscopically small needles, each of which acts like a tiny bar magnet. Information is stored by magnetizing these needles. The *read-write head*, which skims the surface of the disk, can either generate a magnetic field to magnetize the needles, or detect the magnetic field of needles that are already magnetized. The binary digits 0 and 1 are represented by changes in the direction of magnetization.

Data on disks are stored in many concentric circles, each of which is called a *track*. Each track is divided into *sectors*, which are the amount of data that the computer reads into memory in a single step. On a double-sided or multilayer disk pack, the set of tracks in corresponding positions on different layers is known as a *cylinder*. The *directory* of a disk is a special area in which the computer records the names and locations of all the files on the disk. In some operating systems, such as MS-DOS and UNIX, the user can create many directories on a single disk.

As a typical example, the $5\frac{1}{4}$-inch diskettes for the IBM PC have 40 tracks on each of two sides, and each track contains nine 512-byte sectors; with allowances for space taken up by the directory, the capacity of the disk is about 360 kilobytes. Hard disks with capacities ranging from 20 to 300 megabytes are available for the same computer; hard disks for mainframe computers have capacities as large as 2.5 gigabytes (more than 2.5 billion bytes).

Data stored on a magnetic disk cannot be read as quickly as data stored in the main memory of the computer, but disk storage has larger capacity and is not erased when the computer is turned off. Storing data on magnetic tape is even cheaper than using disks, but retrieving data from tape storage takes longer because the computer cannot jump from one location on the tape to another without going through all the tape in between.

In general, two computers cannot read each other's diskettes unless the computers are designed to be compatible. For example, an IBM PC cannot read diskettes recorded by an Apple II. However, the same kind of blank diskettes can be used on many different computers; each computer formats the diskette in its own way before recording on it (see **format**).

In purchasing diskettes for microcomputers, you need to know the following:

1. What size ($3\frac{1}{2}$-inch, $5\frac{1}{4}$-inch, or 8-inch) is needed.
2. Whether the diskettes are single- or double-sided. A double-sided diskette can be used in a single-sided drive, but not necessarily vice versa. Almost all diskettes are now double-sided.
3. Whether the diskettes are to be recorded at single, double, or high density.
4. Whether the diskettes are hard or soft sectored. Almost all microcomputers use soft-sectored diskettes, meaning that the computer decides for itself where each sector is located. A few older computers and word processors use hard-sectored diskettes, in which a ring of small holes near the center is used to line up the sectors.

When in doubt, order $5\frac{1}{4}$-inch, double-sided, double-density, soft-sectored diskettes; these are suitable for the IBM PC, Kaypro, and most other popular microcomputers. The IBM PC high-density $5^{1}/_{4}$-inch diskettes that hold 1.2 MB (see and **PS/2**). There are three common types of $3^{1}/_{2}$-inch diskettes: single-sided double-density (360K to 400K capacity), double-sided double-density (720K to 1 megabyte), and double-sided high density (1.4 to 2 megabytes). The exact capacity depends on the type of computer.

An interesting new development is the *optical disk*, on which information is stored by etching a transparent plastic medium with a laser beam. An optical disk stores about ten times as much information as a magnetic disk of the same size, but it cannot be erased. Optical disks are used mainly for large data files that are often read but seldom changed. (See **CD-ROM; WORM**.)

DISK DRIVE A disk drive is a device that enables a computer to read and write data on disks. (See **disk**.)

DISKETTE A diskette is a removable flexible magnetic disk on which computer programs and data can be stored. The three main sizes are $3^{1}/_{2}$-inch (in a hard shell), $5^{1}/_{4}$-inch, and 8-inch. The $5^{1}/_{4}$-inch and 8-inch diskettes are often called *floppy disks* because the entire diskette, including cover, is flexible. See **disk**.

DITHERING In computer graphics, dithering is the representation of intermediate shades of gray by a pattern of tiny black and white specks. Dithering is used to represent shades of gray on a printer or screen that cannot produce them directly.

DLL In Microsoft Windows and OS/2, a dynamic link library (DLL) contains a library of machine-language procedures that can be linked to programs as needed at run time. See **link** (definition 3). This means that programs don't need to include code to perform common functions because that code is available in the DLL. The program is smaller, and changes can be made once to the DLL routine instead of to each program.

DOCUMENT A document is a file containing a text to be printed (e.g., a letter, term paper, or book chapter) or a drawing.

DOCUMENT MODE In a typical word processor, document mode is the normal way of typing documents that are to be printed. The word processor includes codes that indicate hyphenation, page breaks, and the like, thereby producing a special word processing file rather than a text file. (See **non-document mode; text file.**)

DOCUMENTATION A written description of a computer program is known as documentation. Documentation falls into several categories:

1. Internal documentation, consisting of comments, within the program. (See **comment.**) Internal documentation is addressed mostly to future programmers who may have to make corrections or other modifications.
2. On-line documentation, that is, information that is displayed as the program runs or that can be called up with a command such as HELP. The user should be able to control the amount of information displayed (more for beginners, and less as the user's experience increases). Also, HELP commands should be sensitive to the context in which they are invoked; for instance, typing HELP within an editor should call up information about the editor, not the whole operating system.
3. Reference cards, containing easily forgotten details for quick reference. A reference card assumes that the user is already familiar with the general principles of the program.
4. Reference manuals, setting out complete instructions for the program in a systematic way. Related information should be grouped together, and a good index should be provided.
5. Tutorials, serving as introductions for new users. Unlike a reference manual, a tutorial gives the information in the order in which the user will want to learn it; items are grouped by importance rather than by function or logical category.

DOMAIN ADDRESS A domain address is an Internet address in conveniently readable form, such as "mcovingt@aisun1.ai.-uga.edu." See **Internet; IP address.**

DOS DOS (**D**isk **O**perating **S**ystem) has been used by many computer manufacturers as a name for various operating systems, including an early operating system for the IBM 360; the disk operating system for the Apple II (Apple DOS); MS-DOS, developed by Microsoft for 16-bit microcomputers; and PC-DOS, a version of MS-DOS commonly sold with the IBM PC.

DOS 640K LIMIT See **MS-DOS.**

DOT-MATRIX PRINTER A dot-matrix printer forms characters as patterns of dots. These printers are generally speedy and inexpensive. The quality of the print depends on the number of pins used (for example, a 24-pin printer will produce better looking characters than a 9-pin printer). Some dot-matrix printers allow the user to switch between a fast single-pass mode and a slower double-pass mode that produces higher quality characters. Dot-matrix printers are a good choice for many microcomputer buyers. If you need to print both high-quality text and graphics, consider a laser printer (although laser printers are more expensive than dot matrix printers).

DOTS PER INCH See **resolution.**

DOUBLE-CLICK To double-click a mouse is to depress one button (usually the leftmost button) twice very rapidly. By contrast, see **click** and **press.**

DOUBLE DENSITY A double-density floppy diskette is recorded in a format that puts twice as many bits into a given area as the earlier single-density format. (See **disk.**)

DOUBLE PRECISION Double precision means that the computer will carry out arithmetic calculations keeping track of twice as many digits as it usually does. For example, if a computer normally keeps track of 6 digits for floating point numbers, it will keep track of 12 digits when it is operating in double-precision mode. See **rounding error.**

DOWN A computer system is down when it is not available to users for some reason, such as when it malfunctions or when it is being tested.

DOWNLOAD To download is to transmit a file or program from a central computer to a smaller computer or a computer at a remote site. See **Kermit; XMODEM; FTP.** For contrast, see **upload.**

DOWNWARD COMPATIBILITY A computer program or accessory is downward compatible if it works not only on the machine for which it was designed but also on earlier models. By contrast, see **upward compatibility.**

DPI DPI stands for dots per inch. See **resolution**.

DRAG To drag an object is to move it by using a mouse. To do this, move the mouse pointer to the object, then hold down a mouse button (usually the leftmost button if there is more than one), and move the mouse. The object will move (or drag across the screen) along with the pointer. When you are finished moving it, release the button.

DRAIN The drain is one of the three regions in a field-effect transistor.

DRAM DRAM (<u>D</u>ynamic <u>R</u>andom <u>A</u>ccess <u>M</u>emory) is a computer memory that requires a refresh signal to be sent to it periodically. Most computers use DRAM chips for memory. (See **memory; RAM**.)

DRAW PROGRAM A draw program is one type of program for drawing pictures on a personal computer (see Figure 24). Unlike a paint program, a draw program treats the picture as a collection of objects, each of which will be printed as sharply as the printer can print. Thus, the sharpness of the picture is not limited by the resolution of the screen. Also, individual circles, lines, rectangles, and other shapes can be moved around without affecting other objects they overlap. On the other hand, individual pixels cannot be edited. Draw programs are sometimes called *object-oriented graphics programs.*

  Draw programs are preferred for drawing diagrams, while paint programs are sometimes superior for pictorial artwork.

  Some popular draw programs include MacDraw (for the Macintosh), Corel Draw (for Microsoft Windows), and Draw-Perfect (for the IBM PC). See also **paint program**.

DRIVER See **device driver**.

DROP-DOWN MENU See **pull-down menu**.

DRUM A magnetic drum is a computer storage device in which data items are stored on rotating metal cylinders.

DTE See **DCE**.

DUMP To dump is to transfer data from one place to another without regard for its significance.

A dump (on paper) is a printout of contents of a computer's memory or disk file, shown byte by byte, usually in both hexadecimal and character form. Dumps are usually very hard to read and are used only when there is no other convenient way to get access to the data.

Large-scale copying of files from disk to tape, or vice versa, is sometimes referred to as dumping.

DYADIC OPERATION A dyadic operation requires two operands. For example, addition, multiplication, subtraction, and division are all dyadic operations because each of them operates on two numbers. Negation is not a dyadic operation because it operates on only one number.

DYNAMIC DATA EXCHANGE See **DDE**.

DYNAMIC LINK LIBRARY See **DLL**.

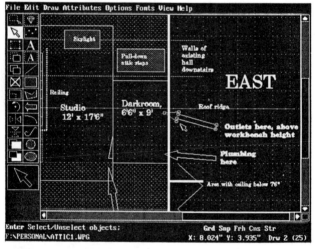

FIGURE 24 Draw program

e _____

e The letter *e* is used in mathematics to stand for a number whose value is approximately 2.71828. The reason why *e* is important is that the function e^x is its own derivative. In BASIC and other programming languages, the function EXP(X) computes e^x. If $y = e^x$, then x is the natural logarithm of y.

E FORMAT See **exponential notation.**

EBCDIC The acronym EDCDIC (Extended Binary Coded Decimal Information Code) refers to the numeric representation of characters on large IBM computers. (By way of contrast, see **ASCII**, which applies to most other computers.) The decimal and hexadecimal numbers corresponding to the most commonly used EBCDIC characters are shown in Table 5. Note that the numbering of the letters of the alphabet is discontinuous. Some EBCDIC devices support a variety of additional characters.

ECHO To echo information is to send it back where it came from. With computers, this refers to two things:

(1) When communicating by modem, a computer echoes typed characters if it sends them to its own screen as well as to the other computer. If you can't see what you're typing, turn echoing on; if what you type appears twice, turn echoing off.

(2) In MS-DOS (PC-DOS) and OS/2, the ECHO command sends a message to the screen. In a BAT file, the command

        ECHO OFF

tells DOS not to print commands on the screen as they are executed. In DOS 3.3 and higher, you can prevent the ECHO OFF command from itself being echoed by prefixing it with '@':

        @ECHO OFF

There is a similar *echo* command in UNIX.

EDIT To edit a file is to examine it and make changes in it, usually with the aid of an editor. (See **editor.**)

EDITOR An editor is a computer program that enables the user to sit at a console or terminal, view the contents of a file, and add material or make other changes. There are two types of editors: full-screen and line.

TABLE 5 EBCDIC (IBM Mainframe) Character Codes

Decimal	Hex	Character	Decimal	Hex	Character
129	81	a	193	C1	A
130	82	b	194	C2	B
131	83	c	195	C3	C
132	84	d	196	C4	D
133	85	e	197	C5	E
134	86	f	198	C6	F
135	87	g	199	C7	G
136	88	h	200	C8	H
137	89	i	201	C9	I
145	91	j	209	D1	J
146	92	k	210	D2	K
147	93	l	211	D3	L
148	94	m	212	D4	M
149	95	n	213	D5	N
150	96	o	214	D6	O
151	97	p	215	D7	P
152	98	q	216	D8	Q
153	99	r	217	D9	R
162	A2	s	226	E2	S
163	A3	t	227	E3	T
164	A4	u	228	E4	U
165	A5	v	229	E5	V
166	A6	w	230	E6	W
167	A7	x	231	E7	X
168	A8	y	232	E8	Y
169	A9	z	233	E9	Z
240	F0	0	64	40	blank
241	F1	1	76	4C	<
242	F2	2	77	4D	(
243	F3	3	78	4E	+
244	F4	4	79	4F		
245	F5	5	80	50	&
246	F6	6	90	5A	!
247	F7	7	91	5B	$
248	F8	8	92	5C	*
249	F9	9	93	5D	)
			94	5E	;
122	7A		96	60	-
123	7B	#	97	61	/
124	7C	@	107	6B	,
125	7D	'	108	6C	%
126	7E	=	109	6D	_
127	7F	"	110	6E	>
			111	6F	?

Full-screen editors use the entire screen as a "window" through which to look at the file; the user can move the cursor around and type anywhere on the screen, or perform scrolling, that is, move the window up or down relative to the contents of the file in order to reach parts of the file that were not originally on the screen. *Line editors* do not allow such free movement of the cursor; instead, line numbers or an imaginary "current line pointer" are used to indicate what line is being worked on, and the user types only at the bottom of the screen.

Full-screen editors are used mostly with microcomputers; practically all word processing packages (e.g., WordStar) include them. It is possible to support full-screen editing at terminals on a large computer (e.g., XEDIT in IBM's VM/CMS), but the data transmission rate must be at least 1,200 baud, since one keystroke may require the entire screen to be retransmitted. Line editors are usually used on slower terminals and are mandatory on terminals that print on paper (e.g., teletypes).

Some questions to ask in evaluating a full-screen editor, particularly on a microcomputer, are the following:

1. What will the editor be used for? Word processing? Modifying existing files? Typing programs? (Does the programming language have fixed margin requirements or a preferred style of indentation?)

2. In the case of a word processor, does it use the operating system's standard file format? (WordStar does not, unless you ask for nondocument mode.) The answer determines whether you can use the editor to create files for purposes other than word processing.

3. Are there limits on the size of the file—either the total size, or the line length? How does the editor handle lines longer than the width of the screen?

4. How fast does the editor run? Does the screen display move fast enough when scrolling? Are there noticeable delays at any point?

5. How easy is it to find and change all occurrences of a particular word or phrase (a *search and replace*)? To move several consecutive lines from one place to another (a *block move*)? Is it possible to shift a column of material sideways (a *column move*)? Can you insert material from another file or view more than one file at a time?

6. Are the keystrokes and commands easy to remember?

7. Does the editor protect your data? Will it prevent you from forgetting to save your file when you end the session? Will it save your file periodically while you are typing?

8. To what extent can you customize the editor to suit your specific needs?

EDLIN EDLIN, the editor provided with MS-DOS, is efficient but not especially easy to use. Some common commands are as follows:

5L	List a screenful of lines beginning with line 5.
5D	Delete line 5.
5,7D	Delete lines 5 through 7 inclusive.
	(Warning! Lines are automatically renumbered whenever any lines are inserted or deleted.)
8I	Start inserting lines after line 8. (End by hitting Ctrl-Break.)
E	Save the edited file and quit.
Q	Quit, ignoring the changes made and leaving the file in its original form.

It is not a full-screen editor; that is, you cannot move the cursor around the screen. In practice, almost all editing today is done with full-screen editors (see **editor**) or with word processors that can create plain text files (see **text file**). In version 5 of MS-DOS, EDLIN has been replaced by a full-screen editor.

EEPROM An EEPROM chip is an electrically erasable programmable read-only memory; that is, its contents can be both recorded and erased by electrical signals, but they do not go blank when power is removed. This contrasts with permanently recorded ROM chips and with EPROMSs that can be programmed electrically but cannot be erased electrically. See **EPROM; ROM**.

EFFICIENCY Efficiency refers to the process of conserving scarce resources. If method A accomplishes the same task as method B, but uses less of every resource, then A is clearly more efficient then B. However, if A uses more of one resource, but B uses more of another resource, then it is not possible to determine which method is more efficient without information about the relative scarcity of the two resources.

With computers, some of the most important resources are:

1. computer execution time;
2. computer memory capacity;
3. auxiliary storage capacity (i.e., disk space);
4. programmer's time.

The general rule is: it is more important to work to conserve a resource if it is more scarce. With early computers, which were very slow and had limited memory (compared to computers available now), it was more important to write programs that would not require much memory and would not require as many steps for the computer to execute. Now that computers are faster and have more memory, it is often the case that the programmer's labor is the most scarce resource. This means that it is more efficient to write software in a way that simplifies the programmer's job, even if it uses more computer time and memory. An added benefit is that if the programmer's job is simplified, errors (bugs) are less likely.

EGA The IBM Enhanced Graphics Adapter (EGA) provides all of the graphics modes of the Color/Graphics Adapter (CGA), as well as additional high-resolution modes and sharper text. (See **video modes [IBM PC]**.)

EIA-232D The RS-232 standard for data communication is now officially known as EIA-232D. See **RS-232**.

EISA Extended industry-standard architecture (EISA) is a proposed standard 32-bit bus for IBM PC-compatible computers using the 80386 or 80486 microprocessor. EISA is not used by IBM; it is an alternative to IBM's Micro Channel. See **ISA; Micro Channel, IBM PC; bus**.

ELECTRONIC CIRCUIT SYMBOLS Figure 25 shows some common symbols used in electronic circuit diagrams. See also **NOT gate; OR gate; AND gate; NAND gate**.

ELECTRONIC DATA INTERCHANGE Electronic data interchange refers to the transfer of information between organizations in machine readable form. Electronic data interchange is becoming more common in the 1990s because it minimizes the errors that can occur if the same information repeatedly needs to be retyped. For example, consider a department ordering an item from a supplier. In a paper-based system, the department will typically fill out a requisition that needs to be approved by

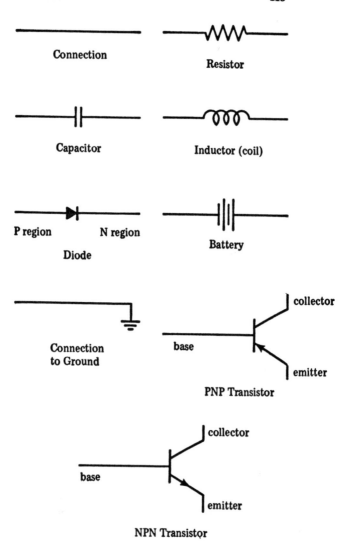

FIGURE 25

the purchasing department, which fills out a purchase order, which is sent to the supplier. The supplier will need to generate its own paperwork to direct the billing and shipment of the item. When the item is received, the receiving department will need to fill out more paperwork for verification. More paperwork will be required for the accounts payable department to receive authorization to pay the bill, and then a paper check must be sent. All that paperwork is required even if the process operates correctly; if an error is made or other inquiry is necessary, still more paperwork will be generated. At each stage of the process, a person can make mistakes typing the relevant information, such as the name of the supplier and the part number of the item being ordered.

In an electronic data interchange system, the basic flow of information is the same, except that electronic messages take the place of paper. These messages are similar to electronic mail, except that there is a standard format for each type of message so that software can read it and automatically generate the next message in the process. The part number, quantity, and supplier get typed only once, at the beginning, and then are automatically transferred from computer to computer. At the end, even the payment may take place by electronic funds transfer rather than by writing a check.

Electronic data interchange systems can work only if all of the companies involved have agreed on the same standards. Extra care must be taken to protect against fraud, and the legal system needs to adjust to the fact that in the absence of paper documents it is not possible to use signatures as evidence of approval. Nevertheless, the advantages of electronic data interchange are such that this type of system will become more common in the future. See also **electronic mail**.

ELECTRONIC MAIL Electronic mail (email) consists of messages that are sent by computer from one person to another, then saved until the recipient chooses to read them.

Email is much more convenient than ordinary mail or telephone calls because it arrives immediately but does not require the recipient to be present, nor does it interrupt anything else the recipient may be doing. Messages are easily printed out, saved on disk, or forwarded to other people.

In email messages, the symbols :) or -) (smiling face or tongue in cheek) denote remarks that are not to be taken seriously; this is important because the recipient cannot hear the sender's tone of voice. Ill-considered angry messages are fairly common and are called *flames.*

All users of email should be aware that backup copies of the messages may be saved on disk or tape and that perfect privacy cannot be guaranteed.

See also **electronic data interchange; local area network; wide area network.**

ELECTROSTATIC PRINTER This printer operates by using an electric charge to deposit toner on paper. Laser printers are electrostatic printers.

ELEMENT An element of an array is one of the items in that array.

ELITE An elite typewriter prints 12 characters per inch. (See **pitch; pica.**)

EM DASH See **dash.**

EMAIL Email is an abbreviation for "electronic mail." (See **electronic mail.**)

EMBEDDED SYSTEM An embedded system is a computer that forms part of a larger machine of some other kind. The microprocessor that controls an automobile engine is an example. Embedded systems must usually be extremely reliable. They must also respond to events in real time (that is, as they happen) without undue delay. See **microcontroller; real-time programming**.

EMITTER The emitter is one of the three areas in a bipolar transistor. (See **transistor.**)

EMS See **expanded memory**.

EMULATION One machine emulates another if it achieves the same results as the machine being emulated. For example, VT-100 emulation means making a computer act exactly like a VT-100 terminal.

Emulation is different from simulation, which involves imitating the internal processes, not just the results, of the thing being simulated.

EN DASH See **dash.**

ENCRYPTION To encrypt information is to convert it into a code or cipher so that people will be unable to read it. A secret key, or password, is required to decrypt (decode) the information.

END The word END is used in several programming languages to indicate the end of a particular program structure. In BASIC the END command tells the computer to stop executing the program. In Pascal the keyword END followed by a period is placed at the end of a program. The word END is also used to mark the end of Pascal procedures, functions, and compound statements that are started with the word BEGIN.

END-OF-FILE MARK In some operating systems, every file ends with a special symbol. For example, in CP/M, ASCII character 26 (control-Z) marks the end of a text file. In MS-DOS and OS/2, control-Z is normally used in the same way, but it is not strictly necessary because the directory keeps track of the exact length of the file in bytes.

END USER An end user of a product is the person ultimately intended to use it, as opposed to people involved in developing or marketing it.

ENIAC The ENIAC (Electronic Numerical Integrator and Calculator), an early computer built in the mid 1940s, was the first electronic computer. It contained about 18,000 vacuum tubes. Initially, the ENIAC was programmed by plugging cables into circuit boards.

ENTER KEY The enter key on a computer terminal is the key you press at the end of each line in order to enter the contents of that line into the computer. On some terminals, this key is called the *return key.*

ENVIRONMENT (1) On a computer, an environment defines what you can do with the computer. For instance, the operating system, a word processor, and a spreadsheet provide (at least) 3 different environments that respond to different commands. For example, if you type a word processing command while you are in the operating system environment, or vice versa, the command will not be understood.

(2) In PC-DOS (MS-DOS) and OS/2, the environment is a data area in which you can leave messages for programs by using the SET command. To see the contents of the environment area, type SET by itself.

EPROM EPROM stands for Erasable Programmable Read Only Memory. A PROM is a memory chip that can be programmed once but cannot be reprogrammed. An EPROM is a special type of PROM that can be erased by exposing the chip to ultraviolet light. Then it can be reprogrammed. See also **ROM; EEPROM.**

EPSON Epson is a prominent Japanese manufacturer of dot-matrix printers, distributed in the United States by Epson America, Inc., of Torrance, California. The Epson MX-80 printer received wide acceptance during the early 1980s and set many standards to which other manufacturers now adhere. Epson printers are capable of many special effects, including dot-by-dot graphics. Table 6 lists a number of control codes that work on the MX-80, RX-80, FX-80, and other Epson-compatible printers.

ERASE In PC-DOS (MS-DOS), the ERASE command deletes a file from disk. See also **recovering erased files.**

ERGONOMICS Ergonomics is the science of designing machines and working environments to suit human needs. An ergonomically designed machine is one whose design is based on the scientific study of human requirements such as vision, posture, and the like.

ERROR TRAPPING See **trapping.**

ESCAPE KEY The escape key is a key on a computer keyboard that has a special meaning depending on what software is being used. In a typical program, such as Lotus 1-2-3, the escape key means "get out of where you are now and get back to where you were before." The escape key is represented by ASCII character code 27, which is a character used to send special messages to devices. (See **escape sequence.**)

ESCAPE SEQUENCE An escape sequence is a special series of character codes that causes a screen or printer to perform some action (such as changing type styles) rather than displaying the characters. (See **ANSI screen control; Epson.**)

TABLE 6 Epson Printer Control Codes

These codes are the same on the MX-80, RX-80, and FX-80; they can be expected to work on virtually all printers claiming Epson compatibility. There are many other codes, each specific to a particular model of printer. In each case, the numbers given below are the ASCII codes for the sequence of characters to be transmitted (see **ASCII**).

7	Sound buzzer on printer.
10	Line feed
12	Go to top of next page.
13	Carriage return
27 48	Set line spacing to $^1/8$.
27 50	Set line spacing to $^1/6$ (normal).
27 51 X	Set line spacing to $^X/216$.
27 67 X	Set form length. X is number of lines.
27 67 0 X	Set form length. X is number of inches.
27 78 X	Skip X lines at perforation between pages.
27 79	Cancel skip-over-perforation.
15	Condensed mode (narrow type) on
18	Condensed mode off
14	Double width mode until end of line
20	Double width mode off
27 87 1	Double width mode on until canceled
27 87 0	Double width mode canceled
27 69	Emphasized (heavy print) mode on
27 70	Emphasized mode off
27 45 1	Underlined mode on
27 45 0	Underlined mode off
27 83 1	Subscript mode on
27 83 0	Superscript mode on
27 84	Subscript or superscript mode off

Some printers also offer italics and/or elite type. All mode combinations are legal except the following:

Emphasized condensed	Emphasized elite
Emphasized subscript	Condensed elite
Emphasized superscript	

In particular, condensed double width is permissible and prints 8.5 characters per inch.

ESDI The Enhanced Small Device Interface (ESDI) was introduced by Maxtor in 1983 as an alternative to the ST-506 standard interface for hard disks. Compared to ST-506, ESDI allows somewhat faster data transfer. See **ST-506; ESDI; SCSI; IDE.**

ETHERNET Ethernet is a type of local area network originally developed by Xerox Corporation. Communication takes place by means of radio frequency signals carried by a coaxial cable. The name "Ethernet" apparently comes from "ether," the nineteenth-century name for the medium through which light waves were thought to travel. (See **local-area network; data communication.**)

On the physical level, there are three types of Ethernet connections. *Thin-wire Ethernet* uses RG-58 coaxial cable. Conventional *baseband Ethernet* uses a thicker cable about 3/8 inch in diameter, and *broadband Ethernet* modulates the whole Ethernet signal on a higher-frequency carrier so that several signals can be carried simultaneously on a single cable, as is the case with TV channels.

The control strategy of Ethernet is called *CSMA/CD* (Carrier Sense, Multiple Access, Collision Detection). Each node listens to see if another node is transmitting. If so, it waits its turn to transmit. If two nodes inadvertently transmit at the same time, the collision is detected and they retransmit one at a time.

Different Ethernet systems use different software protocols, including TCP/IP and DECNET. See **TCP/IP.**

EVENT-DRIVEN PROGRAMMING In event-driven programming, the computer spends its time responding to events rather than stepping through a prearranged series of actions. Computers that control machinery are almost always event-driven. So are computer programs that run under graphical user interfaces such as the Macintosh operating system or Microsoft Windows. Such programs respond to events such as the user choosing an item on a menu or clicking the mouse on an icon. See **object-oriented programming; Visual Basic; graphical user interface; window.**

EXCEL Excel is an integrated program produced by Microsoft that combines a spreadsheet, a database manager, and graphics.

EXE FILE In MS-DOS (PC-DOS), OS/2, and VAX/VMS, an EXE (executable) file is a file that contains a relocatable machine code program and has a name ending with ".EXE." To execute the program, type the name of the file without the final ".EXE"; for example, to execute AAAA.EXE, type AAAA. In VAX/VMS, however, an .EXE file is executed by the RUN command (e.g., RUN AAAAA.EXE.)

Most application programs are distributed as EXE files. Most compilers translate source code into EXE files (see **compiler**).

EXECUTE To execute an instruction is to do what the instruction says to do. A computer alternates between a fetch cycle, when it locates the next instruction, and an execute cycle, when it carries the instruction out. (See **computer design**).

EXP In many programming languages the function EXP(X) calculates the value of e^x. The letter e represents a special number approximately equal to 2.71828.

EXPANDED MEMORY Expanded memory is a method of equipping an IBM PC with many megabytes of memory. Ordinarily, the 8088 processor in the PC can address only one megabyte (1024K) of memory. The upper 384K of this is reserved for special purposes, leaving only 640K available for ordinary use. Expanded memory uses bank switching to swap many different sets of memory chips into a single block of addresses within this 640K region. The Lotus-Intel-Microsoft Expanded Memory Specification (LIM-EMS) specifies how this is done. Special software is required to take advantage of it.

By contrast, extended memory (on the PC AT and PS/2) is directly accessible at addresses higher than one megabyte. This requires an 80286 or 80386 processor and, under DOS, a different type of special software. The OS/2 and UNIX operating systems use extended memory automatically.

EXPERT SYSTEM An expert system is a computer program that uses stored information to draw conclusions about a particular case. It differs from a database, which merely calls up stored information and presents it to the user unchanged. Expert systems are widely used to troubleshoot defects in machines; they have also been used successfully to diagnose diseases or recommend manufactured products.

Every expert system consists of three parts: (1) a user *interface*, which is a way of communicating with the user through such devices as menus, commands, or short-answer questions

(See **user interface**); (2) a *knowledge base* containing stored expertise; and (3) an *inference engine*, which draws conclusions by performing simple logical operations on the knowledge base and the information supplied by the user.

Figure 26 shows a complete (though small) expert system written in Prolog. It has several features that would be hard to implement in a conventional programming language. The entire knowledge base is expressed in a notation that a human being can easily understand and verify. The program asks only the questions that are relevant to the diagnosis being considered, and it never asks the same question twice, even if it is needed for more than one diagnosis. You can easily expand this expert system, or adapt it to other purposes, by changing only the knowledge base, even if you do not know very much about Prolog.

See also **Prolog; artificial intelligence.**

EXPONENT An exponent is a number or letter that indicates repeated multiplication. Thus a^n means to multiply n number of a's together. For example, $3^2 = 3 \times 3 = 9$, $4^5 = 4 \times 4 \times 4 \times 4 \times 4 = 1,024$, and $10^6 = 10 \times 10 \times 10 \times 10 \times 10 \times 10 = 1,000,000$.

Also, $a^2 = a \times a$ is called a to the second power, or a squared. The number that when multiplied by itself gives a is called the square root of a (written as $\sqrt{a}$). That means $\sqrt{a} \times \sqrt{a} = a$. For example, $\sqrt{9} = 3$, since $3 \times 3 = 9$.

EXPONENTIAL FUNCTION An exponential function is a function of the form $y = a^x$, where a can be any positive number except 1 and is called the *base* of the function. The most common exponential function is e^x. (See e.)

EXPONENTIAL NOTATION Exponential notation is a way of expressing very big and very small numbers on computers. It is the same as scientific notation. A number in exponential notation is written as the product of a number from 1 to 10 and a power of 10. The letter E is used to indicate what power of 10 is needed. For example, 5.4E6 means 5.4×10^6, which in turn means 5,400,000. The number of meters in a light year is 9,460,000,000,000,000, which can be written in exponential notation as 9.46E15. The wavelength of red light is 0.0000007 meter, which is 7E –7.

EXPRESSION In a programming language, an expression is a set of symbols that can be evaluated to have a particular value. For

```
/* Demonstration expert system   M. Covington 1988 */

/*************************
 *** INFERENCE ENGINE ***
 *************************/

/* The built-in Prolog inference engine is used. */
/* The following procedure makes it backtrack    */
/* through all possible diagnoses.               */

main :-
  write('This program tells you why your car won''t start.'), nl,
  write('Answer all questions ''y'' or ''n'' (lower case).'), nl,
  nl,
  abolish(recorded_answer/2),
  possible_diagnosis(D),
  give_explanation(D),
  fail.

main.

/***********************
 *** USER INTERFACE ***
 ***********************/

/*
 * answer(Q,A)
 *    checks whether question Q has already been answered,
 *    and if so, whether the answer was A.
 *    If Q has not already been asked, it is asked and
 *    the user's answer is recorded.
 */

answer(Q,A) :- call(recorded_answer(Q,A)).

answer(Q,A) :- not recorded_answer(Q,_),
               question_text(Q,Text), write(Text), nl,
               get_y_or_n(Resp),
               assert(recorded_answer(Q,Resp)),
               !,
               A = Resp.

/*
 * get_y_or_n(Resp)
 *    instantiates Resp to "y" or "n".
 */

get_y_or_n(Resp) :-
        get(Char), nl,
        check_y_or_n([Char],Resp).

check_y_or_n("y","y") :- !.
check_y_or_n("n","n") :- !.
check_y_or_n(_,Response) :-
        write('(Type y or n) '),
        get_y_or_n(Response).
```

FIGURE 26

FIGURE 26 Continued

```
/***********************
 *** KNOWLEDGE BASE ***
 ***********************/

/* Table of questions that can be asked */

question_text(starter_worked,
  'Did the engine turn over when you first tried to start it?').

question_text(starter_still_working,
  'Does the engine turn over when you try starting it now?').

question_text(fuel_in_carb,
  'Is there fuel reaching the carburetor?').


/* Possible diagnoses, with conditions for each */

possible_diagnosis(electrical) :-
        answer(starter_worked,"n").

possible_diagnosis(drained_battery) :-
        answer(starter_worked,"y"),
        answer(starter_still_working,"n").

possible_diagnosis(fuel) :-
        answer(fuel_in_carb,"n").

possible_diagnosis(ignition) :-
        answer(fuel_in_carb,"y"),
        answer(starter_worked,"y").

/* Explanations for the diagnoses */

give_explanation(electrical) :-
  write('The defect may be in the battery, alternator,'), nl,
  write('or voltage regulator. Jump-starting may get'), nl,
  write('the car going temporarily.'), nl, nl.

give_explanation(drained_battery) :-
  write('The battery has become drained during your'), nl,
  write('attempts to start the car. Jump-starting or'), nl,
  write('recharging may be necessary.'), nl, nl.

give_explanation(fuel) :-
  write('Either the car has run out of fuel, or there'), nl,
  write('is a defect in the fuel line or fuel pump.'), nl, nl.

give_explanation(ignition) :-
  write('The defect may be in the ignition system.'), nl, nl.
```

FIGURE 26 Continued

```
C:\>api
Arity/Prolog Interpreter Version 4.0
Copyright (C) 1986 Arity Corporation
?- consult(carstart).

yes
?- main.
This program tells you why your car won't start.
Answer all questions 'y' or 'n' (lower case).

Did the engine turn over when you first tried to start it?
y
Does the engine turn over when you try starting it now?
n
The battery has become drained during your
attempts to start the car. Jump-starting or
recharging may be necessary.

Is there fuel reaching the carburetor?
n
Either the car has run out of fuel, or there
is a defect in the fuel line or fuel pump.

yes
?- halt.
```

example, the following are numeric expressions (i.e., their values are numbers):

3.5
(4/3)*PI*R^3
SQRT(A^2 + B^2)

Some programming languages have expressions whose values are character strings or Boolean (true-false) values. For example,

"WALLA" + "WALLA"

is a character string expression, and

(P OR Q) AND R

is a Boolean expression.

EXTENDED INDUSTRY STANDARD ARCHITECTURE
See EISA.

EXTENDED MEMORY Extended memory is memory at addresses higher than 1 megabyte on IBM PC AT and PS/2 computers. It contrasts with expanded memory, which is bank-switched. Windows, OS/2, and UNIT use extended memory. (See **expanded memory; bank switching.**)

EXTENSION A file name in CP/M, MS-DOS, and some other operating systems can be followed by a three-letter file extension that often indicates the nature of the file. When typing the file name, a period is used to separate the name from the extension. For example, in the file name

    PROG1.BAS

BAS is the file extension. Some file extensions have standard meanings. For example, BAS designates BASIC program files; COM or EXE, command files; and BAK, backup files.

EYEGLASSES FOR COMPUTER USERS Most eyeglasses are designed either for vision at a great distance or for reading at about 18 inches. Neither of these is suitable for looking at a computer screen two or three feet away. As a result, many eyeglass wearers need new glasses for computer work. Some of them think the computer has harmed their vision, although in fact there is no evidence that computer work (or any other kind of close work) harms the eyes.

Computer screens emit tiny amounts of ultraviolet (UV) light and special glasses are available that block this. However, there is much more UV in ordinary sunlight than in the image on a computer screen, so UV-blocking glasses are probably more beneficial outdoors than in the office.

f _____

F KEYS See **function keys.**

FACTORIAL The factorial of a positive integer is equal to the product of all the integers from 1 up to that number. The factorial of a number n is symbolized by an exclamation point:$n!$. For example:

$$2! = 2 \times 1 = 2$$
$$3! = 3 \times 2 \times 1 = 6$$
$$4! = 4 \times 3 \times 2 \times 1 = 24$$
$$5! = 5 \times 4 \times 3 \times 2 \times 1 = 120$$

FAT The file allocation table (FAT) is the part of the disk that contains information about the sizes and locations of the files.

FAT BITS In MacPaint, Fat Bits is a mode in which the user can edit individual pixels (the small black or white squares of which the picture is composed). The pixels are shown greatly magnified on the screen.

FAX A FAX, or facsimile machine, transmits copies of paper documents over telephone lines by converting the appearance of the document into an electronic signal. The output looks much like a photocopy. Some computers have the ability to send and receive FAX signals.

FCC In the United States, the Federal Communications Commission (FCC) regulates all equipment that produces radio-frequency signals, including computers. The FCC issues two levels of approval for computers: Class A (suitable for use in industrial or business areas) and Class B (suitable for use in the home). See **RFI protection.**

FEEDBACK Feedback occurs when a control device uses information about the current state of the system to determine the next control action. For example, when a thermostat controls the temperature in a house, it needs to know the current temperature in the house before it decides whether to turn on the furnace.

FIBER OPTICS A fiber-optic cable carries light rather than electrical energy. It is made of a thin fiber of glass. Large amounts of data can be carried by a single fiber-optic cable.

FIELD A group of adjacent characters is called a field. For example, in a company payroll system the information about a single individual can be stored as one record. Each record will be divided into several fields. One field will contain the employee's name; another field, his Social Security number; a third field, his salary or rate per hour; and so on. See also **record; database**.

FIELD-EFFECT TRANSISTOR A f̲ield-e̲ffect t̲ransistor (FET) is a transistor in which the flow of current from *source* to *drain* is controlled by a charge applied to the gate. This charge attracts electrons into the area between source and drain or repels them away from it, thus changing its semiconductor properties. No current actually flows into the gate (in practice, there is a small current, on the order of 10^{-12} ampere). Thus, field-effect transistors consume little power and can be packed very densely on integrated circuit chips.

MOSFETs (m̲etal-o̲xide s̲emiconductor FETs) have an insulating layer of metal oxide between the gate and the rest of the transistor. They consume the least power of all kinds of transistors. (See **transistor; CMOS; integrated circuit**.)

FIFTH GENERATION COMPUTERS In 1981, Japan announced a national effort to develop a new generation of computers that manipulate data in sophisticated ways and understand human languages. This effort is called the Fifth Generation Project. During the first decade it yielded considerable progress in development of parallel computers and logic programming. (See **parallel processing; Prolog**.)

FILE A file is a block of information stored on disk, tape, or similar media. A file may contain a program, a document, or a collection of data (such as a mailing list or a set of accounting information). (See **text file; binary file; database management; record; disk**.)

FILE-PROTECT RING A file-protect ring is used to prevent the information on a magnetic tape from being accidentally overwritten or erased. Information can be stored on the tape only when the ring is in place. When the ring is removed, recording cannot take place. A similar system works for audiocassette tapes. When the tabs at the end of the tape are broken, recording becomes impossible. (See **write protect**.)

FILE SERVER A file server is a computer that provides file access for other computers through a local area network. This saves disk space because each computer no longer needs its own copy of all the software that it uses. Also, it enables separate computers to share and update a single set of files. (See **local area network; NFS.**)

FILTER See **UNIX.**

FINDER The Finder is part of the operating system of the Apple Macintosh. It allows users to copy and manipulate files by moving icons on the screen.

FINGER On many TCP/IP and UNIX networks, the "finger" command provides information about users of other machines. For example, if you type

```
finger smith@aisun1.ai.uga.edu
```

your computer will connect with AISUN1 at the University of Georgia and look for a user named Smith; if one exists, you will get that person's full name and email address, along with some other information depending on the operating system.

FIRMWARE The term *firmware* refers to software (i.e., computer programs) that are stored in some fixed form, such as a read-only memory (ROM).

FIRST-GENERATION COMPUTERS First-generation computers are the computers that were built in the late 1940s and early 1950s, using vacuum tubes.

FIXED DISK See **hard disk.**

FIXED PITCH Fixed-pitch type is type in which all letters are the same width (e.g., "I" the same width as "M"). Most typewriters, low-cost printers, and computer screens use fixed-pitch type. By contrast, see **proportional pitch**. For illustration, see **typeface.**

FIXED-POINT NUMBER A fixed-point number is a number in which the decimal point is fixed. For example, the population of a city can be represented by a fixed point number with no digits to the right of the decimal point. An amount of money in U.S. currency can be represented by a fixed point number with two digits to the right of the decimal point. By way of contrast, see **floating-point number.**

FLAME See **electronic mail**.

FLAT-FILE DATABASE A flat-file database is like a relational database except that it has only one table. (See **relational database**.)

FLIP-FLOP A flip-flop is the basic component of which computer registers are composed. A flip-flop can flip between two states called 1 and 0. Figure 27 shows how to construct a flip-flop using two NOR gates. (A NOR gate is the opposite of an OR gate.) A simple flip-flop has two inputs; the set input and the clear input. The two outputs correspond to 1 and 0. When the 1 output is at the voltage representing "1," the state of the flip-flop is 1. When the 0 output is at the "1" level, the state of the flip-flop is 0. (Both outputs cannot be at the same level at the same time, because of the way the NOR gates are connected.) The following table describes the operation of the flip-flop:

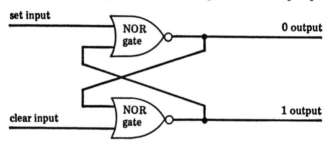

FIGURE 27 Flip-flop

Set Input	Clear Input	Old State	New State
0	0	0	0
0	0	1	1
1	0	0	1
1	0	1	1
0	1	0	0
0	1	1	0

If neither the set input nor the clear input is pulsed, the flip-flop will stay the same way it was. Figure 28 shows what will happen if the set input is at high voltage. The state of the flip-flop will become 1, regardless of its old state. If the clear input is at high voltage, the opposite will happen and the state of the flip-flop will become 0.

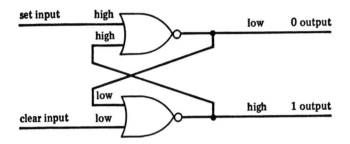

FIGURE 28

When reading information into a flip-flop (see Figure 29), you need to have a data input, telling what state you want the flip-flop to be in, and a control input, telling whether or not you want the flip-flop to pay attention to the data input. If the control input is 0, then neither the clear input nor the set input will be pulsed, so the flip-flop will stay the way it was. if the control input is 1, then the state of the flip-flop will match the state of the data input. This control structure is used to control the transfer of data between different registers. A register, such as the accumulator, is composed of a row of flip-flops.

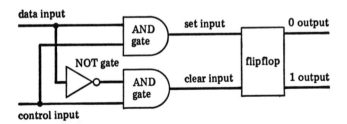

FIGURE 29

FLOATING ILLUSTRATION In desktop publishing, a floating illustration is a picture that should appear near a particular position, but need not be at a particular point in the text. For instance, the figures in this book are floating illustrations; they appear near the articles that refer to them, but not between particular words. The page-layout software places the illustrations wherever it is convenient to put them.

FLOATING-POINT NUMBER A floating-point number is a number in which the decimal point can be in any position. For instance, a memory location set aside for a floating-point number can store 0.735, 62.3, or 1200. By contrast, a fixed-point memory location can only accommodate a specific number of decimal places, usually 2 (for currency) or none (for integers).

Floating-point numbers are often written in scientific notations, such as 4.65E4, which means 4.65×10^4, or 46,500. See **real number; rounding error.**

FLOPPY DISK See diskette.

FLOWCHART A flowchart is a chart consisting of symbols and words that completely describe an algorithm (i.e., how to solve a problem). Each step in the flowchart is followed by an arrow that indicates which step to do next.

The flowchart in Figure 30 shows how to calculate the cube root of a number (a) using Newton's method. If x is the guess for the cube root of a, and δ indicates how accurate the result must be, then the procedure will follow around the loop until $|x^3 - a| < \delta$.

"Start" and "stop" statements are written with ovals; action statements are written with squares; and decision statements are written in diamonds. A decision statement asks a yes or no question. If the answer is yes, the path labeled "yes" is followed; otherwise the other path is followed.

Writing a flowchart often helps to solve a complex programming problem, although flowcharts are used less often now that structured programming has become popular. See **structured programming.**

FLUSH LEFT To align type flush left is to start each line at the same horizontal position, allowing the lengths of the lines to vary.

> This is
> an example of
> flush-left
> type

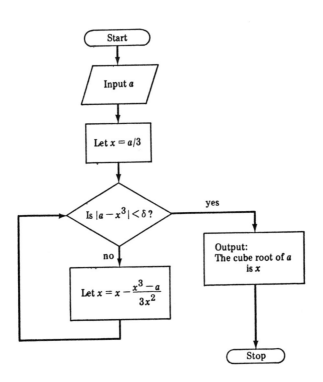

FIGURE 30

Note that the left margin is smooth and right margin is irregular ("ragged").

This is how type is ordinarily arranged on a typewriter. By contrast, see **justification; flush right**.

FLUSH RIGHT To align type flush right is to make each line end at the same horizontal position. The beginnings of the lines are not lined up.

> This is
> an example of
> flush-right
> type.

Flush-right alignment is seldom used except in charts or tables. By contrast, see **flush left; justification**.

FOLDER Subdirectories on the Macintosh are called folders. (See **directory**.)

FONT A font is a collection of characters with a consistent size and style. Most desktop publishing systems allow you to use more than one font in a single document. For example, you could have some words printed in italics and some other words printed in boldface. Figure 31 shows a sample of different fonts (including the internal fonts that come with a Hewlett-Packard LaserJet II printer). (See also **typeface; style; pitch; point; soft font; internal font; font cartridge**.)

FONT CARTRIDGE A font cartridge is a plug-in device for a laser printer or certain other printers that contains additional fonts (kinds of type) recorded on ROM chips. For contrast, see **internal font; soft font**.

FOOTPRINT The footprint of a device refers to the amount of space on a desk it takes up. A smaller footprint is desirable because it leaves more space for other items on your desk.

FOR The keyword FOR is used to identify the beginning of one kind of loop in BASIC and Pascal. (It corresponds to DO in PL/I and FORTRAN.)

A FOR loop causes a certain variable, known as the *loop variable*, to take on several values in sequence. For example, these groups of statements, in BASIC and Pascal, respectively, print out the whole numbers from 1 to 10:

FONT ID	NAME	PITCH	POINT SIZE	SYMBOL SET	PRINT SAMPLE
RIGHT FONT CARTRIDGE					
R15	SPECIAL	16.6	7	0Q	ΑΒΓΔΣεηθικ·α.;ςs҂҂:v●○◆123
R16	SPECIAL	16.6	7	1Q	θθθθ∞♣\√∫∫₂﹢☰☷☳▢\∖ ҂◆Y3τ
INTERNAL FONTS					
I00	COURIER	10	12	8U	ABCDEfghij#$@[\]^'(|)~123 ÀÂ˚ÇÑ¡¿£§êéàèëöÀØåæÄÜßÁÐÒ
I01	COURIER	10	12	10U	ABCDEfghij#$@[\]``(|)¯123 íó|¦¦¬¾¶ª╨╦╧╡▐ ╘╬╥ ╛╫█ ▌απΦ
I02	COURIER	10	12	11U	ABCDEfghij#$@[\]``(|)¯123 íó|¦¦¬¾¶ª╨╦╧╡▐ ╘╬╥ ╛╫█ ▌απΦ
I03	COURIER	10	12	0N	ABCDEfghij#$@[\]``(|)¯123 ¡¢³´¶.³»½ÁÀÈÉÍÎDÒÒ×ØÙÞàãè
I04	COURIER BOLD	10	12	8U	**ABCDEfghij#$@[\]^'(|)~123 ÀÂ˚ÇÑ¡¿£§êéàèëöÀØåæÄÜßÁÐÒ**
I05	COURIER BOLD	10	12	10U	**ABCDEfghij#$@[\]``(|)¯123 íó|¦¦¬¾¶ª╨╦╧╡▐ ╘╬╥ ╛╫█ ▌απΦ**
I06	COURIER BOLD	10	12	11U	**ABCDEfghij#$@[\]``(|)¯123 íó|¦¦¬¾¶ª╨╦╧╡▐ ╘╬╥ ╛╫█ ▌απΦ**
I07	COURIER BOLD	10	12	0N	**ABCDEfghij#$@[\]``(|)¯123 ¡¢³´¶.³»½ÁÀÈÉÍÎDÒÒ×ØÙÞàãè**
I08	LINE_PRINTER	16.6	8.5	8U	ABCDEfghij#$@[\]^'(|)~123 ÀÂ˚ÇÑ¡¿£§êéàèëöÀØåæÄÜßÁÐÒ
I09	LINE_PRINTER	16.6	8.5	10U	ABCDEfghij#$@[\]``(|)¯123 íó|¦¦¬¾¶ª╨╦╧╡▐ ╘╬╥ ╛╫█ απΦ
I10	LINE_PRINTER	16.6	8.5	11U	ABCDEfghij#$@[\]``(|)¯123 íó|¦¦¬¾¶ª╨╦╧╡▐ ╘╬╥ ╛╫█ απΦ
I11	LINE_PRINTER	16.6	8.5	0N	ABCDEfghij#$@[\]``(|)¯123 ¡¢³´¶.³»½ÁÀÈÉÍÎDÒÒ×ØÙÞàãè

FIGURE 31 Fonts on the LaserJet II Printer

```
BASIC: 10  FOR I = 1 TO 10
       20  PRINT I
       30  NEXT I
```

```
Pascal: FOR i:= 1 TO 10 DO WRITELN(i);
```

A FOR loop can be used either to obtain repetition or to make
the values of the variable available for some purpose. For example, here is how to calculate the sum of the whole numbers
from 1 to 100:

```
BASIC: 10  LET T = 0
       20  FOR I = 1 TO 100
       30  LET T = T + I
       40  NEXT I
       50  PRINT T
```

```
Pascal: PROGRAM addup (output);
        VAR i, t : INTEGER;
        BEGIN
            t := 0;
            FOR i:= 1 TO 100 DO t := t + i;
            WRITELN(t)
        end.
```

Although the statements within the loop can examine the value
of the loop variable, they should not attempt to change it, since
the result of doing so is unpredictable.

FORMAT A format is any method of arranging information that
is to be stored or displayed. The word *format* can therefore
refer to many different things relating to computers. Three of
its most common uses are as follows:

(1) The format of a disk or tape refers to how the information is stored on it. (See **disk**.)

(2) To format a disk is to make the computer record a pattern of reference marks on it. A brand-new disk must always be
formatted before it can be used. Formatting a disk erases any
information previously recorded on it.

(3) In FORTRAN, the FORMAT statement specifies the
form in which data items, especially numbers, are to be read or
written. Some examples of format items are:

I8   An integer occupying eight character positions.
F7.2   A floating point (REAL) number occupying seven
           character positions, two of which are to the right of
           the decimal point.
A40   A single string of 40 characters
40A1   Forty character strings, each containing only one
           character.
5X   Skip five blanks before printing the next item.

The following example shows how the items in a FORMAT statement are paired up with the items in the corresponding WRITE statement:

```
WRITE (6,23)   A,      B,      K
               |       |       |
               |       |       |
               |       |       |
  23   FORMAT (1X,F5.2,5X,F8.3,5X,I5)
```

The list of format items begins with 1X because, in FORTRAN, the very first character on a line of printout is not printed; it is interpreted as a code indicating whether the printer should skip a line, begin a new page, or perform some other special action. Using 1X to transmit a blank tells the printer to begin a new line in the normal manner.

FORTH The programming language FORTH was invented by Charles Moore around 1970. FORTH is noted for requiring few machine resources and giving very rapid execution.

In FORTH, the programmer defines her own statements in terms of simpler statements. FORTH is a *threaded interpretive language*, meaning that a program is represented in the computer as a list of addresses of subroutines, each of which is composed of addresses of other subroutines, and so on until the primitive operations of the language are reached. Because it has little to do except read addresses and jump to them, a FORTH interpreter can run very fast; in fact, there is little difference between an interpreter and a compiler for FORTH.

FORTH programs look very unlike programs in other languages. Most data are stored on a push-down stack (see **stack**), and some common FORTH statements include the following:

!   Store a value from the stack into a variable.
@   Push a variable onto the stack.

+   Pop two numbers off the stack, add them, and push
         the result onto the stack.
–   Subtract (similarly).
KEY   Read a character and place its ASCII value on the
         stack.
EMIT   Pop a character and display it (opposite of KEY).

Because of its stack orientation, FORTH uses Polish notation for algebraic expressions. (See **Polish notation**.) In FORTH the expression $(2 + 3) - 5$ is

    2 3 + 5 -

The following line from a FORTH program defines the statement ENCRYPT as "Read a character, subtract its ASCII code from 159, and print out the resulting character":

    :ENCRYPT 159 KEY - EMIT;

In other words, "Place 159 on the stack, read a character placing its ASCII code on the stack, perform the subtraction (removing two numbers from the stack and placing their difference on it), and print the character whose ASCII code is on top of the stack."

FORTRAN FORTRAN (formula translation), developed by IBM in the late 1950s, was the first major programming language that allowed programmers to describe calculations by means of mathematical formulas. Instead of writing assembly language instructions such as

    LOAD A
    ADD B
    MULTIPLY C
    STORE D

the FORTRAN programmer writes

    D = (A+B)*C

where * is the symbol for multiplication. Figure 32 shows a sample FORTRAN IV program.

FORTRAN has existed in several versions, of which the most important are FORTRAN IV (USASI Standard FORTRAN, 1966) and FORTRAN 77 (ANSI FORTRAN, 1977).

The layout of FORTRAN statements is illustrated by the following example:

```
C SAMPLE OF PART OF A FORTRAN PROGRAM
        WRITE (6,123) A, B, C,
       +D, E, F
   123  FORMAT(1X,6I5)
```

```
C     THIS PROGRAM READS A LIST OF NUMBERS
C     AND DETERMINES WHETHER THEY ARE PRIME.
C     THIS IS IBM 360/370 FORTRAN IV.
C
      INTEGER X, HALF, DIV
      REAL    QUOT
C
C     FORMAT STATEMENTS FOR INPUT-OUTPUT
C
 100  FORMAT(I4)
 101  FORMAT(/' ',I4,' IS NOT A NATURAL NUMBER.')
 102  FORMAT(/' ',I4,' IS DIVISIBLE BY ',I4,'.')
 103  FORMAT(/' ',I4,' IS PRIME.')
C
C     THE ALGORITHM ITSELF
C
  1   READ(5,100,END=99) X
      IF (X.GT.0) GO TO 2
      WRITE(6,101) X
      GO TO 1
C
  2   IF (X.EQ.1) GO TO 3
      DIV = 2
      QUOT = FLOAT(X)/FLOAT(DIV)
      IF (QUOT.EQ.FLOAT(INT(QUOT))) GO TO 4
C             (IN FORTRAN YOU CANNOT DO DIVISION OF INTEGERS GIVING
C              NON-INTEGER QUOTIENT, NOR COMPARE INTEGERS TO REALS,
C              WITHOUT INVOKING CONVERSION FUNCTIONS EXPLICITLY.)
C
      HALF = INT(QUOT)
      DO 10 DIV=3,HALF,2
         QUOT = FLOAT(X)/FLOAT(DIV)
         IF (QUOT.EQ.FLOAT(INT(QUOT))) GO TO 4
 10   CONTINUE
C
  3   WRITE(6,103) X
      GO TO 1
C
  4   WRITE(6,102) X,DIV
      GO TO 1
C
 99   STOP
      END
```

FIGURE 32 Sample FORTRAN IV Program

If the first column contains a C (or an asterisk in FORTRAN 77), the line is taken to be a comment, and the computer ignores it. Otherwise, the first column is blank. Columns 2 to 5 contain the statement number, if any. Ordinary statements begin column 7. If column 6 is nonblank, the line is taken to be a continuation of the statement on the preceding line.

FORTRAN variable names contain up to six letters or digits; the first character must be a letter. Variables can be declared as INTEGER, REAL (floating point), DOUBLE PRECISION (like REAL, but with more significant digits), LOGICAL (Boolean), or (in FORTRAN 77) CHARACTER. If a variable is not declared, it is assumed to be INTEGER if its name begins with I, J, K, L, M, or N, and REAL otherwise.

In FORTRAN IV, all input and output operations require references to a FORMAT statement to specify how the data are to be arranged. (See **format**.) The FORMAT statement can be located anywhere in the program and is identified by statement number. For example, the statement

```
WRITE (6,123) A, B, C
```

writes the values of A, B, and C onto device 6 (the printer) using FORMAT statement 123. The PRINT statement is equivalent to WRITE except that it always uses device 6, so that no device number need be specified; the statement

```
PRINT 123, A, B, C
```

is equivalent to the WRITE statement above. Likewise, the READ statement has two forms, one of which specifies the device number:

```
READ (5,112) A, B, C
READ 112, A, B, C
```

In FORTRAN 77, an asterisk can be used in place of the FORMAT statement number; the computer automatically chooses a format suitable for the data:

```
WRITE (6,*) A, B, C
PRINT *, A, B, C
READ (5,*) A, B, C
READ *, A, B, C
```

Comparisons are usually performed with the IF statement.

For example:

```
IF (X.EQ.Y) THEN PRINT *, 'THEY ARE EQUAL'
```

Note that the comparison is written as "X.EQ.Y," not "X = Y." In FORTRAN, an equal sign, =, always indicates assignment, that is, it means that the value of an expression is to be computed and stored in a variable. Thus, it makes sense to say things like

```
Y = Y + 1
```

which means, "Compute the value of Y + 1 and store it in Y."

FORTRAN was the first major programming language to include arrays (see **array**). In addition, portions of a FORTRAN program can consist of subroutines or functions that are compiled separately from the main program (see **compiler; linkage editor**). FORTRAN assumes blindly that each subroutine or function is being called with the right number and types of parameters.

In FORTRAN, blanks within statements are ignored unless they occur within a quoted string. Thus,

```
X       =       A   +   BI G NUM
```

is exactly equivalent to

```
X=A+BIGNUM
```

This creates occasional problems. For example, the statement

```
DO 10 I = 1,10
```

marks the beginning of a DO loop in which the variable I takes on the values 1, 2, 3, 4, . . . , 10. However, if the programmer accidentally leaves out a comma and types

```
DO 10 I = 1 10
```

the computer does not generate an error message. Instead, the compiler ignores the blanks and interprets the statement as

```
DO10I=110
```

assigning the value 110 to the variable DO10I. (Remember that variables need not be declared; the computer will not complain that this is the only place in the program where DO10I is mentioned.) An early Mariner space probe was reportedly lost because of precisely this error.

Compared to FORTRAN IV, FORTRAN 77 includes more sophisticated input-output statements, especially for file handling; the ability to process character-string data; and block-structured IF-ELSE-ENDIF statements to facilitate structured programming (see **structured programming**). All standard FORTRAN IV programs will run under FORTRAN 77, but not vice versa.

FOURTH-GENERATION COMPUTERS Fourth-generation computers are built around integrated circuits with large-scale integration. Some people view these computers as being advanced third-generation computers.

FRACTAL A fractal is a shape that contains an infinite amount of fine detail. That is, no matter how much it is enlarged, there is still more detail to be revealed by enlarging it further.

Fractals are common in nature; they are the shapes of clouds, broken rocks, the edges of torn pieces of paper, and the like. Fractals are important in generating realistic images of everyday objects on the computer.

Figure 33 shows how to construct a fractal called a Koch snowflake: start with a triangle, and repeatedly replace every straight line (___) by a bent line of the form (_∧_). The picture shows the result of doing this 0, 1, 2, and 6 times. If this were done an infinite number of times, the result would be a fractal.

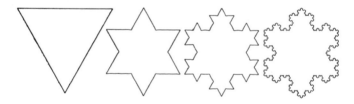

FIGURE 33 Koch Snowflake Generation

Figure 34 shows a Pascal program that can generate this pattern. Note that it uses recursion, since each part of the pattern can be generated by using even smaller repetitions of the same pattern. See **recursion**. See also **Mandelbrot set**.

```
PROGRAM triangles (INPUT,OUTPUT);
uses crt,graph;
  {This is Turbo Pascal 5.0}
VAR maxdepth,graphdriver,graphmode:INTEGER; query:CHAR;

PROCEDURE drawtriangle(x1,y1,x2,y2:REAL;depth:INTEGER);
  VAR x4,y4,x5,y5,x6,y6:REAL;
  BEGIN
    IF depth=maxdepth THEN {draw line}
        LINE(TRUNC(x1),TRUNC(y1),TRUNC(x2),TRUNC(y2));
    x4 := x1*2/3 + x2*1/3;
    y4 := y1*2/3 + y2*1/3;
    x5 := x1*1/3 + x2*2/3;
    y5 := y1*1/3 + y2*2/3;
    x6 := (x4+x5)/2 + (y4-y5)*SQRT(3)/2;
    y6 := (y4+y5)/2 + (x5-x4)*SQRT(3)/2;
    IF depth<maxdepth THEN
      BEGIN
        {here is the recursion: the procedure
           drawtriangle calls itself}
        drawtriangle(x4,y4,x6,y6,depth+1);
        drawtriangle(x6,y6,x5,y5,depth+1);
        drawtriangle(x1,y1,x4,y4,depth+1);
        drawtriangle(x5,y5,x2,y2,depth+1)
      END
  END;

BEGIN  {main block}
  WRITE('Enter how many levels of recursion:');
  READLN(maxdepth);
  graphdriver := detect;
  initgraph(graphdriver,graphmode,'');
  drawtriangle(280.0, 10,164.5,210,1);
  drawtriangle(164.5,210,395.5,210,1);
  drawtriangle(395.5,210,280.0, 10,1);
  READLN(query);
END.
```

FIGURE 34

FRAGMENTATION A disk becomes fragmented when many files are created and erased on it over a long period of time. Files are recorded contiguously on an empty disk, but as files of various sizes get erased, holes develop, which gradually become filled in with parts of newly recorded files. If the file is scattered over many widely separated sectors, access to the file is relatively slow.

A disk can be defragmented by copying all the files to another disk. Programs exist for some machines that will defragment a disk "in place" by carefully rearranging the files without copying to another disk.

FRAME GRABBER A frame grabber is an accessory that takes the image from a video camera and digitizes it, creating a bitmap image. The video image consists of "frames" (successive pictures) transmitted at the rate of 60 per second, and the frame grabber must "grab" and digitize one of these. See **bitmap; scanner.**

FRAMING ERROR A framing error occurs when an asynchronously transmitted character appears to contain the wrong number of bits. (See **asynchronous; RS-232.**) Framing errors usually result from transmitting or receiving at the wrong speed.

FREE SOFTWARE Several kinds of computer software can legally be copied and given free of charge to other users:

1. Public-domain software. This is software that is not covered by any kind of copyright. Few substantial public-domain programs exist, but the term *public domain* is often used incorrectly to refer to other kinds of free software.
2. Software that is copyrighted but is distributed free with permission of the copyright owner. One of the most famous examples is the Kermit communication program (see **Kermit**). Many UNIX utilities are also in this category.
3. Shareware. This is copyrighted software that can be distributed free to anyone, but which requests or requires a payment from satisfied users directly to the author. Shareware is often misleadingly described as "free."

FRONT END A front end is a computer or a program that helps you communicate with another computer or program. For example, supercomputers usually do not communicate with their users directly; instead users submit programs through another computer called the front end.

FTP FTP stand for File Transfer Protocol and is the name of a program that transfers files from one computer to another on the Internet and on other TCP/IP networks. (See **TCP/IP.**)

Normally, to perform an FTP file transfer, you must be authorized to use the computers at both ends, and the FTP software will prompt you for your user name and password on the remote machine. However, some computers support *anonymous* FTP, which means that certain files can be sent to anyone. To use anonymous FTP, give "anonymous" as your user name and give your Internet address in place of your password.

FRICTION FEED PRINTER A friction feed printer relies on the pressure of the platen to move the paper. This method of feeding paper is similar to that found on a typewriter. It makes it possible to use individual sheets of ordinary paper with no sprocket holes.

FULL ADDER A full adder is a logic device that accepts three inputs (two addends and a carry input) and produces two outputs; a sum output and a carry output. The table characterizes the operation of a full adder. (See **binary addition.**)

Input 1	Input 2	Carry Input	Sum Output	Carry Output
0	0	0	0	0
0	0	1	1	0
0	1	0	1	0
0	1	1	0	1
1	0	0	1	0
1	0	1	0	1
1	1	0	0	1
1	1	1	1	1

FULL DUPLEX The term *full duplex* refers to the transmission of data in two directions simultaneously. (See **half duplex; modem.**)

FULL-HEIGHT DRIVE A full-height $5\frac{1}{4}$-inch disk drive is approximately $3\frac{1}{4}$-inches high, twice the height of a half-height drive.

FULL-SCREEN TERMINAL A full-screen terminal allows you to type in characters anywhere on the display screen. By way of contrast, a line-at-a-time terminal allows you to type only at the bottom line of the display.

FULL TEXT SEARCH A full text search occurs when a computer searches through every word in a set of documents to retrieve information you are interested in. An example of a full text search system is Lexis, which is available to lawyers by modem. It allows the user to search through a wide range of legal documents, such as court decisions and law review articles. The user specifies a search target, and the system will find all documents meeting the specific condition. For example, if you are researching computer privacy, you can have the system find all documents that contain "computer" and also contain "privacy" within 25 words of the same place. This is better than searching for the specific phrase "computer privacy" (which might not occur in some documents on computer privacy) or searching for "computer" and "privacy" individually (each of which occurs in too many irrelevant documents).

Targets can also be connected with the word OR. This is most useful when the same item might be referred to more than one way, such as "Holland OR Netherlands" or "Visa OR Bankamericard."

FUNCTION A computer function is like a mathematical function: it is a set of instructions that generate a unique output value for a particular value of the independent variable (or variables). In BASIC, functions are defined using the DEF command. For example:

```
10   DEF FNR(X) = (INT(100*X + .5))/100
```

The name of the function is FNR. This function rounds a number off to the nearest hundredth. X represents the argument of the function. To use the function, type the function name followed, in parentheses, by the number you want rounded. For example, FNR(3.456) will have the value 3.46, and FRN(104.011) will have the value 104.01.

Here is an example of a simple Pascal function that doubles a number:

```
FUNCTION double(a:REAL):REAL;
  BEGIN
    double := 2*a
  END;
```

For example, double (23.4) will have the value 46.8.

Here is an example of a more complicated Pascal function that calculates the factorial of a number (see **factorial**):

```
FUNCTION fact(n:INTEGER):REAL;
VAR z :REAL; i :INTEGER;
   BEGIN
     z := 1;
     IF n>1
       THEN FOR i := 1 TO n DO
                z := z*i;
     fact := z
   END;
```

The top line tells the computer that the name of the function is "fact," the argument is of type INTEGER, and the result is of type REAL. For example, fact (6) has the value 720.

In C and LISP, all procedures are called functions, and the value returned is often ignored. See **procedure**.

FUNCTION KEYS Function keys (F keys) are keys labeled F1 through F12 on the IBM PC and PS/2 keyboards (F1 through F10 on earlier models). Their function depends on the software being run. See also **programmable-function key**.

FUZZY LOGIC Fuzzy logic is a formal system of reasoning developed by Lotfi Zadeh in which the values "true" and "false" are replaced by numbers on a scale from 0 to 1. The operators "and," "or," and the like are replaced by procedures for combining these numbers. See **boolean algebra**.

Fuzzy logic captures the fact that some questions do not have a simple yes-or-no answer. For example, in ordinary English a 6-foot-high man might or might not be described as tall. In fuzzy logic, a 6-foot man might be tall with a truth value of 0.7, and a 7-foot man might be tall with a truth value of 1.0.

A problem with fuzzy logic is that there is often no clear way to come up with the numbers that are used as truth values. For an alternative, see **default logic**.

Fuzzy logic is often used in **expert systems**. See **expert system**. See also **confidence factor**.

g ────────────────────────────────

GANTT CHART A Gantt chart is a diagram that shows the schedule for a series of tasks. (See **project manager**.)

GAS PLASMA DISPLAY A gas plasma display, which works according to the same principle as a neon light, is used for the screens for some laptop computers. Gas plasma screens are easier to read than liquid crystal display (LCD) screens. The screen uses high voltage to ionize a gas. (A "plasma" is a glowing, ionized gas.) A gas plasma display consumes more power than an LCD but less than a CRT.

GATE (1) The gate is one of the three parts of a field-effect transistor.
   (2) Several types of logic circuits are known as gates. (See **AND gate; OR gate; NOT gate**.)

GATEWAY A gateway is a link between two or more computer networks.

GB GB is an abbreviation for GigaByte, approximately one billion bytes (2^{30} = 1,073,741,824 to be precise).

GERMANIUM Germanium is a material used to make semiconductor devices. Each atom in a germanium crystal contains 32 protons and 32 electrons. Of the electrons 28 are bound tightly to the nucleus, while the outer 4 (valence) electrons can be dislodged easily. (See **semiconductor**.) Germanium is the second most popular material (after silicon) for making semiconductor devices.

GIF Graphics Interchange Format (GIF) is a format developed by CompuServe for storing bitmap images on disk. (See **bitmap; CompuServe**.) GIF images can have up to 64,000 pixels and 256 colors. For comparison, see **TIFF; PCX**.

GIGABYTE A gigabyte (GB) is approximately one billion bytes (2^{30} = 1,073,741,824 to be precise).

GLITCH A glitch is an erroneous response that occurs inside a computer because signals that are supposed to be simultaneous ~~~ally arrive at slightly different times.
   ~~ware errors are occasionally called glitches. (See **bug**.)

GLOBAL VARIABLE A global variable is a variable that can be recognized anywhere in a program. For contrast, see **local variable**.

GRAPHICAL USER INTERFACE A graphical user interface (GUI) is a way of communicating with the computer by manipulating icons (pictures) and windows with a mouse. For examples, see **Windows; Macintosh**.

GRAPHICS Computer graphics is the use of computer output devices, such as screens and plotters, to produce pictures. A plotter is a device that draws on paper, usually by moving a pen from point to point.

The application of computer graphics include the following:

1. Generating graphs and charts of mathematical data. This was the earliest use to which plotters were put.

2. CAD/CAM (<u>C</u>omputer-<u>A</u>ided <u>D</u>esign and <u>C</u>omputer-<u>A</u>ided <u>M</u>anufacturing). Using a light pen, a technician sketches the design of a piece of metalwork or a printed circuit board on the computer screen; the computer can straighten the lines, allow the technician to make changes, and then control automated factory equipment to manufacture the product.

3. Typesetting and the graphic arts. A computer can make it easy to edit a drawing by rearranging the components, changing the scale, or inserting extra space. Nowadays, drawing editors (such as MacPaint on the Apple Macintosh) are as common as word processors. Extremely elaborate computers are already being used to generate images for movie animation.

4. Education and entertainment. Graphic illustrations can enhance the value of educational computer programs, and interactive computer graphics forms the basis of all video games.

There are two basic ways to tell a computer how to draw a picture. In *vector graphics*, the computer is told to put a real or imaginary pen in a particular position and then draw a line a certain distance in a certain direction (or draw a line to another specific point). This is how most plotters work. The alternative is *raster graphics*, in which the screen or plotting area is divided into a rectangular array of points (called *pixels*, from "picture cells"), and the computer is told what color each dot should be. This is the usual technique for plotting on the screen of a microcomputer; many dot matrix printers also support it. Many computers allow the programmer to give vector-style instructions even when plotting on raster devices (e.g., all the graphics commands in the language LOGO are based on the vector concept).

The amount of fine detail that a particular graphics device can show is called the *resolution*. For vector devices, the resolution is usually given as a fraction of an inch or millimeter; for raster devices, it is given as the number of pixels in the array. For example, a 640-by-400 array of pixels will contain as much detail as the average monitor screen can reproduce; a 320-by-200 array is quite adequate for most home computers. (See also **three-dimensional graphics; resolution; video modes; IBM PC.**)

GRAPHICS CARD A graphics card is a video card that can display graphics as well as text. (See **video card.**)

GREEKING Greeking is the use of random letters or marks to show the overall appearance of a printed page without showing the actual text. With computers, greeking is used when the page is displayed too small for the text to be readable on the screen.

GREP In UNIX, the "grep" command reads a text file and outputs all the lines that contain a particular series of characters. For example, the command

```
grep abc myfile
```

reads the file *myfile* and outputs every line that contains "abc."

Instead of specifying the exact characters to be searched for, you can give a regular expression that defines them. For example,

```
grep [bB]ill myfile
```

outputs all lines that contain either "bill" or "Bill." See **regular expression; UNIX.**

The origin of the word "grep" is disputed, but it may be an acronym for "Generalized Regular Expression Parser." Grep programs have been written for other operating systems, such as MS-DOS.

GRID In various draw programs and paint programs, a grid is a feature that allows lines to be drawn only in certain positions, as if they were drawn on the lines of graph paper. The grid makes it much easier to draw parallel and perpendicular lines, lay out diagrams, and avoid irregular breaks. However, when the grid is turned on, there are positions in which you cannot draw. (See also **draw program; paint program.**)

GRID SYSTEM The grid system is a way of standardizing the layout of many related pages, such as the pages of a multi-page document. The designer first draws a grid that will define the possible positions of columns, horizontal divisions, and pictures. Not all the possibilities of the grid are used on any single page, but the grid ensures that column positions do not vary haphazardly, and thereby makes the pages look related.

GROUNDING In any electrical device, "ground level" is the voltage level to which all other voltages are compared. In most computers, the ground level is connected to the ground pin (the third, rounded pin) of the power plug, and the power line then connects it to the earth itself, thereby assuring that the ground level for all machines is the same. This helps prevent cables from picking up noise or emitting radio frequency interference. It also reduces the danger of damage from lightning. (See **power line protection; RFI protection.**)

GUI See **graphical user interface.**

GW-BASIC Microsoft GW-BASIC is an interpreter for the same dialect of BASIC as is implemented in ROM on the IBM PC. However, GW-BASIC runs on machines that need not contain the IBM ROM chip. (For contrast, see **BASICA.**)

h_____

HACKER The word *hacker* means at least three things in relation
to computer programming: (1) an exceptionally skilled computer programmer; (2) a person who programs computers for
recreation or as a hobby; (3) a person who "breaks into" computers without authorization, either for malicious reasons or
just to prove it can be done. (See **computer security**.)

HALF ADDER A half adder is a logic circuit that accepts two inputs and produces two outputs, as shown in the table.

Input 1	Input 2	Sum Output	Carry Output
0	0	0	0
0	1	1	0
1	0	1	0
1	1	0	1

(See **binary addition**.)

HALF DUPLEX The term *half duplex* refers to the transmission
of data in only one direction at a time. (See **full duplex;
modem**.)

HALF-HEIGHT DRIVE A half-height 5 $\frac{1}{4}$-inch disk drive is approximately 1 $\frac{5}{8}$-inches high, half the height of a full-height
drive.

HANDSHAKING The term *handshaking* refers to the exchange
of signals between two computers to indicate that data transmission is proceeding successfully. For examples, see **X-OFF,
X-ON** and **XMODEM**.

HARD CARD A hard card is a type of hard disk that is built into
a card that can be plugged into a slot inside the computer.

HARD COPY A hard copy is a printout on paper of computer
output.

HARD DISK A hard disk is a storage medium using rigid aluminum disks coated with iron oxide. Hard disks have much
greater storage capacity than do diskettes. Originally, 10
megabytes was a common size for microcomputer hard disks.
More recently, 120-megabyte hard disks have become common,
and even larger sizes are available. The read-write head travels
across the disk on a thin cushion of air without ever actually

touching the disk. However, hard disks have the disadvantage that they are built into the machine and cannot be removed, as can diskettes. Hard disks are also called *winchester disks*. (See **disk; diskette; hard-disk management**.) For information on the interface between the hard disk and the computer, see **ST-506; IDE; ESDI; SCSI**.

HARD-DISK MANAGEMENT Here are some tips for using a hard disk effectively:

1. Learn how to back up your hard disk, and do it frequently. *Every hard disk in use today WILL break down within just a few years!*
2. Divide the disk into subdirectories (see **directory**) and put related files in each subdirectory (e.g., all word processing files in one directory and all spreadsheet files in another). Use a further level of subdirectories where appropriate, e.g., to separate letters from reports within the word processing directory.
3. Use the MS-DOS PATH command or its equivalent so that commonly used commands will work no matter what directory you are in. You can put the PATH command in your AUTOEXEC.BAT file.
4. In MS-DOS, use the command

   `PROMPT $P$G`

   so that the command prompt will tell you what directory you are in (e.g., "C:\MYDIR>" rather than just "C>"). Again, this command can be in your AUTOEXEC.BAT file.
5. Delete files that you no longer need. Make a directory called \JUNK in which to put files that will not be needed for very long, so that they will not clutter up other directories.
6. Periodically run CHKDSK or its equivalent to check for lost clusters. (See **cluster**.)
7. If possible, run a defragmentation program every few months, or eliminate fragmentation by backing up the whole disk, erasing all files, and restoring all files from the backup. (See **fragmentation**.)

HARDWARE The hardware in a computer system consists of all the physical elements in the computer, such as integrated circuits, wires, and terminals. For contrast, see **software**.

HARDWARE INTERRUPT See **interrupt**.

HASHING Hashing refers to a storage mechanism where data items are stored at locations that are determined by a mathematical function of the data. For example, suppose you need to store a list of 100 numbers in memory locations whose addresses run from 1 to 100. One example of a hashing function is to calculate the remainder when the number is divided by 100 and then to store it at that location. For example, the number 538 would be stored at memory location 38. The use of hashing makes it possible to store and retrieve the data items quickly, since it is not necessary to search through the list in order to find the item. However, there is one complication: A hashing function will sometimes assign more than one data item to the same address. For example, using the rule given above, the number 638 would also be stored in location 38. To avoid that problem, a hashing system needs to be able to resolve collisions by storing the new data item in a separate place.

HAT The character "^" is sometimes called a hat.

HAYES COMPATIBILITY A modem is Hayes compatible if it responds to the same set of auto-dialing commands as the Hayes Smartmodem (made by Hayes Microcomputer Products, Inc., Norcross, Georgia).

Two modems need not be Hayes compatible in order to communicate with each other. Hayes compatibility refers only to the commands used by the computer to control the modem. A sampling of such commands is given in Table 7.

Table 7 Examples of Hayes Modem Dialing Commands

ATDT9W555-1212	Dial 9, wait for another dial tone, and dial 555-1212 (using tone dialing).
ATDP9W555-1212	Same, but use pulse dialing.
ATH0	Hang up.
ATA	Answer an incoming call (right now) with modem.
ATO	Resume communicating (use this after you have typed "+++" to issue commands in the middle of a session). Note that this command uses the Letter O, not the digit 0.
ATS0=1	Answer when the phone rings.

The modem accepts commands whenever it is not connected via phone lines to another modem. To set the modem baud rate, simply start sending commands at the baud rate you desire. To send a command to the modem while communicating to another computer, stop typing for 1 second, type "+++" (without quotes), and again stop typing for about a second. The modem will respond "OK," and you are free to give a command.

Table 8 gives the DIP switch settings for the Hayes Smartmodem 1200. Other modems use similar settings. (See also **modem; RS-232.**)

Table 8 Examples of Configuration-Changing Commands for Hayes Smartmodem 2400

AT&F	Reset modem to factory default configuration
AT&W	Store current configuration in nonvolatile RAM
ATZ	Reset modem to stored configuration
	(Also done when modem is turned on)
ATB0	At 1200 baud, use V.22 protocol (Europe)
ATB1	At 1200 baud, use Bell 212A protocol (U.S.A.)
ATE0	Do not echo (display) commands typed to modem
ATE1	Echo commands
ATL1	Speaker volume low
ATL3	Speaker volume high (also ATL2 in between)
ATM0	Speaker always off
ATM1	Speaker on during dialing, until connected
ATM2	Speaker always on
AT&C0	CD (carrier detect signal) always on
	(Necessary to allow some communication programs to send commands to the modem)
AT&C1	CD on only when connection is present
AT&D0	Modem ignores DTR signal from computer
AT&D2	Modem hangs up when DTR signal turns off
	(e.g., upon exiting from communication program)
AT&D3	Modem hangs up and resets (like ATZ) when DTR turns off

HEAD The head is the part of a disk drive that reads and writes information. A double-sided disk drive or multilayer hard disk has a head for each side of each layer. (See **disk.**)

HELP Many computer programs contain an on-screen help facility that a user can turn to when questions arise. For example, if you have forgotten how a particular command works, you may consult a help facility (if one is available) to refresh your memory. Different programs use different methods for obtaining help. For example, typing the F1 key will bring help if you are using Lotus 1-2-3. (See also **documentation; context-sensitive help.**)

HELVETICA See **typeface.**

HERCULES GRAPHICS CARD The Hercules Graphics Card (HGC) provides all of the functions of the IBM Monochrome Display Adapter (MDA) with the same type of monitor, plus a high-resolution graphics mode. The Hercules Graphics Card is not an IBM product, and its graphics mode is not the same as that of any IBM product. (See **video modes [IBM PC].**)

HEURISITIC The word *heuristic* refers to a method of solving problems that involves intelligent trial and error. By contrast, an algorithmic solution method is a clearly specified procedure that is guaranteed to give the correct answer. (See algorithm.) For example, there is no known algorithm that tells how to play a perfect game of chess, so computer chess-playing programs must use a heuristic method of solution.

HEWLETT-PACKARD Hewlett-Packard, located in Palo Alto, California, makes a wide variety of electronics instruments and calculators, as well as microcomputers, workstations, and the LaserJet series of laser printers (see **LaserJet**).

HEXADECIMAL A hexadecimal number is a number written in base-16. A hexadecimal system consists of 16 possible digits, labeled by 0, 1, 2, 3, 4, 5, 6, 7, 8, 9, A (= 10), B (= 11), C (= 12), D (= 13), E (= 14), and F (= 15). For example, the number A4C2 in hexadecimal means

$$10 \times 16^3 + 4 \times 16^2 + 12 \times 16^1 + 2 \times 16^0 = 42{,}178$$

Hexadecimal numbers provide a good shorthand way of representing binary numbers, since binary numbers can be converted to hexadecimal numbers by looking at only four digits at a time. For example, binary 1 1 1 1 equals hexadecimal F, binary 0 1 0 0 equals hexadecimal 4, and binary 1 1 1 1 0 1 0 0 equals hexadecimal F4:

$$\underbrace{1\ 1\ 1\ 1}_{F} \qquad \underbrace{0\ 1\ 0\ 0}_{4}$$

When converting a binary number to hexadecimal by this method, start by adding zeros at the left to make the number of digits a multiple of 4.

Table 9 shows the hexadecimal equivalents of the four-digit binary numbers, and Table 10 shows the decimal equivalents of the hexadecimal numbers from 00 to FF.

TABLE 9 Hexadecimal Equivalents of Binary Numbers

Binary	Hexadecimal	Binary	Hexadecimal
0000	0	1000	8
0001	1	1001	9
0010	2	1010	A
0011	3	1011	B
0100	4	1100	C
0101	5	1101	D
0110	6	1110	E
0111	7	1111	F

TABLE 10 Decimal Equivalents of Hexadecimal Numbers

00 = 0	20 = 32	40 = 64	60 = 96	80 = 128	A0 = 160	C0 = 192	E0 = 224
01 = 1	21 = 33	41 = 65	61 = 97	81 = 129	A1 = 161	C1 = 193	E1 = 225
02 = 2	22 = 34	42 = 66	62 = 98	82 = 130	A2 = 162	C2 = 194	E2 = 226
03 = 3	23 = 35	43 = 67	63 = 99	83 = 131	A3 = 163	C3 = 195	E3 = 227
04 = 4	24 = 36	44 = 68	64 = 100	84 = 132	A4 = 164	C4 = 196	E4 = 228
05 = 5	25 = 37	45 = 69	65 = 101	85 = 133	A5 = 165	C5 = 197	E5 = 229
06 = 6	26 = 38	46 = 70	66 = 102	86 = 134	A6 = 166	C6 = 198	E6 = 230
07 = 7	27 = 39	47 = 71	67 = 103	87 = 135	A7 = 167	C7 = 199	E7 = 231
08 = 8	28 = 40	48 = 72	68 = 104	88 = 136	A8 = 168	C8 = 200	E8 = 232
09 = 9	29 = 41	49 = 73	69 = 105	89 = 137	A9 = 169	C9 = 201	E9 = 233
0A = 10	2A = 42	4A = 74	6A = 106	8A = 138	AA = 170	CA = 202	EA = 234
0B = 11	2B = 43	4B = 75	6B = 107	8B = 139	AB = 171	CB = 203	EB = 235
0C = 12	2C = 44	4C = 76	6C = 108	8C = 140	AC = 172	CC = 204	EC = 236
0D = 13	2D = 45	4D = 77	6D = 109	8D = 141	AD = 173	CD = 205	ED = 237
0E = 14	2E = 46	4E = 78	6E = 110	8E = 142	AE = 174	CE = 206	EE = 238
0F = 15	2F = 47	4F = 79	6F = 111	8F = 143	AF = 175	CF = 207	EF = 239
10 = 16	30 = 48	50 = 80	70 = 112	90 = 144	B0 = 176	D0 = 208	F0 = 240
11 = 17	31 = 49	51 = 81	71 = 113	91 = 145	B1 = 177	D1 = 209	F1 = 241
12 = 18	32 = 50	52 = 82	72 = 114	92 = 146	B2 = 178	D2 = 210	F2 = 242
13 = 19	33 = 51	53 = 83	73 = 115	93 = 147	B3 = 179	D3 = 211	F3 = 243
14 = 20	34 = 52	54 = 84	74 = 116	94 = 148	B4 = 180	D4 = 212	F4 = 244
15 = 21	35 = 53	55 = 85	75 = 117	95 = 149	B5 = 181	D5 = 213	F5 = 245
16 = 22	36 = 54	56 = 86	76 = 118	96 = 150	B6 = 182	D6 = 214	F6 = 246
17 = 23	37 = 55	57 = 87	77 = 119	97 = 151	B7 = 183	D7 = 215	F7 = 247
18 = 24	38 = 56	58 = 88	78 = 120	98 = 152	B8 = 184	D8 = 216	F8 = 248
19 = 25	39 = 57	59 = 89	79 = 121	99 = 153	B9 = 185	D9 = 217	F9 = 249
1A = 26	3A = 58	5A = 90	7A = 122	9A = 154	BA = 186	DA = 218	FA = 250
1B = 27	3B = 59	5B = 91	7B = 123	9B = 155	BB = 187	DB = 219	FB = 251
1C = 28	3C = 60	5C = 92	7C = 124	9C = 156	BC = 188	DC = 220	FC = 252
1D = 29	3D = 61	5D = 93	7D = 125	9D = 157	BD = 189	DD = 221	FD = 253
1E = 30	3E = 62	5E = 94	7E = 126	9E = 158	BE = 190	DE = 222	FE = 254
1F = 31	3F = 63	5F = 95	7F = 127	9F = 159	BF = 191	DF = 223	FF = 255

HIDDEN FILES In MS-DOS (PC-DOS), hidden files are files that are not listed by the DIR command and are invisible to some programs.

Any boot disk has two hidden files on it, named either IBM-BIO.SYS and IBMDOS.SYS, or IO.SYS and MSDOS.SYS. These files are hidden so that they will not be copied or moved; DOS relies on their being in a specific position on the disk when the machine boots up.

Other programs occasionally use hidden files to implement copy protection.

The COPY and XCOPY commands do not copy hidden files, but the DISKCOPY command duplicates an entire disk, hidden files and all.

HIERARCHICAL Data items have a hierarchical arrangement if a data item can be regarded as "below," or "belonging to," another data item that is at a higher level. At the very top level of the hierarchy is a data item (called the root) that is not below any other items. Hierarchical data items can be thought of as an inverted tree, with the root at the top and other locations (called nodes) branching out below. Hierarchical data structures are common both in ordinary life and when dealing with computers. For example, the executive branch of the U.S. government can be thought of as a hierarchy with the president at the top, cabinet secretaries one level down, and various bureau and office directors and their staffs below the secretaries.

The Lotus 1-2-3 menu structure is arranged hierarchically. If you are in the READY mode, then pressing the / key puts you at the top of the menu tree, with several possible choices you may branch to. If you choose the Range command, you will be presented with a new set of choices that are subcommands of the Range command. If you now choose the Name command, then you will see a new list of subcommands. This part of the command structure can be illustrated as a tree like this:

Worksheet Range Copy Move File Print Graph Data Quit

Format Label-Prefix Erase Name Justify Protect Unprotect Input

Create Delete Labels Reset

For other examples of hierarchical data structures, see **directory; outline; tree.**

HIERARCHICAL FILE SYSTEM The Hierarchical File System is a feature that gives the Macintosh the ability to store files in subdirectories (called *folders*). (See **directory.**)

HIGH DENSITY A high-density diskette records considerably more data per inch than the earlier double-density format. See **disk.**

HIGH-LEVEL LANGUAGE A high-level language is a computer programming language designed to allow people to write programs without having to understand the inner workings of the computer. BASIC, PL/I, FORTRAN, and Pascal are examples of high-level languages. A machine language is at the lowest level, since machine language programming requires detailed knowledge of the computer's inner workings. An assembly language is at a slightly higher level than a machine language.

HIRAGANA See **kana.**

HOLE A hole is a place where an electron is missing from the crystal structure of a P-type semiconductor. A hole acts as a moving positive charge. (See **semiconductor.**)

HOST COMPUTER The host computer is the computer that is in charge of the operations of a group of computers linked in a network.

HOT LINK See **DDE.**

HOURGLASS ICON In Microsoft Windows, the pointer turns into an hourglass when the user needs to wait until the computer has completed an operation. See also **watch icon.**

HYPERCARD Hypercard is a program for data management for the Apple Macintosh. Information is arranged in stacks, which consist of collections of cards. When an individual card is displayed on the screen, the parts of the card will be visible. Each card can contain fields (which contain text), graphics, or buttons. Parts of the card are common to all cards in the stack; other parts of the card are unique to each individual card. A button will appear on the screen as a picture or text that indicates what the button will do. If a button is pressed (by using the mouse), then a specific action will occur, which may involve moving to another card in the same stack or moving to a different stack. In this way it is possible for the data items in HyperCard to be connected to each other. Users of HyperCard may work with stacks obtained from data sources, or users may author their own stacks. For example, HyperCard might be used to keep track of the organization chart for a company. Buttons could be used to move up or down the hierarchy. See also **hypertext**.

HYPERDOCUMENT See **hypertext**.

HYPERTEXT A hypertext document (or hyperdocument) presents information that can be connected together in many different ways, instead of simply sequentially as is done in a book. A hypertext document will typically present a computer screen with information (text, graphics, and/or sound). The user then will have different options as to what related screen to go to next; typically, options are selected by a mouse. Encyclopedia information is especially suitable for hypertext presentation. If this book were in the form of hypertext, then each entry would represent a screen of information; each cross-reference would be a button that you could select if you wished to immediately move to that entry.

The help file that gives information about how to use a piece of software is also suitable for hypertext. The computer user does not need to read the help file information sequentially; instead, the user needs to choose whatever information is helpful at the moment.

There is a danger that the user might become lost in the middle of a hyperdocument. A good hyperdocument should include some form of navigational aid that allows the user to see an overview of the document. Also, it would be helpful if the computer maintains a record of the path that has been followed, both so the user can go backwards and so it is possible to retrace the same path at a future date if so desired. Often a hyperdocument follows a particular sequence automatically if the user does not want to make all of the choices individually.

Hyperdocuments can be difficult to create because of the need to establish all of the connections. Hypercard for the Macintosh is one hypertext-authoring software that has become popular.

A large hyperdocument (an encyclopedia, for example) requires large amounts of storage such as provided by a CD-ROM.

i _____

IBM IBM (International Business Machines) is the industry's largest computer manufacturer. IBM makes other office equipment as well as computers, which it started manufacturing in the 1950s. A decade later, IBM controlled about 80 percent of the computer market with models such as the IBM 360 computer. The company continues to make popular mainframe computers, such as the 390 series. In 1981 IBM introduced the IBM PC, which quickly became one of the most popular microcomputers. Now many other companies produce software or peripherals designed to be used with the IBM PC, and several companies produce computers designed to run the same programs as the IBM PC. In 1987 IBM introduced the PS/2 line of microcomputers, and in 1988 it introduced the AS line of minicomputers. The headquarters of IBM is in Armonk, New York.

IBM 3270 Terminals in the IBM 3270 series are commonly used with IBM mainframe computers. They use the EBCDIC character set. An unusual aspect of 3270 series terminals is that most of the user's interaction is with a terminal cluster controller rather than with the computer itself. The cluster controller maintains the contents of the screen, and when the user presses Enter, the whole screen is sent to the computer.
  See also **IBM 7171**.

IBM 7171 The IBM 7171 communications controller allows ASCII terminals such as the VT-100 (or personal computers emulating ASCII terminals) to take the place of IBM 3270 EBCDIC terminals. The 7171 performs ASCII-to-EBCDIC translation and takes the place of the 3270 cluster controller.

IBM PC, PS/1, AND PS/2 The IBM Personal Computer (PC), introduced in 1981, was the first of a family of very popular microcomputers, including not only IBM products but also "clones" (imitations) made by other companies. The original IBM PC used very little proprietary technology, and it was easy to build compatible machines without violating patents. (See **clone; PC compatibility**.)
  IBM has maintained a high level of "upward compatibility" within the PC, PS/1 and PS/2 line. This means that later-model

machines in this line will run virtually all software written for earlier models.

IBM's two original machines, the PC and PC XT, are virtually identical, featuring 4.77-MHz 8088 microprocessors with an 8-bit bus. The XT had a 10-megabyte hard disk.

The PC AT, introduced in 1984, was the first machine to use the 80286 microprocessor, enabling programs to run much faster. The PC AT had what is now known as the ISA (industry standard architecture) bus; it accepted both 8-bit (PC-style) and 16-bit plug-in cards.

The PS/2 machines were introduced in 1987. They are much more compact than comparably configured PCs or ATs, and all but the lowest models use the Micro Channel bus, which will make it possible in the future to use more than one CPU in a single machine. Unlike the PC, XT, and AT, the PS/2 machines have built-in video adapters.

In 1990, IBM introduced the PS/1 as a low-priced, self-contained, ready-to-run home computer, which was sold complete with software.

All the computers in the PC, PS/1, and PS/2 line can run appropriate versions of DOS (PC-DOS, also known as MS-DOS). Those with 80286, 80386, or 80486 microprocessors can also run Microsoft Windows and OS/2. See **MS-DOS; microprocessor; Windows; OS/2.** Table 11 shows the types of diskettes used by these machines.

These computers use the ASCII character set (see ASCII). In addition, they define printed representations for all character codes from 0 to 255, even those that are not defined by the ASCII standard. Some of these characters can never be printed because they are equivalent to codes such as Return or Line Feed.

Figure 35 shows special characters that can be printed on most IBM printers, along with their numeric codes. These characters are typed by holding down the Alt key and typing the appropriate number on the numeric keypad at the right side of the keyboard. For example, to type a shaded block, hold down Alt, type 178, and then release Alt.

An unusual characteristic of all IBM PCs, ATs, PS/1s, and PS/2s, but not of clones, is that if the machine is unable to load an operating system from disk, it calls up a BASIC interpreter that is stored on a ROM chip. This BASIC interpreter ("Cassette

Table 11 IBM PC Family Diskette Formats

Size	Capacity	Used by
5¼" single-sided double-density	160K	Earliest PCs (DOS 1.0)
5¼" single-sided double-density	360K	Most PCs
5¼" single-sided	1.2MB	PC AT, XT 286 (These drives can also read, write, and format conventional double-density disks. There is a small chance that after being written on by a high-density drive, such a disk will not be readable in a double-density drive.)
3½" conventional	720K	PS/2 25 and 30
3½" high density	1.4 MB	PS/2 50 and up (Can also read, write, and format 3½" conventional diskettes)

á	160	é	130	í	161	ó	162	ú	163
à	133	è	138	ì	141	ò	149	ù	151
â	131	ê	136	î	140	ô	147	û	150
ä	132	ë	137	ï	139	ö	148	ü	129
å	134	É	144			ö	153	Ü	154
Ä	142			æ	145				
Å	143			Æ	146			ÿ	152

ç	135	¢	155	α	224	Ω	234	∫	244
Ç	128	£	156	β	225	δ	235		245
ñ	164	¥	157	Γ	226	∞	236	÷	246
Ñ	165	₧	158	π	227	φ	237	≈	247
		ƒ	159	Σ	228	ε	238	°	248
¿	168			σ	229	∩	239	·	249
¡	173	⌐	166	μ	230	≡	240	·	250
«	174	⌐	167	τ	231	±	241	√	251
»	175	¬	169	Φ	232	≥	242	η	252
		¬	170	Θ	233	≤	243	²	253

218	⌐	191	201	⌐	187	213	⌐	184
192		217	200		188	212		190
214	⌐	183	220	⌐	220	■ 219		▒ 177
211		189	221		222			
			223		223	▓ 178		176

│	179	┤	180	║	186	╢	185	╫ 215
─	196	├	195	=	205	╞	204	
┼	197	┴	194	╬	206	╥	203	╪ 216
		┬	193			╨	202	

FIGURE 35 IBM PC Special Characters, Grouped by Function

BASIC") was originally implemented so that low-budget computer hobbyists could use IBM PCs without disk drives, storing their programs on cassette tape. The same ROM code was included in later machines because it is used by the BASIC interpreter that runs under DOS. (See **BASICA; GWBASIC.**)

IBM RS/6000 See **workstation.**

IC See **integrated circuit.**

ICON An icon on a computer screen is a picture that represents a particular object, command file, or group of files. For example, on a Macintosh computer, the picture of a trash can stands for "delete." Use the mouse to move a file to the trash can, and it will be deleted. (See **mouse; Windows.**)

IDE An IDE (integrated device electronics) hard disk is one that has most of the controller circuitry built into it, to save space. IDE controllers are functionally similar to the older ST-506 standard. See **ST-506; ESDI; SCSI.**

IDENTIFIER An identifier is a symbolic name used in a program and defined by the programmer. Most identifiers stand for variables (see **variable**); however, some languages allow the use of identifiers to represent constants, so that the value of a particular constant, wherever it occurs in the program, can be changed by changing the statement that defines the identifier. (See **constant.**)

IF In many programming languages the keyword IF is used to specify an action that is to be executed only if a specified condition is true. Here is an example of an IF statement in BASIC:

```
100  PRINT "INPUT PRICE"
110  INPUT P
120  IF P< 0 THEN PRINT "PRICE CAN'T BE < 0!":
     GOTO 100
```

If the condition "P<0" is true, then the two commands:

```
PRINT "PRICE CAN'T BE < 0!"
GOTO 100
```

will be executed.

Here is an example of an IF command in Pascal:

```
IF hours <= 40
    THEN BEGIN
        pay := hours * wage;
        WRITELN('No overtime hours')
    END
ELSE BEGIN
        pay := wage * 40 + 1.5 * wage * (hours - 40);
        WRITELN('Overtime wages paid')
    END;
```

If the condition "hours $<=40$" is true, then the two statements between the first BEGIN/END pair will be executed. If the condition is false, then the two statements between the BEGIN/END pair following the word ELSE will be executed.

IMPEDANCE The impedance of an electrical circuit is a measure of how easily an alternating current can pass through it. The impedance of a resistor is the same as its resistance. Capacitors and inductors also affect impedance.

The characteristic impedance of coaxial cable results from the interaction of its inductance and capacitance. It is not a resistance and cannot be measured with an ohmmeter. (See **coaxial cable**.)

INCREMENTAL BACKUP An incremental backup is one that only copies files that have not already been backed up. (See **backup**.)

INCREMENTAL COMPILER An incremental compiler compiles the lines of a program as they are typed into the computer, rather than compiling the whole program at once. (See **compiler**.)

INDEXED FILE In an indexed file, the order of the items is recorded in a separate file called the *index*. For example, if the computer is looking for John Smith's billing records, it would first look up "Smith, John" in the index, and then the index would tell it where to look in the billing record file.

Indexed files have two advantages. First, the index can be sorted (alphabetized) without moving the contents of the main file. This saves time because the index is much smaller. Second, it is possible to maintain multiple indexes to the same file—for example, to index by name and also by account number, ZIP code, or date.

INDUSTRY STANDARD ARCHITECTURE See **ISA**.

INFERENCE ENGINE See **expert system**.

INFORMATION HIDING See **structured programming**.

INHERITANCE In object-oriented programming, one object type is said to *inherit* from another if the second type is defined to be the same as the first type except for components that are specified to be different. See **object-oriented programming**.

INK JET PRINTER An ink jet printer forms characters by firing tiny dots of ink at the paper. Advantages include speed, high resolution, and silence. An ink jet printer is often an economical alternative to a laser printer. The Hewlett-Packard DeskJet is a popular monochrome printer and the PaintJet is a color ink jet printer.

INPUT The input to a computer is the data that are fed into the computer for it to process. (Note that the terms *input* and *output* are always used from the computer's point of view.) The input data may be either numbers or character strings (e.g., a list of names). The computer receives input through an input device, such as a keyboard, or from a storage device, such as a disk drive.

INSERTION POINT The insertion point in a full-screen editor or drawing program is the place where characters will appear if you start typing. The insertion point is usually indicated with a cursor or a thin vertical bar.

INSERTION SORT The insertion sort algorithm is a way of placing the elements of an array in ascending or descending order. This method is efficient if the list is already close to being in order. Suppose we wish to sort the following list of numbers:

2404   8653   1354   5781

To perform an insertion sort, we examine every item in the list except the first. Whenever we find an item whose immediate neighbor on the left should be to the right of it, we pick up the current item, shift its neighbor on the left one space to the right, and see whether we can put the current item in the space thus vacated. If not, we shift that item to the right and try again. Here is an example, using ascending order:

Step 1.   Examine 8653. Its neighbor on the left is 2404, which should indeed be to the left of 8653, so all is well; proceed to the next item.

Step 2.   Examine 1354. Its neighbor on the left is 8653, which should be to the right of it. Pick up 1354:

                    2404   8653   5781

Shift 8653 one space to the right:

                    2404   8653   5781

Can 1354 be put into the empty space? No; its neighbor on the left would be 2404, a larger number. Therefore we shift 2404 one space to the right:

                      2404   8653   5781

Now we can put 1354 into the empty space:

                    1354   2404   8653   5781

Step 3.   Examine 5781. Its neighbor on the left, 8653, should be to the right of it. We pick up 8653 and shift it one space to the right then put 5781 into the empty space:

                    1354   2404   8653   ....
                    1354   2404   8653
                    1354   2404   5781   8653

Now all the elements are in order, and the process is complete. Here is a Pascal program to perform an insertion sort:

```
PROGRAM insertionsort;

VAR
  a: ARRAY [1..10] OF INTEGER;
  i, value, position: INTEGER;

BEGIN
  { Read in the data }
    FOR i := 1 TO 10 DO
```

FIGURE 36

FIGURE 36 Continued

```
      BEGIN
        write('Enter item ',i:2,':');
        readln(a[i])
      END;

{ Perform the insertion sort }
  FOR i := 2 TO 10 DO
    BEGIN
      value := a[i];
      position := i;
      WHILE (position > 1) AND
            (a[position-1] > value) DO
        BEGIN
          a[position] := a[position-1];
          position := position-1
        END;
      a[position] := value
    END;

{ Print the results }
  FOR i := 1 TO 10 DO write(a[i]:5);
  writeln
END.
```

INSTANCE VARIABLES In object-oriented programming, the instance variables are the variables (fields) that contain data unique to each object. See **object-oriented programming**.

INTEGER An integer is a whole number or the negative of a whole number, such as 1, 2, 3, 0 , −10, −26, 157, 567, or −2,397. An integer does not contain a fractional part.

INTEGRATED CIRCUIT An integrated circuit is an electronic device consisting of many miniature transistors and other circuit elements on a single silicon chip. The first integrated circuits were developed in the late 1950s, and since then there has been continued improvement. The number of components that can be placed on a single chip has been steadily rising.

The advantages of integrated circuits include the fact that they are very small (less than $1/4$ inch square), their internal connections are more reliable, they consume much less power, they generate much less heat, and they cost less than similar circuits made with separate components.

Integrated circuits are classified by their level of complexity. "Small-scale integration" refers to circuits containing fewer than 10 logic gates; "medium-scale integration," to circuits containing 10 to 100 gates; and "large-scale integration," to circuits with more than 100 gates.

The pattern of components to be placed in an integrated circuit is first mapped out by a computer. It is necessary to add impurities to the silicon-crystal to create either P-type or N-type regions. (See **semiconductor**.) An evaporated metal is engraved on the circuit by photographic techniques in the places where electrical conducting paths are needed. Integrated circuits are mass produced by making many identical circuits at the same time from a single wafer of silicon. Each circuit must be individually tested, however, because a single defect in the crystal can completely ruin the circuit.

The ultimate integrated circuit is the microprocessor, which is a single chip that contains the complete arithmetic and logic unit of a computer.

INTEL Intel Corporation produces many of the microprocessors that are used in microcomputers such as the 8088, 80286, 80386, and 80486. See **microprocessor**. Intel developed the first microprocessors (4004, 8008) and the microprocessor for which CP/M was developed (the 8080, soon superseded by Zilog's Z80). The company is headquartered in Santa Clara, California.

INTERACTIVE SYSTEM In an interactive computer system the user communicates with the computer through a keyboard and a CRT screen. The computer presents the results almost immediately after an instruction has been entered, and the user can type in new instructions after seeing the results of the previous ones. See, for contrast, **batch processing**.

INTERBLOCK GAP An interblock gap is a blank space on a magnetic tape between two adjacent blocks. The presence of the gap makes it easier to keep track of the locations of the blocks when the tape is started and stopped.

INTERLACING A video display is said to be interlaced if the CRT scans all the odd-numbered rows first, then all the even-numbered rows, or vice versa. This is supposed to reduce flicker because the whole screen is scanned twice as often as it would be if the rows were scanned in order.

In practice, interlacing reduces flicker only if adjacent rows are similar so that they can blend together. Thus interlacing works well with an ordinary TV picture but not so well on a computer screen, where a horizontal line, for example, might occupy only one row. With computer graphics, best results are obtained with a non-interlaced display that scans the whole screen at least 50 times per second. See **monitor; CRT**.

INTERNAL FONT An internal font is a description of a kind of type to be printed on a printer. Unlike soft fonts and font cartridges, internal fonts are permanently built into the printer, where they reside on ROM chips. For contrast, see **font cartridge; soft font.**

INTERNAL RATE OF RETURN The internal rate of return of an investment project is the hypothetical interest rate such that the present value of the project is zero. (See **present value**.) If the internal rate of return for the project is greater than the actual interest rate, then the present value is positive and the project is profitable. Many spreadsheets will automatically calculate the internal rate of return. However, there is no formula to do this; it must be done by an iterative process where different interest rates are tried until a zero present value is found.

INTERNAL STORAGE The internal storage of a computer is the memory that is built in (see **memory**). For contrast, see **auxiliary storage.**

INTERNATIONAL BUSINESS MACHINES See **IBM.**

INTERNET The Internet is an immense network of networks, connecting computers at universities, research labs, and commercial and military sites around the world. Users of the Internet can exchange electronic mail, send files from any computer to any other via FTP, and even use each other's computers directly via Telnet or rlogin if they have appropriate passwords. See **electronic mail; FTP, Telnet; rlogin; finger.**

Every user of every machine has an address. Here is an example showing the meaning of each of its components:

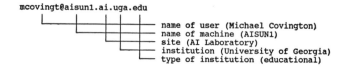

```
mcovingt@aisun1.ai.uga.edu
```

name of user (Michael Covington)
name of machine (AISUN1)
site (AI Laboratory)
institution (University of Georgia)
type of institution (educational)

Here "aisun1.ai.uga.edu" is a *domain address* which gets translated into a numeric *IP address*, in this case 128.192.12.9.

The Internet grew out of the original ARPAnet as well as BITNET and several other networks (See **ARPAnet; BITNET; wide area network.**)

INTERPRETER An interpreter is a program that executes a source program by reading it one line at a time and doing the specified operations immediately. Most BASIC systems are interpreters. For contrast, see **compiler.**

INTERRUPT An interrupt is an instruction that tells a microprocessor to put aside what it is doing and call a specified routine. The processor resumes its original work when the *interrupt service routine* finishes.

Interrupts are used for two main purposes:

1. To deal with hardware events such as a key being pressed or a character arriving through a serial port. These events cannot be ignored; the incoming data must be either processed immediately or stored in a buffer.
2. To call subroutines that are provided by the hardware or operating system. On the IBM PC, most DOS and BIOS services are called through interrupts rather than through the ordinary instruction for calling a subroutine. OS/2 services, on the other hand, are called as ordinary subroutines.

These correspond to the two main ways of causing an interrupt: by receiving a signal from outside the microprocessor (a *hardware interrupt*) or by executing a machine instruction (a *software interrupt*).

INTERRUPT SERVICE ROUTINE See **interrupt.**

INVERTER (1) A NOT gate is often called an inverter. (See **NOT gate.**)

(2) A device that converts direct current to alternating current for power supply purposes (e.g., to power a computer from a car battery) is called an inverter.

IP ADDRESS An IP (Internet Protocol) address is the numeric address of a machine, in the format used on the Internet. For example, the IP address of one of the University of Georgia's computers is 128.192.12.9. See **Internet.**

ISA Industry-standard architecture (ISA) is a term often used to describe the conventional IBM PC (8-bit) and IBM PC AT (16-bit) bus, as opposed to the Micro Channel Architecture. See **EISA; Micro Channel; IBM PC; bus.**

ISDN An ISDN (integrated services digital network) telephone line is an all-digital line that offers the ability to transmit digital data as well as voice, without a modem. ISDN service began in the U.S. in 1988 and may eventually replace conventional telephone service. (See **modem.**)

ISO ISO stands for International Standards Organization. There are ISO standards for many industries.

   The most important ISO standard related to computers is the official standard version of the Pascal language, ISO Pascal. Most actual implementations of Pascal contain all of the features of ISO Pascal plus some others added by the implementor. However, the most popular implementation, Turbo Pascal, lacks some ISO features and therefore will not run all ISO Pascal programs. (See **Turbo Pascal.**)

ITERATION Iteration is the process of repeating a particular action. A definite iteration occurs when the specified action will be repeated a fixed number of times. For example, you can find the sum of all the integers from 1 to 100 with the following BASIC program, which uses iteration:

```
10   T = 0
20   FOR I = 1 TO 100
30   T = T + I
40   NEXT I
```

(See **loop.**) An indefinite iteration occurs if the repetitions stop when a particular condition is met, but you don't know in advance how many repetitions will take place before the condition is met. An example of an indefinite iteration is a binary search routine. (See **binary search.**) In that case the iteration will continue until the item you're looking for has been found, or you establish that it is not in the list.

j ————————————————

JACKET A diskette is encased in a stiff plastic jacket that contains holes giving the disk drive access to the information on the disk. The disk should never be removed from the jacket.

JAPANESE WRITING See **kana.**

JCL The Job Control Language of a computer is the command language used in batch jobs to tell the computer what to do. (See batch processing.) The acronym JCL usually refers to the job control language used on large IBM computers, but sometimes designates very different languages used for the same purpose on other computers.

The following is an example of JCL for an IBM 360; the language is the same for all IBM mainframe computers running operating systems derived from OS/360, such as OS/VS2 and MVS:

```
//JONES JOB 123456,TIME=5
// EXEC PLIXCG
//PLI.SYSIN DD DSN=JONES.SAMPL.PL1,DISP=SHR
//GO.SYSIN DD *
 1234
/*
//
```

The first statement is the JOB card, which gives the job a name, specifies the user's account number, and establishes a CPU time limit of 5 minutes for the whole job. The EXEC PLIXCG statements calls up the procedure to compile and execute a PL/I program; its operation happens to consist of two steps, PLI (compile) and GO (execute). The SYSIN (standard system input) file for the PLI step is defined as a catalogued disk data set named JONES.SAMPL.PLI; the SYSIN for the GO step is given in the job itself, beginning after DD * and ending with /*. The // card marks the end of the job.

In IBM JCL, each statement has up to four fields, as in this example:

```
//GO.SYSIN DD * INPUT FILE
```

Here GO.SYSIN is the name field, DD is the operation field, * is the operand field, and INPUT FILE is the comment field. The rules for coding the fields are as follows:

1. The fields are separated by at least one blank. Only the first 71 characters of every line (not 72, as you might expect) are significant.
2. The name field is immediately adjacent to the two slashes at the beginning of the line. Often the EXEC statement has no name field; when this is the case, be sure to type

```
// EXEC
```

and not

```
//EXEC
```

The name field cannot contain any blanks.

3. The next field after the name field is the operation field, usually JOB, EXEC, or DD. The operation field also cannot contain any blanks.
4. The next field after the operation field is the operand field; this too cannot contain any blanks unless they are in quotation marks.

   If the operand field will not fit on one line, it can be continued to a second line, as in this example:

```
//GO.SYSIN DD DSN=JONES.OLD.DATA,
//              DISP=SHR,
//              DCB=(LRECL=80,BLKSIZE=3120)
```

Here every line except the last ends with a comma. Every line except the first begins with two slashes followed by from 1 to 13 blanks. (A common error is to include too many blanks.)
5. Anything after the operand field is considered to be a comment and is ignored by the computer.

JCL also includes a null statement (consisting of // by itself), which marks the end of a job, and a comment statement, which begins with //*. Comment statements are ignored by the operating system itself but are often used to convey information to utilities that have been added onto the operating system for various purposes (e.g., automatic allocation of tape drives).

The details of JCL vary considerably from installation to installation; consult local manuals for more information.

JOB See batch processing.

JOB CONTROL LANGUAGE See **JCL**.

JOIN See **relational database**.

JOULE The joule is a unit for measuring amounts of energy. 1 joule equals 1 kilogram-meter^2/second^2. See **watt; watt-hour; volt**.

JOYSTICK A joystick is a computer input device especially helpful when playing computer games. The joystick consists of a handle that can be pointed in different directions. Because the computer can sense in which direction the joystick is pointed, the joystick can be used to control the movements of objects displayed on the computer screen.

JUNCTION The junction is the part of a diode or transistor where two opposite types of semiconductor material meet. (See **diode; transistor**.)

JUSTIFICATION Justification is the insertion of extra space between words in lines of type so that both the left and right margins are even and smooth. Most of the type in this book is justified.

On a typewriter, the only way to justify is to insert extra spaces equal to the width of whole characters, thereby lengthening most lines. This makes the text harder to read because of the large, irregular spaces between words.

A better way to justify is to use *microspacing*, i.e., to insert small, equal amounts of space between all the words. Some printers will do this. But with fixed-pitch type, the results can still be hard to read (see **pitch**).

The best justification is obtained with microspacing and proportional-pitch type. Even then, justification is only practical when the columns are wide enough that the extra space does not look awkward or conspicuous.

See also **river**.

k

K K is the symbol for the unit used to measure the size of a computer's memory; a computer with memory of 1K can store 1,024 characters. The number 1,024 is significant because $2^{10} = 1,024$. K is short for *kilobyte*, which is approximately 1,000 bytes. The maximum memory size (without bank switching) is 64K for older 8-bit systems and 640K for the IBM PC. Some more recent microcomputers have several megabytes of memory.

KANA Kana is the Japanese phonetic writing system and is usually used when printing Japanese on computers. There are two styles, *hiragana* and *katakana*. Kana contrasts with *kanji*, the Chinese-derived symbols for whole words. Printed Japanese books use a mixture of kana and kanji.

KANJI See **kana**.

KATAKANA See **kana**.

KAYPRO Kaypro Corporation of Solona Beach, California, manufactures the Kaypro 286 and Kaypro 386 microcomputers, which contain 80286 and 80386 microprocessors, respectively, and come with word processing and other software. In the early 1980s, Kaypro manufactured 8-bit computers using the CP/M operating system (the Kaypro 2, Kaypro 4, and Kaypro 10).

KERMIT Kermit is the name of a protocol for transferring files from one computer to another. It is also the name of a program (distributed free by Columbia University) that implements this protocol. (Other communications programs also implement part or all of the Kermit protocol.)

Like XMODEM, Kermit makes an exact copy of the original file even when transmitting over a noisy line. All data packets are error-checked and erroneous packets are retransmitted.

Kermit is slightly slower than XMODEM. Its advantages include the following:

1. The file name is sent along with the file.
2. A group of files can be sent by using wild card characters in file names (see **wild card**).
3. Eight-bit communication is not required. Kermit can be implemented on mainframe computers that transmit only 7 bits per byte. (See **RS-232**.)

4. Kermit is implemented on a very wide variety of machines, including many that have no other file-transfer protocol.

KERNING Kerning is a reduction in the amount of space between certain combinations of letters in proportional-pitch type. If the combination "Ty" is typeset with the same letter spacing as "Th," the letters seem to be too widely spaced. "Ty" looks better if the top of the "T" is allowed to overhang the "y" slightly. See Figure 37.

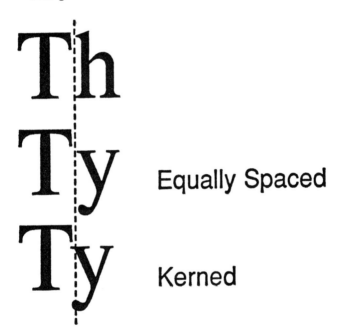

FIGURE 37 Kerning

KEY (1) The buttons on a keyboard are called keys.

(2) The item by which a data file is sorted or searched is called the key. For instance, if a file of names and addresses is sorted by ZIP codes, then the ZIP code is the key.

(3) The password or other secret information needed to decode an encrypted message is called the key. (See **encryption.**)

KEY DISK Some copy protection systems require that a particular noncopyable disk be inserted in the computer to start a program, even if the program is not actually on that disk. Such a disk is called a key disk.

KEYWORD A keyword is a word that has special meaning in a particular programming language. For example, GOSUB is a keyword in BASIC, and BEGIN is a keyword in Pascal.

KILOBYTE See **K**.

KILOWATT-HOUR One kilowatt-hour is 1000 watt-hours. See **watt-hour**.

KLUDGE A kludge (pronounced "klooge") is an improvised, jury-rigged, poorly thought out solution to a problem, usually intended only for temporary use. The word kludge may be derived from German *klug*, "clever."

KNOWLEDGE BASE See **expert system**.

KOCH SNOWFLAKE See **fractal**.

L

LABEL (1) In some programming languages a *statement label* is a name that represents a particular statement.

(2) A file stored on tape is preceded by an *identifying label*, containing information about the file.

(3) In MS-DOS (PC-DOS) and OS/2, disks have identifying names ("volume labels") recorded on them.

LAN See **local-area network**.

LANDSCAPE Landscape orientation refers to paper oriented so that it is wider than it is high, like a landscape painting. This results from turning the paper sideways relative to the way it is most commonly used ("portrait orientation"). Laser printers typically offer a choice of portrait or landscape orientation.

LAP-B LAP-B (link access procedure—balanced) is a method for detecting and correcting errors in data transmission. (For a description of another method in detail, see **XMODEM**.) LAP-B error correction is built into some high-speed modems so that erroneous data are never sent to the computer.

LAPTOP A laptop computer is a small, lightweight computer (under 8 pounds) with a flip-up screen that can be powered by batteries and is easily portable. Laptops are especially valuable for people who travel frequently and need to be able to work on a computer while on the road.

LARGE-SCALE INTEGRATION The term *large-scale integration* refers to integrated circuits that contain more than 100 logic gates. (See **integrated circuit**.)

LASER PRINTER A laser printer uses a laser beam to generate an image, then transfers it to paper electronically. (See **electrostatic printer**.) Laser printers provide letter-quality output for text. They also can print graphics and are quieter and faster than printers that mechanically strike the paper (see **dot-matrix printer** and **daisywheel printer**.) Laser printers are often used in desktop publishing. However, they are more expensive than other printers that are commonly used on microcomputers. For specific examples, see **Laserwriter** and **LaserJet**.

LASERJET The LaserJet is a popular laser printer produced by Hewlett-Packard. The main LaserJet models are the LaserJet Plus, LaserJet II, and LaserJet III. Each of these incorporates improvements in the command language and the built-in fonts. Software designed for earlier models will work with later models, but not vice versa.

LaserJet printers have space for plug-in font cartridges; it is also possible to use software-provided fonts loaded into the printer directly from the computer. Commands to the LaserJet can be sent with escape sequences (a sequence of ASCII codes beginning with code 27). Table 12 shows some of the common sequences. (Note that a LaserJet-compatible software program will send these codes automatically to the printer.)

LASERWRITER The Apple Laserwriter is a laser printer commonly used with the Macintosh computer. It uses the Postscript command language. (See **Macintosh; Postscript**.)

LCD A liquid crystal display (LCD) is the type of display used on most digital watches, calculators, and laptop computers. LCDs

Table 12 Some LaserJet Command Codes

ASCII code numbers	Action
27 38 108 ## 80	set page length to ## lines per page
27 38 108 ## 69	set top margin to ## lines
27 38 97 ## 76	set left margin to column ##
27 38 97 ## 77	set right margin to column ##
27 38 108 54 68	set vertical spacing to 6 lines per inch
27 61	half line feed
27 38 97 ## 82	position cursor at row ##
27 38 97 ## 67	position cursor at column ##
27 38 108 48 79	switch orientation to portrait
27 38 108 49 79	switch orientation to landscape
27 40 56 85	switch font to internal Roman-8
27 40 115 ## 72	set primary pitch to ## characters per inch
27 40 115 ## 86	set primary point size to ##
27 40 115 48 83	set primary style to upright
27 40 115 49 83	set primary style to italics
27 40 ## 88	set primary font to number ##

consume much less power than any other kind of display, but they are sometimes hard to read because of a lack of contrast ("black" is not much darker than "white"). "Supertwist" LCDs have more contrast than earlier types.

LCDs use liquid crystals, which are chemicals whose optical properties change in the presence of an electric field. A polarizing filter is built into the LCD; through this filter, the liquid crystal compound looks light or dark depending on its electrical state.

LEADING Leading (pronounced "ledding") is the insertion of extra space between lines of type. On old printing presses, this was originally done by inserting strips of lead between rows of type cast in lead. (See **typeface**.)

LED The acronym LED stands for Light-Emitting Diode. An LED device will light up when the proper current is passed through it. The display on some digital clocks is made of LEDs.

LETTER QUALITY A letter-quality printer produces print equal in quality to that of the best typewriters. All laser printers and daisywheel printers are letter quality; so are some ink-jet printers and dot-matrix printers.

LIBRARY A library is a collection of files, computer programs, or subroutines. A loader library is a file containing subroutines that can be link-edited into a machine language program.

LIGHT-EMITTING DIODE See **LED**.

LIGHT PEN A light pen consists of a light-sensitive detector and is used to control pictures on a computer terminal. By using the light pen the operator can change the appearance of the lines on the screen.

LIM-EMS See **expanded memory**.

LIMITS OF COMPUTER POWER Computers can perform only tasks that can be reduced to mechanical procedures (algorithms). They are therefore inapplicable to tasks that cannot or should not be reduced to mechanical form, such as judging the greatness of a work of art or administering psychotherapy.

Rather surprisingly, however, there are some tasks that are mathematically precise but that present-day computers cannot perform. These fall into two major types: (1) problems with no known algorithmic solution, and (2) problems whose best known algorithmic solutions require unreasonable amounts of time. (Some mathematical problems can be proved to have no algorithmic solution, but they seldom turn up in practical work.)

An example of a problem of the first type (i.e., one with no presently known algorithmic solution) is how to get a computer to recognize the structures of sentences in a human language such as English. Obviously, this is something computers will have to be able to do if we are ever to be able to communicate with them in English, and there is no reason to think it impossible. The difficulty is simply that English (and all other human languages) are so complicated that complete algorithms for processing them have not yet been discovered.

A good example of the second type of problem, one that takes an unreasonable amount of time to solve, is the so-called *traveling salesman problem*. The task is to find the shortest route by which a salesman can visit a particular set of cities (in any order). The only known way to solve this problem is to try all possible routes. A few shortcuts are possible—for instance, the testing of each route can be abandoned as soon as its length exceeds the shortest length already found, without pursuing it to the end—but the number of steps is never substantially fewer than N factorial, where N is the number of cities (see **factorial**).

Suppose the fastest imaginable computer could perform one step in this algorithm by moving an electric charge a distance of 1 millimeter at the speed of light. This would mean that it could perform 3×10^{11} steps per second. Then the times required to solve the traveling salesman problem (in N! steps) would work out as follows:

Number of Cities	Number of Steps	Time Required
5	120	0.36 picosecond
10	3,628,800	12 microseconds
15	1.3×10^{12}	4.4 seconds
20	2.4×10^{18}	94 days
25	1.6×10^{25}	1.6 million years
30	2.7×10^{32}	2.8×10^{13} years

And this is with a computer millions of times faster than any that presently exist. Obviously, it will never be feasible to solve the traveling salesman problem for more than a few cities unless a much better algorithm is found.

Another interesting class of computational problems, known as *NP-complete problems*, has been proved to be equivalent to the traveling salesman problem; if a better algorithm is found for any NP-complete problem, it will be applicable to all of them.

LINE PRINTER A line printer is a high-speed printer for computer output. A line printer consists of a separate chain of type elements for each column, so it is capable of printing an entire line of output at one time. Fast line printers are capable of printing output at rates of up to 1,400 lines per minute.

LINK (1) Any kind of communication path between two computers can be called a link.

(2) Under Microsoft Windows or OS/2, a DDE communication path between programs is called a hot link or cold link. See **DDE**.

(3) To link a program is to combine the machine instructions for the program itself with the machine instructions for any predefined procedures that it uses. For example, a program that does trigonometric calculations might use predefined procedures to find sines, cosines, and tangents.

Some compilers perform linking automatically; others require you to execute a linker as a separate command.

(4) The pointers in a linked list or tree are called links. See **linked list; tree**.

LINKED LIST A linked list is a way of organizing data items in the computer so that they are retrievable in a particular order that is not necessarily the same order of the physical locations in which they are stored. Each data item consists of two parts: the data itself, and a number giving the location of the next item; Figure 38 shows how this is usually diagrammed. To read the items in order, you need only know which item is in the beginning (the *head*) of the list; having located it, you can go next to the item whose address was stored with it; and so on.

Linked lists allow items to be added or removed without requiring that other items be moved to make room. For instance, the list A-D-E of Figure 38 can be changed into A-B-C-D-E by

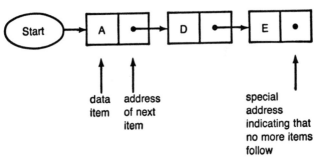

data item — address of next item — special address indicating that no more items follow

FIGURE 38

adding two items. As Figure 39 shows, the newly added items B and C can be placed in the unused area after the E, and "inserted" into the list by changing the address associated with

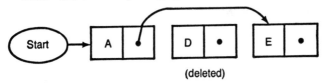

(deleted)

FIGURE 39

item A. Figure 40 shows that an item can be "deleted" by changing the addresses so that there is no longer a path to that item. In either case, using linked lists can eliminate the need to move hundreds or thousands of data items when an insertion or deletion takes place.

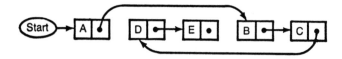

FIGURE 40

Figure 41 shows a way to construct a linked list in an ordinary two-dimensional array; this can be done in practically any

item no.	data item	address of next item
1	A	4
2	D	3
3	E	0
4	B	5
5	C	2

FIGURE 41

programming language. Each row of the array contains a data item and an integer indicating which row the next item is on (or zero, to indicate that there are more items). In the example, it is assumed that the first item in the list will always be in row 1; if you wish to be able to delete the first item, you can use a separate integer, outside the array, to keep track of where the list starts. See also **data structure**.

LIQUID CRYSTAL DISPLAY See LCD.

LISP The programming language LISP (List Processor) was developed in the early 1960s at MIT under the direction of John McCarthy. Because of the ease with which it can handle complex data structures, LISP is used for artificial intelligence research and for writing programs whose complexity would render them intractable in other languages.

A LISP program is easy to recognize because of the accumulation of closing parentheses at the end of the program. All LISP statements and data structures are linked lists, written as lists of elements in parentheses (see **linked list**). The programmer builds a complex program by defining her own statements (actually functions) in terms of those previously defined: For example, a function that computes the factorial of X is:

```
(DEFUN FACTORIAL (X)
       (COND ((= X 0) 1)
             (T      (* X (FACTORIAL (- X 1)))))))
```

Translating into English, we have the following: "This is the definition of a function called FACTORIAL whose parameter is X. If X is zero, its factorial is 1; otherwise, its factorial is equal to X times the factorial of X–1." Here COND introduces a series of lists to be tried in succession until one beginning with a true predicate is found, and T means "true" (thereby introducing a clause that executes if (= X 0) is false). This function calls itself recursively; recursion is the normal way of expressing repetition in LISP.

LIST A list is a set of data items that are to be accessed in a particular order; for instance, a list of the students in a class might be accessed in alphabetical order. Lists are stored in arrays or linked lists. (See **array**; **linked list**.)

LIST BOX In a dialog box, a list box is an area in which the user can choose among a list of items, such as files, directories, printers, or the like. For picture, see **dialog box.**

LIST PROCESSING (1) The manipulation of linked lists is called list processing. See **linked list; LISP.**

(2) The processing of mailing lists is also sometimes called list processing. See **database management.**

LITERAL A literal is a symbol in a computer program that stands for a particular value and is not programmer-defined (i.e., cannot possibly stand for any other value). For example, in the following BASIC program:

```
10    LET A = 2.4
20    LET B$ = "THE ANSWER IS"
30    PRINT B$, A
```

the literals are "THE ANSWER IS" and 2.4.

LN The function LN(X) in Pascal and some other languages calculates the natural logarithm of X. (See **logarithm.**)

LOAD To load is to transfer information from an auxiliary storage device into a computer. For contrast, see **save**.

LOCAL-AREA NETWORK A local-area network connects together several machines that are located nearby (in the same room or building) allowing them to share files and devices such as printers. For example, see **Ethernet; token ring**.

A local-area network can be very valuable if several people must constantly enter data into a single database. Some database programs, such as Paradox, have network versions designed specifically for this purpose. For example, several workers might work on the same inventory-control system, one of them logging new merchandise as it comes in, the other logging sales as they take place.

For an example of a popular local-area network system, see **Novell NetWare**.

LOCAL VARIABLE A local variable has meaning only within a particular function or subroutine. The name of a local variable can be used in another subroutine elsewhere in the program, where it will mean something totally different.

Most programming languages contain provisions to make a particular variable a local variable. In Pascal, a variable is local to a particular procedure if it is declared within that procedure. Here is an example of a Pascal program where *a* is a global variable, *c* is a local variable inside procedure pl, and the name *b* represents two variables—a global variable and a local variable inside procedures pl:

```
PROGRAM example(INPUT,OUTPUT);
   {This program demonstrates the use of local
    and global variables}
  VAR a,b:INTEGER;

PROCEDURE p1;
   VAR b,c:INTEGER;
    BEGIN
      a := 500;
      b := 100;
      c := 200;
      WRITELN('We are now in procedure p1');
      WRITELN('a=',a,' b=',b,' c=',c)
    END;
```

```
BEGIN {main program}
  a := 10;
  b := 20;
  WRITELN('We are in the main program block');
  WRITELN('a=',a,' b=',b);
  p1;
  WRITELN('We are back in the main block');
  WRITELN('a=',a,' b=',b)
END.

  ---OUTPUT ---:
We are in the main program block
a=10 b=20
We are now in procedure p1
a=500 b=100 c=200
We are back in the main block
a=500 b=20
```

FIGURE 42

Note that, when we change the value of a in procedure pl, the change affects the global variable a. Changing the value of b in procedure pl changes only the local variable, and so does not affect the value of b in the main block. We could not include the statement WRITELN(c) in the main block because c is a local variable that will be recognized only inside procedure pl.

The advantage of using local variables is not obvious in short programs. However, it is a good idea when writing a long program to make as many variables as possible into local variables, because then there will be no problem if you wish to use the same name to mean something else at another point in the program. This rule is even more important if several different people are writing subroutines that will be combined into one main program. (See also **side effect**.)

LOG In many versions of BASIC and other languages, the function LOG(X) calculates the natural logarithm of X. However, in some versions, LOG(X) is the common logarithm and LN(X) is the natural logarithm. (See **logarithm**.)

LOGARITHM If $y = a^x$, then x is the logarithm of y to the base a (written as $x = log_a y$). The most common bases for logarithm functions are 10 and *e*. Base-10 logarithms are called *common logarithms*; base-*e* logarithms, *natural logarithms*. For example, the common logarithm of 10,000 is 4 ($\log_{10} 10,000 = 4$) because $10^4 = 10,000$.

LOGIC GATE A logic gate is a device that accepts binary digits (bits) as inputs and produces an output bit according to a specified rule. For examples, see **AND gate; OR gate; NOT gate.**

LOGIC PROGRAMMING Logic programming is the use of computers to draw conclusions from data by reasoning logically, much as humans do. For examples, see Prolog; **expert system.**

LOGO LOGO is a programming language developed by Seymour Papert of MIT for use in teaching programming to children. Papert's fundamental insight was that computer-aided instruction is of little use unless the pupil can control the computer, rather than the other way around. To experiment with this idea, he designed a language that is markedly easier to use than BASIC and does not share BASIC's preoccupation with numerical calculation.

Although LOGO offers a full range of computer functions, most elementary LOGO exercises revolve around the "turtle," originally a robot that rolled around on a sheet of paper making marks with a pen. (The present-day turtle is more often a triangle that moves around the screen, drawing a line if told to do so.) Drawing shapes with the turtle appeals to children who would not be attracted to mathematical calculation or verbal input-output; at the same time, it serves as a good medium for teaching geometry and logical problem solving.

LOGO is an extensible language; that is, programs are constructed by defining statements in terms of previously defined statements. For example, the following procedure draws a square:

```
TO SQUARE
   CLEARSCREEN
   FORWARD 50
   RIGHT 90
   FORWARD 50
   RIGHT 90
   FORWARD 50
   RIGHT 90
   FORWARD 50
END
```

In other words, "Clear the screen (and put the turtle in the center), go forward (up) 50 units, do a 90-degree right turn, go forward 50 units, do a 90-degree right turn," and so forth.

Since LOGO procedures can call themselves recursively, complicated snowflake-like patterns are relatively easy to generate.

LOG ON To log on to a computer is to establish a connection from your terminal to the computer and to identify yourself as an authorized user.

LOOP A loop in a computer program is a set of statements that are to be executed repeatedly. For example, the BASIC program

```
10 FOR I = 1 TO 5
20     PRINT I,I∧2
30 NEXT I
```

contains a loop. Statement 20 will be executed five times, first with I equal to 1, then with I equal to 2, and so on. The output from the program will look like this:

```
1      1
2      4
3      9
4      16
5      25
```

The program above contains a loop that will always be executed the same number of times. It is also possible to establish a loop that will be executed until a particular condition occurs. See also **repeat; while.**

LOST CLUSTER In MS-DOS (PC-DOS) and other operating systems, a lost cluster is a group of disk sectors that are not marked as free but are not allocated to a file. Lost clusters result when the operation of creating a file is interrupted. They waste space and should be cleaned up periodically; this is done with the CHKDSK /F command.

LOTUS 1-2-3 Lotus 1-2-3, an integrated software package produced by Lotus Development Corp., has become one of the best selling business decision-making tools. Lotus 1-2-3 combines the functions of a spreadsheet program with data management capabilities and graphics. See **spreadsheet; database management,** and **graphics** for information on these topics.

Work in 1-2-3 is based on a worksheet of rows and columns that appears on the screen. The rows are numbered, and the columns are identified with letters. Each individual cell can be identified by specifying its row and column; for example, C4 is the cell in the third column and the fourth row. Numbers, text, or formulas can be entered into cells. The arrow keys on the keyboard are used to move the cell pointer to new locations. The start of a 1-2-3 command is signaled by typing "/", which causes a command list menu to appear on the top of the screen.

Here is an example of a 1-2-3 spreadsheet. We will enter information on the personal finances of an individual with money in four places; a checking account, a savings account, an Individual Retirement Account (IRA), and cash. We will use the first row to display a label that identifies the table, and we will enter the labels for each category in column A. The numbers themselves will go in column B.

Figure 43 shows what the spreadsheet looks like. The symbol B3: at the upper left corner indicates that the cell pointer is currently pointing at cell B3, and this cell currently holds the value 450.53. You can tell that we have just pressed the "/" key in this case because the command menu has appeared in the second and third lines of the screen.

```
B3: 450.53                                                              MENU
Worksheet  Range  Copy  Move  File  Print  Graph  Data  Quit
Global, Insert, Delete, Column-Width, Erase, Titles, Window, Status
        A        B         C        D        E        F        G        H
 1  Personal Financial Data
 2               Today
 3  Checking     450.53
 4  Saving       832.52
 5  IRA         3040.11
 6  Cash          83.43
 7
 8
 9
10
11
12
13
14
15
16
17
18
19
20
```

FIGURE 43

The value of the spreadsheets stems from their ability to store formulas in cells and then automatically calculate the values given by these formulas. We would like to calculate the total amount of money in the four places. To do that we will enter the formula @SUM(B3..B6) into cell B7. The @ symbol is put in front of all 1-2-3 functions. The SUM function automatically calculates the sum of all cells in the indicated range. The notation B3..B6 means to take all cells from B3 to B6. Figure 44 shows the result.

```
B7: @SUM(B3..B6)                                                 READY

         A       B       C       D     E     F     G     H
1   Personal Financial Data
2            Today
3   Checking   450.53
4   Saving     832.52
5   IRA       3040.11
6   Cash        83.43
7   Total     4406.59
8
9
10
11
12
13
14
15
16
17
18
19
20
```

FIGURE 44

If we change one of the numbers in cells B3 to B6, then 1-2-3 will automatically calculate the new total and display that value in cell B7. (Note that we included a label for the total in cell A7.)

It is often helpful to enter a formula in one cell and then copy that formula into several other cells. For example, if you wish to compare your financial position today with your position in 1972, you need to divide each amount by the price level (which measures the amount that prices have risen because of inflation since 1972). Enter the value 2.23 for the price level into cell E3. Then enter this formula into cell C3: (B3/$E$3); the "/" is used to represent division. The dollar signs in the cell address $E$3 indicate that this is an absolute address, that is, this address will always refer to cell E3 even if we copy this formula into a cell at a different location in the worksheet. The B3 in the formula does not contain dollar signs, so this is a relative address. Since B3 is one cell to the left of C3 (where we put the formula), the computer treats B3 as meaning "the cell that is one cell to the left." If we then copy the same formula to cell C4, the computer will automatically change the B3 to B4, since B4 is the cell that is one cell to the left of C4.

To copy a formula, type /C; 1-2-3 will ask you for the range to copy from and to. We would like to copy the formula in cell C3 into cells C4 to C7. After we have copied the formulas, 1-2-3 will automatically calculate the values in column C. The result is shown in Figure 45.

```
C4: (B4/$E$3)                                                    READY

        A        B        C        D      E       F      G      H
1    Personal Financial Data
2             Today    1972 $              Price Level
3    Checking   450.53 202.0313              2.23
4    Saving     832.52 373.3273
5    IRA       3040.11 1363.278
6    Cash        83.43 37.41255
7    Total     4406.59 1976.049
8
9
10
11
12
13
14
15
16
17
18
19
20
```

FIGURE 45

If we now move the pointer to cell C4, the top of the screen will display the formula stored in cell C4, which is (B4/$E$3). Note that $E$3 is the same as it was in the formula for cell C3, but the first part of the formula is now B4, since B4 is the cell that is one cell to the left of C4. If we change the value in cell E3, then 1-2-3 will automatically recalculate all of the values in column C.

A big advantage of 1-2-3 is its ability to draw graphs representing the information contained in the worksheet. There are several types of graphs that can be drawn: line diagrams, bar graphs, x-y scatter diagrams, and pie charts. Let's draw a pie chart showing the fraction of the total in each category. Type /G to enter the graphics menu; a list of graphics commands will appear at the top of the screen. Type T to indicate that you wish to select the type of graph, type P to indicate that you will draw a pie chart, and type A to indicate that you are defining which cells will be part of the data range that 1-2-3 calls the "A" range. Then 1-2-3 will ask you to enter the range of cells, which will be B3..B6 in the present case. (For some types of graphs you will have more than one data range. The other data ranges are indicated by the letters B to F.) In a pie chart the data are contained in the A range, and the labels for the sector data are contained in the X range. Type X and then respond to the question by entering the cells A3..A6 for the X range. Now type V (for view), and the graph will appear on the screen. (See Figure 46.)

FIGURE 46

Several versions of 1-2-3 have been released. Newer versions contain numerous improvements. See **three dimensional spreadsheet.**

LOTUS DEVELOPMENT CORP. Lotus, a software company located in Cambridge, Massachusetts, produces Lotus 1-2-3, the integrated program Symphony, and the information-management program Agenda.

m

MACAPP MacApp, introduced in 1986, is a programming tool for developing application programs on the Macintosh. MacApp is essentially an "empty" program; it knows how to use the graphical user interface but does not do any actual work. To create a real application, the programmer adds menus and supplies procedures to do whatever the application program is supposed to do.

MacApp uses object-oriented Pascal. It is similar to object-oriented Turbo Pascal and to Visual Basic, both of which came later. See **object-oriented programming; Visual Basic.**

MACDRAW See **draw program.**

MACHINE-DEPENDENT PROGRAM A machine-dependent program works on only one particular type of computer.

MACHINE-INDEPENDENT PROGRAM A machine-independent program can be used on many different types of computers.

MACHINE LANGUAGE A machine language contains instructions that a computer can execute directly. Machine language statements are written in a binary code, and each statement corresponds to one machine action.

An assembly language is a language in which each statement corresponds to one machine language statement, but the statements themselves are written in a symbolic code that is easier for people to read. (See **assembly language**.) A single statement in a high-level language such as BASIC may contain many machine instructions.

MACHINE-READABLE DATA Machine-readable data are data in any form that can be fed into a computer through an input device. Examples of machine-readable data include data stored on magnetic tape or punched cards, and data on forms that can be read by an optical scanner.

MACINTOSH The Macintosh computer, introduced by Apple in 1984, was the first personal computer to use a graphical user interface with a mouse. Users copy files and activate software by pointing to symbols (icons) on the screen rather than by typing commands. The screen is always in graphics mode; it is divided into windows and can display all the typefaces that the printer can print. The Macintosh user interface was derived from that of Xerox workstations; it has been imitated by a number of other operating systems, including Microsoft Windows and OS/2 Presentation Manager.

Most importantly, the mechanisms for using windows, icons, and mouse menus are provided by the operating system, which means they look virtually the same in all programs. Thus, anyone who knows how to use any Macintosh software package will also know how to perform similar operations in any other software package.

The original Macintosh used a 7.80-MHz Motorola 68000 microprocessor with 128K of RAM (see **microprocessor**). This was not enough for the software to perform well, and all present models have at least one megabyte of RAM. The Macintosh II, introduced in 1986, is a completely different machine with an IBM-PC-like keyboard and a color display. It runs five to ten times faster than the original Macintosh and is one of the most powerful microcomputers available. (See **workstation.**)

Current Macintosh models feature the 3.5-inch "Super-Drive," which can read and write not only Macintosh diskettes but also 3.5-inch IBM PC and Apple II diskettes.

For serial port pinouts, see **RS-232.**

MACPAINT See **paint program.**

MACRO A macro is an instruction that stands for a sequence of simpler instructions.

(1) In assembly language, a macro instruction is a user-defined abbreviation for one or more lines of code.

(2) A macro is also a group of keystrokes that have been combined so that they can be easily accessed. Many software packages make it possible to define macros for commonly used keystroke combinations. For example, in Lotus 1-2-3, a macro is defined by entering characters into a cell (or range of cells) and then giving that cell a name. Suppose we frequently wish to format a group of cells to have currency format with two decimal places. The commands to do this are / Range Format Currency. To spare yourself from typing these characters each time, enter the expression ' /RFC2~ into a convenient cell. The quotation mark at the beginning indicates that this is a label; the 2 indicates that two decimal places are to be taken, and the ~ symbol represents the return key. Use the / Range Name Create command to give this cell a name, consisting of a backslash followed by a letter. We could give the macro the name \F, since F stands for format. The macro has now been defined. In order to execute the macro, press the ALT key and then the letter that names the macro (in this case F). The result will be the same as if we had pressed each of the keys / R F C 2 (RETURN) individually.

Macros can become much more complicated. For example, it is possible to create a macro that pauses at some point to obtain input from the user.

MACRO ASSEMBLER An assembler translates assembly language programs into machine code (see **assembly language**). A macro assembler is one that allows the programmer to define macro instructions (see **macro**).

MAGNETIC BUBBLE MEMORY Magnetic bubble memory can be used in the same way as RAM but does not go blank when power to it is turned off. At present, bubble memories are more expensive than disks; they are used in very lightweight, portable computers when a disk drive would be too bulky or too fragile.

MAINFRAME COMPUTER A mainframe computer is a large computer occupying a specially air-conditioned room and supporting typically 100–500 users at a time. The IBM 370 and IBM 3090 are examples of mainframe computers.

MAKE Typically, a large machine-language program is made by compiling several different source files, producing a group of object files, and then linking the object files together. (See **source code; object code.**) The "make" command manages this process. It looks at a *makefile* (Figure 47), which tells it how to create each of the files needed to generate the complete program. Then it looks at the date on which each file was last modified. If any file is newer than the other files made from it, "make" will do whatever is needed to update those files (typically compiling or linking). By using "make," the programmer avoids recompiling anything that has not been changed.

The "make" command can actually manage any process in which files are made from other files. All it needs is a makefile containing the appropriate commands.

```
#
#  Example of a makefile
#
#  Each entry consists of:
#   A filename
#   A list of other files that the file depends on
#   A command to generate it from them
#
myprog:        myprog1.o  myprog2.o
               cc myprog1.o myprog2.o -o myprog
#
myprog1.o:     myprog1.c
               cc -c myprog1.c
#
myprog2.o:     myprog2.c
               cc -c myprog2.c
```

FIGURE 47

MANAGEMENT INFORMATION SYSTEMS The study of Management Information Systems (MIS) deals with effective systems for the development and use of information in an organization. The complete information system includes not just the computers but also the people. Any effective information system must determine:

1. what the goals of the organization are
2. what information is needed to accomplish those goals
3. how that information is originated
4. how the information needs to be stored and transferred to accomplish those goals.

MANDELBROT SET The Mandelbrot set, discovered by Benoit Mandelbrot, is a famous fractal, i.e., a shape containing an infinite amount of fine detail. It is the set of values of c for which the series $z_{n+1} = z_n^2 + c$ converges, where z and c are complex numbers and z is initially $(0,0)$.

The detail in the Mandelbrot set fascinates mathematicians. Figure 49 shows the whole set and an enlargement of a small area. On the plot, x and y are the real and imaginary parts of c. The Mandelbrot set is the black bulbous object in the middle; elsewhere, the stripes indicate the number of iterations needed to make $|z|$ exceed 2.

Figure 48 is an IBM PC BASIC program to plot the Mandelbrot set. A complete plot takes several hours to generate.

MAPPING SOFTWARE A mapping software package contains data making it possible to create various types of maps for different applications. The map data is stored in digital form, consisting of the coordinates describing where to draw lines and labels. (See **vector graphics**.) The map can be viewed at different scales, and other information could be displayed, such as using different colors to illustrate sales figures for each district.

Map data typically require a large amount of memory and disk space. If maps consisted of straight lines, it would be necessary to store only the end points of the lines, but a realistic description of a curvy coast can require thousands of bytes.

PC-Globe is an example of a popular commercially available mapping package that contains data about the countries of the world (see Figure 50). Maps are often provided as clip art with draw programs.

MATH COPROCESSOR See **coprocessor**.

```
100 ' Choose area to be plotted
110 XMIN = -2
120 XMAX = 2
130 YMIN = -1.5
140 YMAX = 1.5
150 ' Select 320x200 4-color graphics
160 SCREEN 1
170 KEY OFF
180 ' Plot the Mandelbrot set
190 FOR IX = 0 TO 319
200    FOR IY = 0 TO 199
210       ' Locate this point
220       X = (IX/319)*(XMAX-XMIN) + XMIN
230       Y = (IY/199)*(YMAX-YMIN) + YMIN
240       ' Does the function converge?
250       COUNT = 0
260       QX = X
270       QY = Y
280       WHILE COUNT < 128 AND (QX*QX + QY*QY) < 4
290          COUNT = COUNT + 1
300          TEMP = 2*QX*QY + Y
310          QX = QX*QX - QY*QY + X
320          QY = TEMP
330       WEND
340       ' Plot point in color depending on count
350       PSET (IX, IY), (COUNT MOD 4)
360    NEXT IY
370 NEXT IX
380 END
```

FIGURE 48

X = -2.00 to 1.25   Y = -1.50 to 1.50   X = -0.30 to 0.00   Y = 0.85 to 1.10

FIGURE 49 Mandelbrot Set

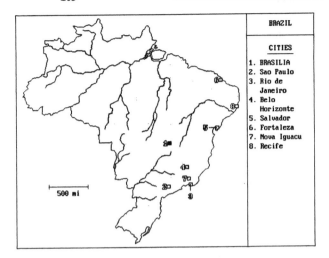

FIGURE 50

MATRIX See **array**.

MATRIX PRINTER A matrix printer forms letters and other symbols by patterns of dots. (See **dot-matrix printer**.)

MAXIMIZE To maximize a window is to make it take over the whole screen. To do this, click the mouse on the maximize button (see **window**). See also **minimize; restore**.

MB See **megabyte**.

MCGA The IBM M̲onochrome/C̲olor G̲raphics A̲dapter (MCGA) is built into the PS/2 Model 25 and 30. It offers all the features of the MDA and CGA, plus some additional video modes of its own. However, it lacks some of the modes supported by the EGA and VGA. (See **video modes [IBM PC]**.)

MDA The IBM PC M̲onochrome D̲isplay A̲dapter (MDA) provides very sharp, readable text, but no graphics, on a monochrome screen. (See **video modes [IBM PC]**.)

MEDIUM-SCALE INTEGRATION The term *medium-scale integration* refers to an integrated circuit that contains from 10 to 100 logic gates. (See **integrated circuit**.)

MEGABYTE A megabyte (MB) is an amount of computer memory equal to $2^{20} = 1,048,576$ bytes = 1,024 kilobytes. One megabyte can store more than one million characters. The internal memory (RAM) of a microcomputer is often measured in megabytes: one MB, two MB, or more have become common sizes. Hard disk capacity is also measured in megabytes; 20 MB, 40 MB, 80 MB, or more have become common sizes.

MEGAHERTZ Megahertz means "million hertz" or "million cycles per second." (See **clock; microprocessor.**)

MEGAPIXEL A megapixel image is an image containing about one million pixels or more. For example, a 1024×1024-pixel image is often referred to as a megapixel. See **bitmap.**

MEMORY The memory, formerly called the *core*, is the space within a computer where information is stored while being actively worked on. Most microcomputers have a small amount of read-only memory (ROM), containing the built-in programs that start the operation of the computer when it is turned on, and a large amount of random-access memory (RAM) for user's programs and data. Except for ROM, memory goes blank when the computer is turned off; any data in it must be copied to disk or tape if they are to be saved.

The memory requirements of a computer are dictated by the software that is to be run on it. In the early 1980s, 64K was a common size for a microcomputer memory. The memory requirements of newer software continued to increase, however, so by the end of the decade 640K became the minimum amount of memory necessary for a business microcomputer. Memory sizes of one or two megabytes or more became common. See also **expanded memory; extended memory; MS-DOS.**

MEMORY CHIPS Memory is often added to a computer simply by plugging RAM chips into sockets. This entails checking the following things:

1. The type of memory chips required. Each chip holds a particular number of bits (e.g., 64K, 256K, or 1 megabyte). Some computers allow use of different types of chips (e.g., 64K or 256K) by setting a switch to indicate which kind are installed. Check that you actually have space to install additional chips; you may need to buy an additional board to hold them.

2. The number of chips needed. A byte is 8 bits (even on a 16- or 32-bit processor), so if you are adding 64K bytes of memory, you will need eight 64K chips to hold the data, plus (on most computers) a ninth 64K chip for parity checking.
3. The speed rating of the chips, typically 120 or 150 nanoseconds. This is a measure of how quickly the chip can return valid data to the CPU. If you install chips that are too slow, you will get memory errors; if your chips are faster than needed, you may be wasting money, because the CPU controls the speed at which the chips actually run.
4. How to tell the computer that additional memory has been installed. This usually involves setting switches or running a configuration program.

MEMORY-MAPPED VIDEO The video display of a computer is memory-mapped if the contents of the screen are controlled by storing appropriate value in a block of memory that is directly accessible to the CPU. (See **video memory**.) For example, the IBM PC has memory-mapped video; most UNIX systems do not.

MEMORY RESIDENT A memory resident program is one that remains in memory after being run, so that it can be called up later. Memory resident programs are often called TSRs ("terminate-and-stay-resident").

Memory resident programs extend the capabilities of the operating system or provide "pop-up" functions, such as a calendar or calculator, that can be called up in the middle of another program without disturbing it. You can then return to the original program as if nothing had happened.

MENU A menu is a list of choices that appears on the screen while a particular program is being executed. By typing the number or letter that corresponds to a particular command operation, you can cause the command to be executed. The presence of menus in a program makes it easy for people to use the program because they don't need to memorize all the commands. By looking at the menu, they can see all their options.

The problem with menus is that it often takes a substantial amount of time to work through them. Many programs, including Lotus 1-2-3 and Word Perfect, provide two ways to execute commands: by choosing them for menus or by hitting specific keys. This enables experienced users to work faster.

MENU BAR A menu bar is a horizontal menu at the top of the screen or window. Depending on the software, the items in the menu bar are chosen by clicking on them with a mouse, or by typing the first letter on each item, or possibly by typing the first letter while holding down Alt. Usually, each item is a further menu. For picture, see **window**. See also **pull-down menu**.

MERGE SORT The merge sort algorithm is a technique for sorting data (see **sort**). Merge sort takes advantage of the fact that it is easy to combine two lists that are already sorted: just keep looking at the first element of each list and taking whichever element comes first. For example, to combine the lists

Adams	Bush
Buchanan	Johnson
Lincoln	Kennedy

do the following: Compare Adams to Bush; take Adams. Then compare Buchanan to Bush and take Buchanan. Then compare Lincoln to Bush and take Bush, and so on. This will give you a list of all six names in alphabetical order.

To perform a complete merge sort, first divide your data into several small sorted lists. These can be sorted with some other sorting algorithm; or they can be two-element lists which are sorted by swapping the two elements where needed; or they can even be one-element lists, which do not need sorting. Then combine these lists, two at a time, until all have been put together into a single sorted list.

A big advantage of merge sort is that you never need to see more than the first element of any list. Thus, merge sort can take its data from tapes or from linked lists, which cannot easily be sorted by any other algorithm. See **sequential-access device; linked list**.

MESSAGE BOX A message box (Figure 51), also called an *alert box*, is a small window that appears in order to give a message to the user. When the user acknowledges reading the message by pressing a mouse button, the message box disappears.

FIGURE 51 Message Box

MESSAGE SENDING In object-oriented programming, a message is a call to a procedure associated with an object type. See **object-oriented programming**.

METALANGUAGE A metalanguage is a language used to describe another language. For example, Backus-Naur Form can be used as a metalanguage to describe the syntax of programming languages. Lisp and Prolog have the interesting property that programs can read and modify themselves, so these programming languages can be put to practical use as metalanguages for themselves. See **Backus-Naur Form; Prolog; Lisp**.

METHOD In object-oriented programming, a method is a procedure associated with an object type. See **object-oriented programming**.

MFM Modified frequency modulation (MFM) is the conventional way of recording data magnetically on disks. See **ST-506**. For contrast, see **RLL**.

MHz See **megahertz**.

MICRO The prefix *micro-* means one millionth (10^{-6}). For example, a microsecond is one millionth of a second (0.000001 second), and a microfarad is one millionth of a farad.

MICRO CHANNEL The Micro Channel is the bus design used in the IBM PS/2 computers, model 50 and higher (see **bus**). It contrasts with the bus design of the IBM PC, XT, and AT, which is also used in the lowest PS/2 models. Plug-in cards designed for one bus cannot be used with the other.

Unlike the original bus, the Micro Channel is designed to allow use of more than one CPU in a single computer. See also **EISA**.

MICROCOMPUTER A microcomputer is a computer whose CPU consists of a single integrated circuit known as the *microprocessor*. Ordinarily, a microcomputer is used by only one person at a time. All home computers are microcomputers. (See **integrated circuit; microprocessor**.)

MICROCONTROLLER A microcontroller is a microprocessor designed specifically for controlling equipment. Microcontrollers often contain some memory and input-output circuitry on the same chip with the microprocessor. This enables the microcontroller to work as a self-contained unit. Microcontrollers are used in consumer products such as telephones, automobiles, and microwave ovens, as well as in industrial equipment. See **embedded system**.

MICROPROCESSOR A microprocessor is an integrated circuit containing the entire CPU of a computer, all on one chip, so that only the memory and input-output devices need to be added. The first popular microprocessor, the Intel 8080, came out in 1973 and cost approximately $400; it now sells for about $1.

Microprocessors are commonly described as "8-bit," "16-bit," or the like. The number can refer either to the number of bits in each internal data register, or to the number of bits on the data bus (see **bus**); these two numbers are often, but not always, the same. Other things being equal, larger registers and a larger bus enable the processor to do its work faster.

Clock speed is also important. The *clock* is the oscillator that causes the microprocessor to proceed from one step to the next in executing instructions. (Each machine instruction takes several clock cycles.) Clock speed is measured in megahertz (MHz); 1 MHz is 1 million cycles per second. Higher clock speeds result in faster computation—but only if exactly the same machine instructions are being executed; this is why it is misleading to compare the clock speeds of processors of different types. It is even possible for two microprocessors with the same instruction set and clock speed to perform computations at different rates because of differences in internal design. An 8-MHz 80286, for example, is much faster than an 8-MHz 8086.

Table 13 describes a number of popular microprocessors. The processors in each group (e.g., the 68020 and 68030) use the same machine language and run the same programs.

MICROSOFT Microsoft, one of the leading software-producing companies, was founded by William Gates and Paul Allen in 1975, when they wrote a version of BASIC. Microsoft BASIC, sold with the IBM PC as PC BASIC, is one of the most commonly used versions of BASIC. (See **BASICA**; **GW-BASIC**.) Microsoft's most widespread product is the operating system MS-DOS, sold with the IBM PC as PC-DOS and also used on many other computers based on the 8088 microprocessor. In 1987 Microsoft introduced OS/2, which is designed to be

Table 13 Commonly Used Microprocessors

Manufacturer	Type number	Register size (bits)	Bus size (bits)	Clock speed (MHZ)	Where used/Comments
Zilog	Z80	8	8	2	Kaypro, other CP/M systems
MOS	6502	8	8	1	Apple II
Tech-nology	6502A	8	8	2	Commodore VIC-20
Intel	8088	16	8	4.77-8	Original IBM PC chip
	8086	16	16	8	Like 8088, wider bus
	80286	16	16	8	IBM PC AT
	80386	32	32	25	Newer PC's
	80386SX	32	16	25	Slower, cheaper 386
	80486	32	32	33	Faster 386, built-in math coprocessor
	80486SX	32	32	20	Slower 486, no math coprocessor
NEC	V20	16	8	8	Replaces 8088, slightly faster
	V30	16	16	8	Replaces 8086, slightly faster
Motorola	68000	32	16	8	Original Macintosh
	68020	32	32	16	Macintosh LC
	68030	32	32	40	Macintosh IIfx
	68040	32	32	50	68030 with math coprocessor

*These processors are manufactured for a variety of clock speeds in the range 16-25 MHz. The manufacturers offer faster speeds as the design is refined.

downward compatible with MS-DOS while at the same time taking advantage of the multitasking features available on microcomputers based on the 80486, 80386, or 80286 microprocessors (such as the IBM PS/2 line). However, acceptance of OS/2 has been slowed considerably because of the large amount of memory it requires to run well.

In 1990 Microsoft introduced version 3.0 of Windows, a much improved version of an earlier product that provided a graphical user interface for computers in the IBM PC line. Windows 3.0 rapidly became a best seller, and many other software makers wrote programs to operate within the Windows environment. (See **Windows**.)

Microsoft is also a big seller of applications software; two major products are the spreadsheet Excel and the word processing program Microsoft Word. Microsoft also produces compilers for several different programming languages. New products introduced in 1991 include version 5.0 of MS-DOS and Visual BASIC, a version of BASIC that allows the programmer to take advantage of the graphical environment of Windows 3.0

Microsoft is headquartered in Redmond, Washington.

MICROSOFT WORD Microsoft Word is a word processing program produced by Microsoft, Inc. It can be used with a mouse that allows you to move the cursor around the screen while editing (see **mouse**). It also allows you to work on more than one area of text at a time by dividing the screen into different windows. Microsoft Word is a powerful, sophisticated word processor and is best suited for complex work.

MICROSPACING Microspacing is the insertion of extra space in a printed document in units smaller than the size of one character. (See **justification**.)

MIDI MIDI stands for M̲usical I̲nstrument D̲igital I̲nterface, which is a standard way for communicating information about music between different electronic devices, such as computers and sound synthesizers. A device with a MIDI out port can be connected to a device with a MIDI in port, and the music can be transmitted between the devices by using a standardized system of codes.

MILLI- The prefix *milli-* means one-thousandth (10^{-3}). For example, a millisecond is one-thousandth of a second (0.001 second), and a millimeter is one-thousandth of a meter.

MINICOMPUTER A minicomputer is a computer intermediate in size between a mainframe computer and a microcomputer; two examples are the Digital Equipment Corporation VAX and the IBM AS/400. A minicomputer typically occupies a large area within a room and supports 10 to 100 users at a time. Minicomputers are typically used by medium-sized business and academic institutions.

MINIFINDER On the Macintosh, the MiniFinder is a menu of commonly used pieces of software. By configuring the MiniFinder appropriately, the user can find commonly used pieces of software without searching through all the files on the disk.

MINIMIZE To minimize a window is to make it as small as possible; usually this means that it becomes an icon rather than a window. To do this, click the mouse on the minimize button (see **window**). This is a handy way to get one piece of software out of the way temporarily while you turn your attention to something else. You can then restore the window when you want to resume working with it. See also **maximize; restore.**

MIPS MIPS stands for <u>m</u>illion <u>i</u>nstructions <u>p</u>er <u>s</u>econd and refers to the speed with which computer programs are run. Because different instructions take different amounts of time, speed measured in MIPS depends on the exact program that the computer is running. For this reason, speed tests are usually done with standard programs such as "Whetstone" and "Dhrystone."

Another problem is that equivalent programs take different numbers of instructions on different CPUs. To compare different computers meaningfully, it is common practice to calculate MIPS using the number of instructions that a program would require on a VAX rather than on the computer actually being tested. This way, equivalent programs are always reviewed as having the same number of instructions and the speed of the computer under test is the only variable.

MIS See **management information systems.**

MNEMONIC A mnemonic is a device that helps you remember something. For example, the expression "Spring forward, fall back" helps you remember which way to adjust your clocks in the spring and the fall for daylight saving time.

A *mnemonic variable name* is a variable name that helps the programmer remember what the variable means. For example, in a payroll program the variable to represent the hours worked could be named X312W17HK, but it would be much better to give the variable a mnemonic name such as HOURS.

MNP MNP (<u>M</u>icrocom <u>N</u>etworking <u>P</u>rotocol) is a method for detecting and correcting errors in data transmission. (For a description of another method in detail, see **XMODEM**.) MNP error correction is built into some high-speed modems so that erroneous data is never sent to the computer. MNP level 5 and above also includes data compression.

MODEM A modem (short for <u>mo</u>dulator-<u>dem</u>odulator) is a device that encodes data for transmission over a particular medium, such as telephone lines, coaxial cables, fiber optics, or microwaves.

The modems commonly used with computer terminals and microcomputers transmit RS-232 serial data over telephone lines. (See **RS-232; serial**.) Since the RS-232 interface is standard, practically any modem can be used with any terminal or computer. (An exception is an *internal modem*, which mounts inside the computer and contains its own RS-232 port.)

To be used with a modem, a microcomputer must run a program that makes it act like ("emulate") a communications terminal.

Some important features of modems include the following:

1. Baud rate. The original Bell 103 method for transmitting data on telephone lines works only for transmission rates of 300 baud (30 characters per second) and slower. At 1,200 baud (120 cps), a different system, known as Bell 212A, is used. Most 1,200 baud modems support both kinds of transmission; less expensive modems can be used only at 300 baud and below. At higher baud rates, the applicable standards are CCITT V.22 bis (2400 baud) and V.32 (4800 and 9600 baud).

2. Originate and answer modes. When two modems are linked together, they transmit at different frequencies so that each one receives signals from the other, rather than from itself. The two sets of frequencies are known as *originate mode* and *answer mode*. Normally, terminals and microcomputers use originate mode, and the mainframe computer that they are calling uses answer mode. Inexpensive modems support only originate mode, since it is usually the only one needed. However, if two microcomputers are to be linked together by telephone, one of the modems must be in originate mode and the other in answer mode (it doesn't matter which is which).

3. Auto-answer capability. An auto-answer modem can be set up to answer incoming telephone calls. This is necessary if

it is to be used with a computer that will receive calls from outside, rather than just making calls under the control of the user.

4. Auto-dial feature. With some modems, the user must dial a telephone number on an ordinary telephone, and then turn on the modem once the other computer answers. An auto-dial modem, however, can do its own dialing in response to special commands transmitted to it by the computer or terminal.

5. Full- and half-duplex modes. This is normally a switch setting on the modem, the computer terminal, or both. In full-duplex mode, characters typed by the user do not appear on the screen until the other computer receives them and transmits them back. This provides visible proof that they are being received correctly. In half-duplex mode, characters appear on the screen when typed and are not repeated by the computer on the receiving end.

If what you are typing does not appear on the screen, switch to half-duplex. If each character appears twice, switch to full-duplex. If there are half-/full-duplex switches on both the terminal and the modem, at least one of them should always be set to full-duplex.

See **Hayes compatibility; ISDN.**

MODEM ELIMINATOR An RS-232 cable that interchanges conductors 2 and 3 is known as a modem eliminator because it allows two computers to be connected together without modems. (See **DCE**; for diagram, see **RS-232.**)

MODEM, NULL See **null modem; modem eliminator.**

MODULA-2 The programming language Modula-2 was developed by Niklaus Wirth in the late 1970s as a replacement for Pascal, which Wirth had developed some 10 years earlier. Modula-2 replaces an earlier version, called simply Modula. As its name suggests, Modula-2 is designed to encourage modularity (see **structured programming**). Modula-2 is very similar to Pascal, especially the extended versions of Pascal that most compilers now implement. The main differences are:

1. In Modula-2, routines can be compiled separately and linked at load time. Compiled units are called MODULES.

2. The IMPORT and EXPORT declarations control recognition of names. IMPORT means "Recognize names here that

are declared in another module;" EXPORT means "Allow other modules to IMPORT names that are declared here."

3. Modula-2 allows the programmer to divide the program into concurrent tasks that run simultaneously. (See **timesharing**.)

4. The BEGIN and END statements are used only to mark the beginning and end of the program. Within the program, each IF, WHILE, or FOR construct is terminated with an END. (As in Pascal, REPEAT is terminated with UNTIL.)

5. Each standard input-output statement handles only one item of a specific type. For instance, the Pascal statement

```
WRITELN('The answer is ',A)
```

is replaced by the sequence:

```
WriteString('The answer is');
WriteReal(A);
WriteLn
```

This feature makes it easier for users to write their own replacements for input-output routines.

6. As in PL/I, procedures can determine, at run time, the size of arrays passed to them as parameters. This makes it practicable to handle variable-length character strings.

7. The CASE statement has an ELSE clause (as it already has in most implementations of Pascal).

8. Upper and lower case are distinguished throughout the program; reserved words must be entirely in upper case, and names differing only in case (e.g., WRITELN vs. WriteLn) are not equivalent. An entire name is significant, not just its first eight characters.

Here is a sample program in Modula-2:

```
MODULE Demo;
FROM InOut IMPORT WriteInt;
VAR k : INTEGER;
BEGIN
   k := 1;
   REPEAT
     WriteInt(k,4);
     k := k * 2
   UNTIL k>1000
END.
```

MODULE A module is a part of a larger system. A module in a computer program is a part of the program that is written and tested separately and then is combined with other modules to form the complete program. (See **top-down programming.**)

MONADIC OPERATION A monadic operation requires only one operand. For example, negation (finding the negative of a number) is an operation that requires only one operand and is therefore monadic.

MONITOR (1) A monitor is a computer program that supervises the activity of other programs.

(2) A device similar to a television set that accepts video signals from a computer and displays information on its screen is known as a monitor. The monitor itself does no computing at all.

The first generation of personal computers used TV-type *composite video* monitors. The sharpness of the image on the screen depended on the *bandwidth*, or frequency response, of the monitor. Users were quick to note that color-TV monitors had much poorer bandwidth than black-and-white (monochrome) monitors.

Several additional kinds of monitors are now in wide use. These include *TTL monochrome monitors*, which give a very sharp image and accept the same signal voltages as TTL integrated circuits; *RGB color monitors*, which accept digital signals for red, green, and blue on separate wires; *analog color monitors*, in which the intensities of red, green, and blue range along a continuum, making a larger number of colors possible; and *multiscan (multisync) monitors*, which can scan the screen at different rates when in different video modes. See **TTL; RGB monitor; video modes (IBM PC); eyeglasses for computer users.**

MONOCHROME MONITOR A monochrome monitor is a computer monitor that can display only one color. Monochrome monitors generally are better when working with text because they provide sharper resolution for numbers and letters than do color monitors. However, a color monitor is needed if you would like your computer to do color graphics. A monochrome monitor usually displays white, green, or amber characters on a black background. Different people have different preferences as to which arrangement is easiest on the eyes.

MONTE CARLO Monte Carlo is a type of simulation method that uses random numbers to determine the evolution of a system. Suppose that you know the probability that a particular event will happen, but it is too difficult to calculate the probability that a complicated combination of events will occur. In the Monte Carlo method you use a random number generator to calculate a random number between 0 and 1, and then compare that number with the probability of the event. For example, if the probability of the event is .62, and the random number generated is .58, then the program will simulate that the event has occurred. The name Monte Carlo comes from the fact that this method is a bit like a game of chance.

MOTOROLA 68000 See **microprocessor.**

MOUSE A mouse is a computer input device that is used by rolling it around on your desk and pressing one or more buttons. Graphical user interfaces such as Microsoft Word and the Apple Macintosh operating system are built around the mouse. So are paint and draw programs. See **Windows; Macintosh; paint program; draw program; trackball.**

There are two basic ways to add a mouse to a computer that was not originally wired for one: to connect a *bus mouse* to the bus via a special adapter card, or to connect a *serial mouse* to a serial port.

MS ms is an abbreviation for millisecond, which is one-thousandth of a second. (See **access time.)**

MS-DOS (PC-DOS) Microsoft Disk Operating System (MS-DOS, marketed by IBM as PC-DOS; often called simply DOS) is the usual operating system for IBM PC-compatible computers. (See **IBM PC.**) MS-DOS originated as a CP/M-like operating system for 8086 and 8088 microprocessors. Since version 2.0, however, DOS has included UNIX-like tree-structured directories and pipes.

DOS file and directory names have the form XXXXXXXX.XXX (i.e., up to 8 letters and/or digits, a period, and up to 3 more letters or digits). The part after the period is called the *extension.*

At any time there is a particular *default disk* (*current disk*) and a particular *default directory* on each disk. These are where a file is assumed to be if there is no indication to the contrary.

Here are some examples of file names with and without directory information:

XXXXX.XXX	File XXXXX.XXX in current directory on current disk
A:XXXXX.XXX	File XXXXX.XXX in current directory of disk A
A:\XXXXX.XXX	File XXXXX.XXX in main (root) directory of disk A
A:ZZZ\XXXXX.XXX	File XXXXX.XXX in directory ZZZ, which is in the current directory of disk A
A:\ZZZ\XXXXX.XXX	File XXXXX.XXX in directory ZZZ, which is in the main (root) directory of disk A

Crucially, if the directory information (the *path*) starts with a backslash (\), it is understood as beginning in the root directory; otherwise it begins in the current directory of the appropriate disk.

Here are some common DOS commands:

A:	Make disk A the default disk
CD C:\PROGS	Make \PROGS the default directory on disk C
DIR B:	List the files on disk B
COPY A:ZZZ B:	Copy file ZZZ from disk A to disk B

To understand how DOS processes commands, imagine you've just typed QWERTY at the command prompt. The following things happen:

1. DOS looks for a built-in command named QWERTY. A few commands, such as DIR, are built in. Of course QWERTY isn't.
2. DOS looks for a file that may be named QWERTY.BAT, QWERTY.COM, or QWERTY.EXE in the current directory of the current disk.
3. DOS looks for files with those names in the search path (a list of directories stored in memory with the PATH or SET PATH command).

If DOS doesn't find QWERTY in any of these places, you get the message "Bad command or file name."

The output of most commands can be redirected to a file or to the input of another command. For example,

DIR C: > B:DIRECTRY

writes the output of DIR C: onto file B:DIRECTRY, and

DIR C: I SORT I MORE

sends the output of DIR C: through the sort program to put lines in alphabetical order, and then through the command MORE, which displays it one screenful at a time.

DOS runs with the microprocessor in real mode, so that memory space is limited to 1,024K, of which addresses above 640K are reserved for video memory. This is the famous "DOS 640K limit" that is actually an artifact, not of DOS, but of the IBM PC video architecture. See **real mode**. See also **BAT; COM; EXE; OS/2; Windows**.

MULTIMEDIA Multimedia refers to the combination of sound and visual information. In the future it will likely be common for people to use computers to display artwork, listen to music, and retrieve related information. A large amount of memory will be required. See **CD-ROM; hypertext**.

MULTIPLE INHERITANCE In object-oriented programming, multiple inheritance is what happens when an object type is defined to be the combination of two or more preexisting types. Some programming languages permit this and others do not. See **object-oriented programming**.

MULTIPLE VIRTUAL MODE See **virtual 8086 mode**.

MULTIPROCESSING Multiprocessing is the use of more than one CPU in a single computer system.

MULTIPROGRAMMING Multiprogramming is the apparently simultaneous execution of more than one program on a single computer through timesharing.

MULTISCAN, MULTISYNC See **monitor**.

MULTITASKING Multitasking is the execution of more than one program apparently at the same time on the same computer. In reality, the CPU rapidly switches its attention among the various programs (see **timesharing**). Multitasking makes it possible to print one document while editing another, or to perform lengthy computations "in the background" while working on something else on the screen. (See **OS/2; Windows; UNIX**.)

The programs that run concurrently are called *processes* or *tasks*. (See **process**.) An important concern is to keep tasks from interfering with each other. For example, two tasks cannot use the same area of memory or the same input-output device, such as a printer, at the same time. (See **protected mode**.) If tasks communicate with each other, it is important to prevent *deadlocks*, in which two tasks are each waiting for the other to do something, so that neither one can make any progress.

A more primitive form of multitasking allows you to switch from one program to another, but only one program at a time actually runs; the others are frozen until you return to them.

MVS MVS (<u>M</u>ultiple <u>V</u>irtual <u>St</u>orage) is an operating system for IBM mainframe computers; from the user's point of view, it is almost completely compatible with OS/360. (See **OS/360; JCL; TSO**.)

n

N-TYPE An N-type semiconductor region is formed by doping a silicon crystal with an impurity that contains five outer-level electrons. (See **semiconductor**.)

NAK In XMODEM and some other protocols, ASCII code 21 (CTRL-U) stands for "not acknowledged" (abbreviated "NAK"); it is sent when a data packet is received incorrectly or is not received when expected.

NAND GATE A NAND gate (Figure 52) is a logic gate whose output is 0 if both of the inputs are 1, and is 1 otherwise, as shown in the table.

input 1
input 2
output

FIGURE 52

Input 1	Input 2	Output 3
0	0	1
0	1	1
1	0	1
1	1	0

A NAND gate is equivalent to an AND gate followed by a NOT gate (Figure 53).

FIGURE 53

Figure 54 shows how other gates can be constructed from combinations of NAND gates. This is commonly done in designing TTL and CMOS digital integrated circuits.

NANO- The prefix nano- means one billionth (10^{-9}). For example, 1 nanosecond is one billionth of a second.

NATIONAL CHARACTER The national characters on a computer are those whose appearance varies from country to country. For example, on IBM mainframes, the characters $, #, and @ are called national characters because they may be replaced by other characters such as £ or ¥ for use outside the United States.

NATURAL LANGUAGE PROCESSING At present, all human communication with computers is done in artificial languages such as BASIC and Pascal. Computers would be much more useful if they could understand instructions in ordinary human languages (natural languages) such as English and French. In the early days of computers, it was assumed that successful natural language processing programs would be easy to construct, given sufficient computing power. However, progress has been slow. There are three main problem areas:

1. Syntax. No one has yet produced a complete, mathematically precise description of the possible sentence structures of any human language. There are a number of promising approaches (all derived, directly or indirectly, from the work of

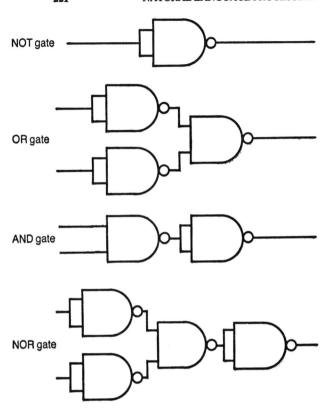

FIGURE 54 Other Gates Constructed from NAND Gates

Noam Chomsky in the 1950s), but all of them run into diffi-
culties with some types of sentences. The correct interpreta-
tion of pronouns such as *himself* and *each other* is especially
problematic; human beings seem to know intuitively how to
use such words in a sentence as soon as they learn what they
mean, but no one has ever captured this knowledge in a completely satisfactory set of explicit rules. Facts such as this
have led Chomsky and his followers to suspect that the
human brain is genetically "preprogrammed" in quite specific ways for certain features of human language.

2. Semantics. If the computer is to understand sentences, it must have some kind of internal representation of their meanings. The most straightforward way to represent meanings in a computer is to decompose them into a finite set of primitive elements; for example, *grandfather* can be rendered as MALE PARENT OF PARENT OF SELF, where MALE, PARENT, OF, and SELF are part of a small "built-in" vocabulary.

There are, however, many words whose meanings defy representation in this form. For example, as Geoffrey Sampson has pointed out, the word *picturesque* cannot be broken up into simpler elements; but one would hardly want to say that the human brain acquired a new "built-in" primitive concept, PICTURESQUE, just a couple of centuries ago when the word first came into use. Many meanings seem to consist of mental images or sets of associated ideas that admit of considerable vagueness.

3. Phonetics. Although computers can now produce reasonably intelligible synthetic speech, it is difficult to get them to recognize human speech. The problem is that, although speech seems to consist of strings of distinct sounds (*m*, *a*, and *n* for *man*), in reality the sounds are merged together, even in the clearest radio-announcer speech. (The *a* and *n* in *man*, for instance, are almost completely simultaneous.) In addition, variations between speakers often lead to ambiguity; for instance, many New Yorkers pronounce *man* almost exactly the way Southerners pronounce *men*. There are even substantial differences between the sound waves produced when the same person pronounces the same word twice. The best speech-recognition systems available today recognize only a few hundred words and usually have to be "tuned" to the speech of a particular person.

There are many approaches to natural language processing. Some programs attempt to model processes in the human brain, while others use any available procedure to obtain practical results, even if it is something human speakers could not possibly do (e.g., processing the words of each sentence in reverse order). There is some controversy over whether it is better to try to determine the sentence structure first, and then the meaning, or whether the computer should construct a representation of the meaning of a sentence in one step; the latter approach results in programs that are less neatly organized, but that can use information about meaning to help make decisions about sentence structure.

The best currently available natural language processors often perform impressively (e.g., Yale University has developed one that reads incoming news stories from a teletype line and prepares summaries of them), but none of them is highly reliable; each program misinterprets certain types of sentences, often producing ludicrously incorrect results. Natural conversations between human beings and computers are still several years away. (See also **parsing.**)

NATURAL LOGARITHM See **logarithm.**

NEAR LETTER QUALITY A near-letter-quality (NLQ) printer produces output that resembles the print of an old cloth-ribbon typewriter. Near-letter-quality printing is completely satisfactory for student papers, magazine articles, and book manuscripts, but not for dissertations or correspondence on corporate letterheads.

NEST To nest structures is to put a structure inside another structure of the same kind. For example, in BASIC, three nested FOR loops look like this:

```
FOR I=1 TO 100
  FOR J=1 TO 100
    FOR K=1 TO 100
      ...statements to be repeated go here...
    NEXT K
  NEXT J
NEXT I
```

NETWARE See **Novell Netware.**

NETWORK A network is a set of computers connected together. (See **local-area network; wide-area network.**)

NEURAL NETWORK A neural network is a computer program that models the way nerve cells (neurons) are connected together in the human brain. Neural networks enable a computer to train itself to recognize patterns in a strikingly human-like way. Like the human brain, neural networks give only approximate results, but they can do things that no other kind of computer program can do.

Figure 55 shows how a neural network is set up. Each neuron has several inputs but only one output. Some of the inputs *excite* (activate) the neuron while others *inhibit* it, each with a particular strength. The idea is that each output neuron will be activated when one particular kind of pattern is present at the input. In the computer, the neurons and connections are simulated by arrays of numbers.

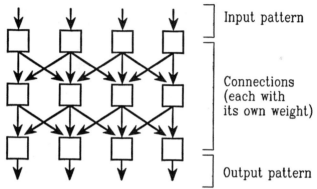

Input pattern

Connections
(each with
its own weight)

Output pattern

FIGURE 55 A Neural Network.

Training a neural network is like training an animal. Patterns are applied to the input and a simple algorithm adjusts the weights of the connections to try to get the desired output. After many training runs, in which this is done with many different patterns, the neural network "learns" to recognize patterns of a certain kind. Even the programmer need not know exactly what these patterns have in common. The patterns are analyzed by the neural network, not by the programmer.

Neural networks are good at recognizing inputs that are vague, ill-defined, or likely to contain scattered variation. For example, a neural network can recognize images of human faces, or patterns of weather data, or trends in stock market behavior. However, a neural network is never 100 percent reliable, and even simple calculations can be quite slow.

NEWSGROUP A newsgroup is a public forum or discussion area on a computer network. All users of the network can post messages, and every user can read all the messages that have been posted.

The most famous newsgroups are those distributed world-wide by the Usenet organization, covering thousands of topics. See **Usenet.**

NFS Network File System (NFS) is an extension to UNIX that enables computers on a network to share disk drives. NFS was developed by Sun Microsystems but is available on computers from a wide variety of manufacturers. See **local area network; file server.**

NIBBLE A nibble consists of 4 bits, or half of 1 byte.

NICAD Nicad stands for nickel-cadmium, a type of rechargeable battery often used in laptop computers.

NODE (1) A node is an individual computer (or occasionally another type of machine) in a network. (See **local-area network; wide-area network.**)

(2) A node is a location in a tree where branches connect. (See **tree.**)

NONDESTRUCTIVE READ A nondestructive read occurs when information is transferred from a memory location without erasing the information that is stored in that memory location.

NONDOCUMENT MODE In WordStar and other word processors, the nondocument mode is used for typing files that are to be used for some purpose other than printing—for example, computer programs. Nondocument mode produces plain-text files with no special codes for hyphenation, page breaks, or the like. (See **document modes; text file.**)

NONINTERLACED See **interlacing.**

NOR GATE A NOR gate (Figure 56) is a logic gate whose output is 0 when either or both of the two inputs are 1, as shown in Figure 56.

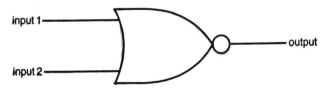

input 1 ──────────────── output

input 2 ────────────────

FIGURE 56

Input 1	Input 2	Output 3
0	0	1
0	1	0
1	0	0
1	1	0

A NOR gate is equivalent to an OR gate followed by a NOT gate (Figure 57), but its circuit is no more complex than that of a single OR gate (Figure 58). In fact, the circuit shown here is more reliable than the circuits illustrated in the articles on AND and OR gates, since the emitters of both transistors are grounded, and their input impedances therefore do not vary with changes in the state of the rest of the circuit. For this reason, it is common to construct all the other gate circuits from combinations of NOR gates (Figure 59). (This type of circuitry, known as RTL (resistor-transistor logic) is now obsolete for everything except demonstration circuits. TTL and CMOS logic circuits are often built up in an analogous way from combinations of NAND gates.)

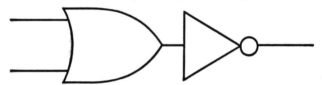

FIGURE 57

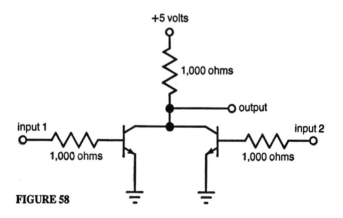

FIGURE 58

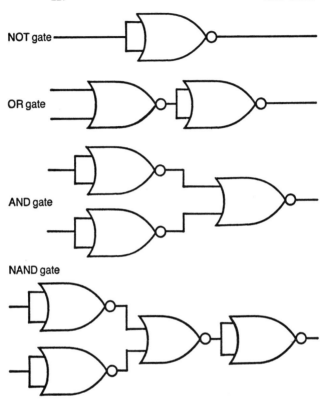

FIGURE 59 Other Gates Constructed from NOR Gates

NORTON UTILITIES The Norton Utilities, by Peter Norton, are a set of programs for the IBM PC. Their most important function is to recover erased files and correct other problems with disks. (See **recovering erased files.**)

NOT GATE A NOT gate (Figure 60) is a logic gate whose output is 1 if the input is 0, and vice versa, as shown in the table.

Input	Output
0	1
1	0

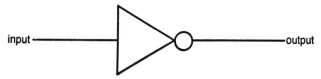

FIGURE 60

A NOT gate can be constructed with a switch (see Figure 61). If the switch is closed, representing 1, then the output voltage will be the same as the ground voltage (0 volt). If the switch is open, then the output voltage is the same as the power supply voltage (which represents 1).

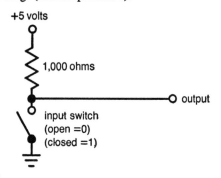

FIGURE 61

The same idea can be used to build a NOT gate with a transistor (see Figure 62). If the input is at 0, the transistor does not conduct, and the output is 5 volts (representing 1). But if the input is 5 volts, the transistor conducts, and the output voltage is zero.

NOTEBOOK A notebook computer is about the size of a looseleaf notebook, weighing some five to eight pounds. It is slightly smaller than a laptop computer.

NOVELL NETWARE Novell NetWare is a very popular software package for networking IBM PC-compatible computers. It is produced by Novell, Inc. of Provo, Utah. NetWare runs with many kinds of network hardware and communications protocols (including Ethernet, Arcnet, and IBM token ring) and enables computers to share files and printers.

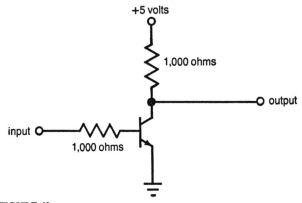

+5 volts

1,000 ohms

output

input

1,000 ohms

FIGURE 62

One of the machines in the network is the server. It is possible for the server to also perform as an ordinary computer, but if the network is very busy, it is more efficient if the server is solely dedicated to the task of being server.

Each individual computer on the network needs to have a part of the network software copied onto its hard disk. This software (called the NetWare shell) will take over the function of the operating system. The software also provides a way for the user to connect to the data on the server machine. This is where the computer in the network will start to behave differently from the stand-alone computer. NetWare assigns a particular drive letter to the file server. It is common in microcomputers for drive letters A and B to refer to floppy disk drives and C, D, and E to refer to hard disks, so NetWare typically uses the letter F for the server. To access the server, the user needs to login—that is, establish a connection to the server. Type F: to change the active disk drive to F, and then enter the command LOGIN. The prompt ENTER YOUR LOGIN NAME will be displayed on the screen. Type that name, and you're in. (If your network has more than one server, you also need to type the name of the server to which you wish to be connected.) For security you may be required to give a password.

Managing the hard disk of the file server is more complicated than managing the hard disk of a stand-alone machine because you need to determine the rules governing access to the data.

When you use the hard disk of your personal stand-alone computer, you have the authority to do whatever you want. In the case of the hard disk of the file server machine, all users cannot do whatever they wish to the hard disk. One user cannot erase files that others will need, or fill up so much hard disk space that other users are crowded out, or browse through confidential files from other users. A network must have a supervisor to control the allocation of rights. There are four levels of access that a user might have to a particular directory:

- unlimited access, meaning the user can read data from files in the directory and write new information to the directory.
- modified write access, meaning the user has limited ability to make changes in some files.
- read-only access, meaning the user can read data from files in the directory but cannot write any new information or cannot change the existing files in any way.
- no access.

All users could be given their own subdirectory on the file server disk, and they would then be given unlimited access to that directory. When a user's job involves entering updates for data, each would be given the right to modify files in that directory. Other users would be given read-only access to the files containing the company data. Most users would also be given read-only access to directories containing software. Individual users should not be able to modify or erase valuable software or data. For directories with data from other departments, the user could be prevented from gaining any access.

In order to send your printing to a network printer, use the NetWare CAPTURE command to tell your computer to intercept output destined for the printer port and instead send it along the communications line to the network. The capture command, part of the NetWare shell, is designed so that your applications software doesn't realize that anything different is happening; it will generate the same codes that it would generate if it was sending output to a printer connected directly to the printer port of your computer.

When the output from the printer command reaches the server, it will be stored in the print queue—that is, a line of jobs waiting to be printed. The network printer will not always be ready for you in the same manner that a printer connected to your own computer will be. In general, the jobs will be printed in the order received by the server, although the order could be modified if one job has a high priority or another large but less urgent job can be run during off-peak hours.

NP-COMPLETE PROBLEM See **limits of computer power**.

NULL MODEM A null modem is a cable for connecting two computers together without a modem. (See **modem eliminator**.) For diagram, see **RS-232**.

NUMBER CRUNCHING To crunch numbers is to perform massive amounts of arithmetic, especially for scientific or engineering calculations.

NUMERIC KEYPAD A numeric keypad is a separate set of keys beside the main alphabetic keypad that contains the digits 0 to 9 and a decimal point key. The digits are arranged in the same way as they are on an adding machine. If you have to type large quantities of numeric data, a numeric keypad is quicker to use than the number keys on the regular keypad.

NUMERICAL INTEGRATION Numerical integration is the process of finding the area under a particular curve by dividing the area into many tiny rectangles, adding up the heights of individual rectangles, and then multiplying the sum by their common width. Numerical integration is the kind of task that is best left to a computer.

For example, in probability it is important to find the area under the curve.

$$y = \frac{1}{\sqrt{2\pi}} e^{-(1/2)x^2} \text{ from } x = -\infty \text{ to } x = b$$

This area can be found with the following BASIC program, which uses a loop to perform a numerical integration:

```
10      INPUT B
20      A = 0
25      P = SQR(2 * 3.14159)
30      FOR I = 1 TO INT(100 * B)
35      X = I/100 - .005
40      Y = EXP(-X * X/2)
45      A = A + Y
50      NEXT I
55      PRINT .5 + A/(100 * P)
60      END
```

As you might imagine, it would take a long time to perform this calculation with a calculator, since you would have to re-type all the instructions each time.

O

OBJECT-ORIENTED GRAPHICS See **draw program**.

OBJECT-ORIENTED PROGRAMMING Many programming languages let the programmer define new data types such as records, arrays, and linked lists (see **data structures**). In object-oriented programming, the programmer can associate a set of procedures (*methods*) with each type. Crucially, the same name can be given to different procedures that do corresponding things to different types; this is called *polymorphism*. For example, there could be a "draw" procedure for circles and another for rectangles.

Some uses for object-oriented programming include the following:

1. *Graphical objects.* A program that manipulates lines, circles, rectangles, and the like can have a separate "draw" procedure for each of these types.
2. *Mathematical objects.* In order to work with vectors, matrices, or other special mathematical objects, the programmer has to define not only data structures for these objects, but also operations such as addition, inversion, or finding a determinant.
3. *Input-output devices.* The procedure to draw a line might be quite different on a printer or plotter than on the screen. Object-oriented programming provides a simple way to ensure that the right procedure is used on each device.
4. *Simulation.* In a program that simulates traffic flow, for example, cars, trucks, and buses might be types of objects, each with its own procedures for responding to red lights, obstructions in the road, and so forth. This, in fact, is what object-oriented programming was invented for. The first object-oriented programming language was Simula, introduced in 1967.

Here is an example of object-oriented programming in Turbo Pascal. Imagine a program that manipulates points, lines, and circles. A point consists of a location (*x* and *y* coordinates), plus a procedure to display it (just draw a dot). So the programmer defines a type called *pointtype* as follows:

```
type pointtype = object
                 x, y: integer;
                 procedure draw;
               end;
```

This is just like a record declaration except that it refers to procedure draw, defined like this:

```
procedure pointtype.draw;
begin
  PutPixel(x,y,white)
end;
```

Now variables of type pointtype can be declared, for example:

```
var  a, b: pointtype;
```

Here the objects *a* and *b* are like records each containing an *x* and *y* field; *x* and *y* are called the *instance variables*. In addition, *a* and *b* are associated with the *point.draw* procedure. Here's an example of how to use objects:

```
a.x := 100;
a.y := 150;
a.draw;
```

This sets the *x* and *y* fields of *a* to 100 and 150, respectively, and then calls the draw procedure associated with *a* (namely *pointtype.draw*).

Now let's process circles. A circle is like a point except that in addition to *x* and *y*, it has *a* radius. Also, its *draw* method is different. We can define *circletype* as another type that *inherits* from *pointtype* (i.e., contains everything that *pointtype* contains) except that it adds an instance variable called *radius* and substitutes a different *draw* method. Here's how it's done:

```
type circletype = object(pointtype)
                  radius: integer;
                  procedure draw;
                end;
```

```
procedure circletype.draw;
begin
  Circle(x,y,radius)
end;

var c: circletype;

  ⋮
c.x := 200;
c.y := 250;
c.radius := 49;
c.draw;
  ⋮
```

It is important to remember that instance variables belong to individual objects such as *a*, *b*, and *c*, but methods (procedures) belong to object types. The advantage of object-oriented programming is that it automatically associates the right procedures with each object: *c.draw* uses the circle draw procedure because object *c* is a circle, but *a.draw* uses the point draw procedure because object *a* is a point.

Object types are often called *classes*. The act of calling one of the object's methods is sometimes described as "sending a message" to the object (e.g., *c.draw* "sends a message" to *c* saying "draw yourself"). All object-oriented programming systems allow one class to inherit from another (like *circletype* and *pointtype* above); some also allow *multiple inheritance*, in which a class can be defined as the combination of two or more pre-existing classes.

See also **C++; Smalltalk**.

OBJECT PROGRAM An object program is a program that has been translated into machine language and is ready to be run. (See **compiler**.)

OCR See **optical character reader**.

OCTAL An octal numbers system is a base-8 number system. Octal numbers use only the digits 0, 1, 2, 3, 4, 5, 6, and 7.

OFFSET (1) On a microprocessor such as the 8088, each memory address is given as two numbers, a segment and an offset. To find the actual address, the segment is shifted one hexadecimal digit to the left and the offset is added to it. For instance, the address F123:1114 (segment F123, offset 0004) means:

$$
\begin{array}{r}
F123 \\
+ \quad 1114 \\
\hline
F2344
\end{array}
$$

where F2344 is the *absolute address*. Note that F000:2344 refers to exactly the same address; so does F200:0344, and so on. See also **segment**.

(2) Offset printing is printing on paper by means of ink transferred by a rubber roller from another surface. Most print shops use offset printing to produce large numbers of high-quality copies from camera-ready art. (See **camera-ready**.)

OHM The ohm is the unit of measure of electric resistance. If an object has a resistance of 1 ohm, then an applied voltage of 1 volt will cause a current of 1 ampere to flow through the device. (See **Ohm's law**.)

Impedance is also measured in ohms. Impedance is similar to resistance but is defined in terms of alternating current rather than direct current. (See **impedance**.)

OHM'S LAW Ohm's law states that the current that will flow through a circuit element is equal to the voltage applied across that element divided by the resistance of that element: $I = V/R$, where I = current, in amperes; V = voltage, in volts: and R = resistance, in ohms.

ON-LINE SYSTEM In an on-line system, data are entered into a device, such as a terminal, that is connected directly to a computer.

OOP See **object-oriented programming**.

OPEN (1) In some editing, word processing, and drawing programs, to open a file or document means to call it up from disk in order to work with it.

(2) In several programming languages, a file is said to be open when it is ready to have data transferred into or out of it.

(3) A switch is open when it is turned off so that no current can flow.

OPEN SYSTEMS INTERCONNECTION See **data communication.**

OPERANDS The items on which a mathematical operation is performed are called its *operands*. For example, in the expression

2 + 3

the plus sign is the operator, and 2 and 3 are the operands.

OPERATING SYSTEM An operating system is a program that controls a computer and makes it possible for users to enter and run their own programs.

A completely unprogrammed computer is incapable of recognizing keystrokes on its keyboard or displaying messages on its screen. Most computers are therefore set up so that, when first turned on, they automatically begin running a small program supplied in read-only memory (ROM), or occasionally in another form (see **boot**). This program in turn enables the computer to load its operating system from disk or tape, though some microcomputers have complete operating systems in ROM.

Under the control of the operating system, the computer recognizes and obeys commands typed by the user. In addition, the operating system provides built-in routines that allow the user's program to perform input-output operations without specifying the exact hardware configuration of the computer. A computer running under one operating system cannot run programs designed to be run under another operating system, even on the same computer. For articles on specific operating systems, see **CP/M; MS-DOS; UNIX; DOS; MVS; OS/2; VM/SP.**

OPERATIONS RESEARCH Operations research is concerned with the development of mathematical models of repetitive human activities, such as those involved in traffic flow, assembly lines, and military campaigns. Operations research makes extensive use of computer simulation.

OPTICAL CHARACTER READER An optical character reader is a device that can recognize typed or handwritten characters on paper.

OPTICAL DISK An optical disk is a high-density storage device that uses lasers to create patterns to represent the information. (See **CD ROM; WORM.**)

OPTION BUTTON In a dialog box, option buttons are small circles only one of which can be chosen at a time. The chosen button is black and the others are white. Choosing any button with the mouse causes all the other buttons in the set to be cleared.

Because options buttons work like the buttons on older car radios, they are sometimes called *radio buttons*. For picture, see **dialog box**.

OR GATE An OR gate (Figure 63) is a logic gate whose output is 1 when either or both of the inputs are 1, as shown below:

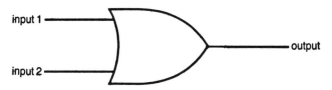

FIGURE 63

Input 1	Input 2	Output 3
0	0	0
0	1	1
1	0	1
1	1	1

An OR gate can be constructed by using two switches in parallel (Figure 64). The output signal will be present (nonzero) if either switch 1 or switch 2 is closed.

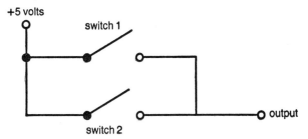

FIGURE 64

The same concept can be used to construct an OR gate with transistors (see Figure 65). In this circuit, logic level 0 is

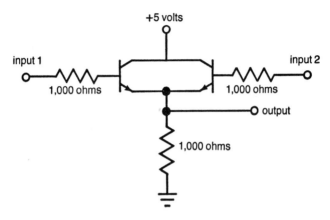

+5 volts

input 1

1,000 ohms

input 2

1,000 ohms

output

1,000 ohms

FIGURE 65

represented by 0 volts, and logic level 1 is represented by 5 volts. A positive voltage at the input of either transistor causes it to conduct; the output voltage is approximately 5 volts if either or both of the transistors are conducting.

ORPHAN The last line of a paragraph is an orphan if it appears by itself as the first line of a page. Some word processors automatically adjust page breaks to avoid orphans. See also **widow**.

OS/2 The OS/2 operating system was developed by Microsoft for the IBM PC AT and PS/2 computers. It runs only on machines with 80286, 80386, or 80486 microprocessors. Version 1.0 of OS/2 uses a command language almost identical to that of MS-DOS (PC-DOS); Versions 1.1 and up use Presentation Manager, a mouse-and-window-oriented user interface similar to that of Microsoft Windows. Version 2.0 can run all DOS and Windows software as well as OS/2 software.

OS/2 is a multitasking operating system. That is, it enables the computer to shift its attention rapidly back and forth between several processes, seemingly running several programs at the same time. This has several advantages:

1. A user can have more than one program active at the same time (e.g., a word processor and a spreadsheet), switching back and forth between them. It is not necessary to save and quit in one program before starting another.

2. Slow computations and data transfers can be done "in the background" while the user works with another program.
3. Multitasking can lead to better performance with complex programs such as word processors. The manufacturer can divide the word processor into tasks that are managed by the operating system, such as a task that checks for keyboard input, a task that updates the screen, and a task that sends output to the printer. The user need never know that multi-tasking is going on.

OS/2 uses the same disk formats as DOS, except that every disk should have a label (labels are permitted but not required under DOS).

Unlike DOS, OS/2 can swap to disk, using extra disk space as a substitute for RAM. Thus, although OS/2 requires about 4 megabytes of RAM for good performance, there is no fixed amount of RAM needed to run a particular program.

OS/360 OS/360, the operating system released with the IBM 360 in the early 1960s, formed the basis of many subsequent operating systems (OS/VS2, MVT, MVS, etc.) See also **TSO; JCL.**

OS-9 OS-9 is a multitasking operating system developed for real-time control computers and also used extensively on the Tandy Color Computer.

OSI See **data communication.**

OUTLINE An outline program makes it possible to organize your ideas into a hierarchical outline. People generally need to arrange large amounts of information into hierarchies. For example, a long book is divided into chapters, and each chapter may be further divided into sections. Outlining programs are available that allow you to organize information you write in this form. When working with an outline, you will sometimes want to see only the broadest points—say, the top two or three levels of the outline. At other times you will want to look at all of the specific information for part of the outline.

For example, suppose you are writing a book about different types of animals. It would help to enter the information about the classification of animals as an outline. If you start at the top level and display four levels down, here is what part of the outline will look like:

Animals
    Invertebrates
    Arthropods
    Vertebrates
        Fishes
            Teleostei (bony fishes)
            Holostei
            Chondrostei
        Amphibians
            Urodela (salamanders and sirens)
            Anura (frogs and toads)
        Reptiles
            Chelonia (turtles)
            Sauria (lizards)
            Crocodilia (crocodiles)
            Serpents (snakes)
        Birds
            Sphenisciformes (penguins)
            Anseriformes (Waterfowl)
            Falconiformes
        Mammals
            Carnivora (dogs, cats, others)
            Aritodactyla (cattle, pigs, others)
            Rodentia (rats, mice, others)
            Chioptera (bats)
            Lagomorpha (rabbits, hares)
            Insectivora (shrews, moles, others)
            Perissodactyla (horses and others)
            Cetacea (whales, dolphins, porpoises)
            Proboscidea (elephants)
            Primates

(Note that not all categories of animals have been included in this outline.) Now, suppose you want to focus on Cetacea. If you move to the Cetacea location and display four levels down from there, the outline looks like this:

      Cetacea (whales, dolphins, porpoises)
        Odontoceti (toothed)
          Physeteridae
            Sperm whale
          Monodontidae
            Narwhal
            Beluga
          Phocoenidae
            Porpoise

        Delphinidae
            Dolphin
            Killer whale
    Mysticeti (baleen)
        Eschrichtiidae
            Gray whale
        Balaenidae
            Right whale
        Balaenoteridae
            Humpback whale

The outline is structured as a tree (see **tree**). Each data item (node) is displayed below the item above it, and lower levels are indented more than upper levels. Recursion can be used in the program to display the outline. The part of the outline below each data item can be displayed as if it were a complete outline on its own. (See **recursion**).

OUTPUT The output of a computer is the information that the computer generates as a result of its calculations. Computer output may be either printed on paper, displayed on a terminal, or stored on magnetic tapes or disks.

OVERFLOW An overflow error condition arises when the result of a calculation is a number too big to be represented on the computer.

OVERLAID WINDOWS Overlaid windows can overlap; when they do, one window hides the parts of others that are behind it. To bring another window to the front, move the mouse pointer into it and click the button. For contrast, see **tiled windows; cascaded windows**.

P ————————————————————————

P-TYPE A P-type semiconductor region is formed by doping a silicon crystal with an impurity that contains three outer-level electrons. (See **semiconductor**.)

PACKET A packet is a group of consecutive characters sent from one computer to another over a network. For an example, see XMODEM. On many local-area networks, all communications are in the form of packets that begin with labels indicating the machine to which they are addressed. See **X.25**.

PACKET RADIO Packet radio is the transmission of data (in packets) by radio. It is a fast-growing hobby among radio amateurs ("hams") and also has commercial applications as a way of linking computers without wires.

A typical amateur packet system consists of a computer linked by a terminal-node controller (TNC) to a radio transmitter and receiver. The TNC constructs and recognizes packets. The packet radio protocol effectively prevents two systems from transmitting at the same time, and all data are error-checked. Packet systems are often used to run bulletin boards (See **BBS**). Unlike telephone-line BBSs, packet BBSs are inherently multiuser systems, because each packet contains a label indicating its sender and receiver. Thus, the computer can keep track of many users concurrently.

Commercial packet systems involve portable computer terminals carried by delivery or service personnel. The terminals are linked by radio to a main computer many miles away. See also **AX.25**.

PACKET SWITCHING Packet switching is a technique that enables many computers to share a single communication channel, such as a cable, by transmitting all data in packets which specify the machine to which they are addressed. See **packet**.

PAGE See **virtual storage**.

PAGE FAULT See **virtual storage**.

PAGEMAKER PageMaker, produced by Aldus Corporation, was one of the pioneering programs used for desktop publishing when it was introduced for the Apple Macintosh in 1984. Its capabilities include the ability to move text or graphics around the page and to use style sheets so that all subheads will have the same form automatically. Updated versions have been released for the Windows 3 environment on the IBM PC. (See **desktop publishing**.)

PAINT PROGRAM A paint program is one type of program for drawing pictures on a personal computer. The user draws with the mouse pointer (see **mouse; pointer**), and commands are provided for drawing circles, lines, rectangles, and other shapes, as well as for drawing freehand and creating shaded areas.

Paint programs treat the picture as a grid of pixels (see **pixel**). Shadings are easy to produce simply by making individual pixels black or white, but the pixel grid puts a fundamental limit on the sharpness of the picture. By contrast, see **draw program**.

Some popular paint programs include MacPaint (supplied with the Apple Macintosh) and Paintbrush (supplied with Microsoft Windows).

PALETTE A palette is a set of colors chosen from a much larger set. For instance, the IBM VGA can display more than 250,000 different colors, but the programmer or user must choose a palette of no more than 256 to use at a time. The whole set of displayable colors is also sometimes called a palette.

PARALLEL (1) Two electronic circuit elements are connected in parallel if the electric current will reach the same destination by flowing through either element. Figure 66 shows two resistors connected in parallel.

(2) Parallel data transmission is the transmission of several bits at the same time over different wires; it is usually faster than serial transmission (see **serial**). In connecting a printer to a microcomputer, it is important to know whether the printer requires parallel or serial (RS-232) data.

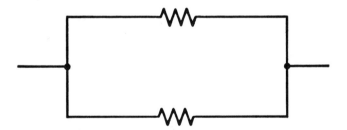

FIGURE 66

PARALLEL PORT A parallel port is a connection by which a computer can transmit data to another device using parallel transmission—that is, several bits sent simultaneously over separate wires. It is common for a microcomputer to have a parallel port that is connected to a printer. For contrast, see **serial port**.

PARALLEL PRINTER A parallel printer is a printer that connects to a computer's parallel port. See **parallel port; serial port**.

PARALLEL PROCESSING Parallel processing is what a computer does when it carries out more than one computation at the same time on different CPUs. By contrast, most multitasking is accomplished by making a single CPU switch its attention among several tasks. This is called **concurrent processing or timesharing**.

PARAMETER A parameter in a procedure is a symbol that will be replaced by a supplied value when the procedure is called. The use of parameters allows you to make your instructions much more general. For example, here is a set of cooking instructions that uses parameters:

1. Put the object in the oven.
2. Set the temperature to the temperature listed in the recipe.
3. Set the timer to the time listed in the recipe.
4. Wait until the timer goes off.
5. Take the object out of the oven.
6. Turn the oven off.

There are three parameters here: "object," "the temperature listed in the recipe," and "the time listed in the recipe." Before you can actually execute the instructions, you must be given specific values for these three items. Here is how the instructions look once you have some specific values:

1. Put the tuna casserole in the oven.
2. Set the temperature to 375 degrees.
3. Set the timer to 30 minutes.
4. Wait until the timer goes off.
5. Take the tuna casserole out of the oven.
6. Turn the oven off.

Here is a Pascal program containing a procedure called swap. The procedure uses two parameters: *x* and *y*. The first time the procedure is called, the variables *a* and *b* are substituted for the parameters. The next time *b* and *c* are used.

```
PROGRAM swapnum (INPUT, OUTPUT);
  VAR
    a, b, c : INTEGER;
    PROCEDURE swap(VAR x, y : INTEGER);
      VAR temp : INTEGER;
      BEGIN
        temp := x;
```

```
 x := y;
 y := temp
END;
BEGIN {Main program}
 READLN(a, b, c,);
 WRITELN('a=',a,' b=',b,' c=',c);
 swap(a,b);
 WRITELN('a=',a,' b=',b,' c=',c);
 swap(b,c)
 WRITELN('a=',a,' b=',b,' c=',c)
END.
```

Here is a sample run of this program with the numbers 239, 535, and 66 as input:

```
a=239 b=535 c=66
a=535 b=239 c=66
a=535 b=66  c=239
```

The names that are used for the parameters in the procedure declaration (*x* and *y* in this case) are known as the *formal parameters*. The names used when the procedure is called (*a*, *b*, and *c* in this case) are the *actual parameters*.

PARITY (1) The parity of a number is its quality of being odd or even. Often, when groups of bits (1's and 0's) are being transmitted or stored, an extra bit is added so that the total number of 1's is always odd (or, alternatively, always even). This is called the parity of the data. An error in transmission has a 50 percent chance of changing the parity, so that if errors are frequent, the recipient of the information will have some warning that they are present.

If you are setting up a computer terminal and do not know how to set the parity and related parameters, try the following, which is the most popular combination:

Baud rate:	1200
Parity:	Even
Data bits:	7
Stop bits	1
Duplex:	Full (FDX) (Change to half duplex if you cannot see what you type.)

A terminal set to the wrong parity can often be recognized because about half of the characters are incorrect, while the rest are received normally.

(2) The memory of IBM PC compatible computers is parity checked. The message PARITY ERROR 1 or PARITY ERROR 2 means that a memory chip is defective.

PARK To park the head of a hard disk drive means to disengage it so that the disk will be protected from possible damage if the computer is moved.

PARSING Parsing is the analysis, by computer, of the structure of statements in a human or artificial language. For instance, MS-DOS (PC-DOS) has to parse the command

    dir b: /p

to determine that "dir" is the name of the command, that "b:" specifies the files to be shown, and that "/p" is another parameter (in this case, it means "pause when the screen is full"). Compilers and interpreters have to parse statements in programming languages. (See **compiler; interpreter**.) Programs that accept natural-language input have to parse sentences in human languages.

Parsing is done by comparing the string to be parsed to a *grammar*, which defines possible structures. For example, Figure 67 shows the structure of the sentence "The dog chased the black cat." Figure 68 shows a small part of a grammar of English.

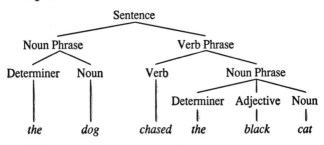

FIGURE 67 Structure of a Simple English Sentence

Parsing can be done either *top-down* or *bottom-up*. In top-down parsing, the computer starts by looking for a particular constituent. It consults the grammar to determine what this constituent consists of, then looks for those constituents instead, thus:

Look for Sentence
Rule 1: Sentence consists of Noun Phrase + Verb Phrase
    Look for Noun Phrase
    Rule 2: Noun Phrase consists of Determiner + Noun
        Look for Determiner
            Accept Determiner *the* from input string
        Look for Noun
            Accept Noun *dog* from input string
    Look for Verb Phrase   (etc.)

(1)	Sentence	→	Noun Phrase + Verb Phrase
(2)	Noun Phrase	→	Determiner + Noun
(3)	Noun Phrase	→	Determiner + Adjective + Noun
(4)	Verb Phrase	→	Verb + Noun Phrase
(5)	Determiner	→	*the*
(6)	Noun	→	*dog*
(7)	Noun	→	*cat*
(8)	Adjective	→	*black*
(9)	Verb	→	*chased*

FIGURE 68 A Small Part of a Grammar of English. Each rule states that the constituent named on the left can consist of the constituents named on the right, in the specified order.

The process is complete when the input string is empty and all of the elements of a sentence have been found.

In bottom-up parsing, the computer accepts elements from the input string and tries to put them together, thus:

Accept *the*, which is a Determiner
Accept *dog*, which is a Noun
Determiner + Noun make a Noun Phrase
Accept *chased*, which is a Verb
Accept *the*, which is a Determiner
Accept *black*, which is an Adjective
Accept *cat*, which is a Noun
Determiner + Adjective + Noun make a Noun Phrase
Verb + Noun Phrase make a Verb Phrase
Noun Phrase + Verb Phrase make a Sentence

Parsing algorithms must be able to *backtrack* (back up and try alternatives) because the grammar provides alternatives. For example, a noun phrase may or may not contain an adjective; and a word like *leaves* may be a verb or a noun. Further, parsing algorithms usually use *recursion* to handle the recursive structure of human languages. For example, a noun phrase can contain a noun phrase, which can contain another noun phrase, as in *the discoverer of the solution to the problem.* (See **recursion; backtracking; natural language processing.**)

PART 15 DEVICE This term refers to radio transmitters that are allowed to operate without a license under the terms of Part 15 of the Federal Communications Commission (FCC) Rules and Regulations. Examples include cordless telephones, wireless intercoms, and some kinds of wireless computer communication devices (wireless LANs). Because individual Part 15 transmitters are not licensed, there is no way to guarantee that they will not interfere with each other. By contrast, licensed transmitters can be given exclusive use of a particular frequency in a particular area.

PASCAL Pascal, a programming language developed by Niklaus Wirth, is designed to encourage programmers to write modular and well-structured programs. Pascal has become one of the most popular languages for microcomputers, and there are several common versions. Here are some of its features:

1. The first word in a Pascal program is PROGRAM, followed by the program name. The first line also normally includes the words (INPUT,OUTPUT). The first part of the program is a declaration section for constants, variables, procedures, and functions. Every variable used in a Pascal program must be declared. The action part of the program starts with the word BEGIN, and the program concludes with the word END, followed by a period. Statements are separated from each other by semicolons.

2. Pascal provides four standard data types: real, integer, Boolean, and char. *Integer* variables can take on only values that are whole numbers or the negatives of whole numbers. *Real* variables can take on numerical values that include fractional parts, such as 23.432. *Boolean* variables are logic variables that can only have two possible values: true or false. *Char* variables can take on single character values.

   Here is an example of a declaration section:

```
VAR
   count, total : INTEGER;
   average : REAL;
   error : BOOLEAN;
   c : CHAR;
```

3. An assignment statement in Pascal looks like this:

```
x : = 3;
```

Note that a colon followed by an equal sign is the symbol used for assignment. This statement will cause the variable x to take on the value 3. For integers and real numbers, + means addition, – means subtraction, * means multiplication, and ** means exponentiation (although exponentiation is not available in all Pascal versions). Division for real numbers is represented by /. There are two separate division commands for integers. The expression a DIV b will be the quotient of *a* divided by *b*, ignoring the remainder. The expression a MOD b will be the remainder when a is divided by b. For example, 14 DIV 5 is 2, and 14 MOD 5 is 4.

4. The two input commands are READ and READLN. If you are using Pascal interactively, the statement READ(x) will cause the computer to stop and wait for you to type a value for x at the keyboard. READLN (which stands for "read line") works the same way except that after a READLN is executed the computer will start looking at the next data line when it reaches the next input statement.

The two output commands are WRITE and WRITELN. The command WRITE(x); causes the value of the variable x to be displayed. The command WRITE ('Hello'); causes the word *Hello* to be displayed. The command WRITE (x:6) causes the value of x to be displayed in a field that is six characters wide, and the command WRITE(x:7:3) causes the value of x to be displayed in a field that is seven characters wide and three characters to the right of the decimal point displayed. After a WRITE command is executed, the output for subsequent output statements will be displayed on the same line. After a WRITELN statement, the output from subsequent output statements will be displayed on a new line.

5. The IF/THEN/ELSE statement can be used to control the actions of a program. For example:

```
IF x > 0 THEN WRITELN ('x is positive')
ELSE WRITELN ('x is negative');
```

If you would like more than one action to be executed if the condition is true, you may form a compound statement that starts with the word BEGIN and concludes with the word END. For example:

```
IF x > 0 THEN
   BEGIN
      WRITELN ('The value of x is a positive');
      WRITELN ('The square root of x is',SQRT(x))
   END;
```

Pascal provides for three types of loops: REPEAT, WHILE and FOR loops. Each of the following program segments causes the numbers from 1 to 10 to be printed:

```
number := 0;
REPEAT
   number := number + 1;
   WRITELN(number);
UNTIL number >= 10;
. . .
number := 1;
WHILE number <= 10 DO
   BEGIN
      WRITELN(number);
      number := number + 1
   END;
. . .
FOR number := 1 TO 10 DO WRITELN(number)
```

6. Arrays are declared by listing the highest and lowest allowable values for their subscripts. For example, the declaration

`VAR officenum : ARRAY [1 .. 20] OF INTEGER;`

defines officenum as being a 20-element one-dimensional array, and the declaration

`VAR table: ARRAY [0 .. 10, 0 .. 15] OF REAL;`

defines tables as being a two-dimensional array with 11 rows (labeled 0 to 10) and 16 columns (labeled 0 to 15).

7. One of the most valuable features of Pascal is the capability it provides for writing modular programs. A procedure is a mini Pascal program defined in the declaration section of the main program. The procedure can be executed from the main program simply by listing its name. A procedure may have parameters, and any variables that are declared within the procedure are local to that procedure. (See **procedure**.) Pascal also provides for functions that return values to the calling program. (See **function**.)

8. A special feature of Pascal is that it provides the capability for the programmer to define new data types that can be used in addition to the four standard types. Pascal also allows the programmer to define sets, and then perform a set operation such as union or intersection. By using a structured data type called a *record*, it is possible to organize related data of different types. (See **record**.)

9. Comments in Pascal begin with a left brace, {, and end with a right brace, }. On some systems comments begin with (* and end with *). A Pascal program can be very readable if it consists of several procedures that all have meaningful mnemonic names.

Here is a sample program written in Pascal:

```
PROGRAM primecheck (INPUT,OUTPUT);
   {*This program reads in an integer n and then
   n determines whether or not it is prime.*}
VAR n,i,max : INTEGER;
   continue : BOOLEAN;
   status : CHAR;
BEGIN
   READLN (n);
   status := 'Y';
   continue := TRUE;
   i := 1;
   max := TRUNC(SQRT(n));
WHILE continue
   DO BEGIN
      i := i + 1;
      continue := (i < max);
      IF (n MOD i) =0 THEN BEGIN
          status := 'n';
      continue := FALSE
      END
   END;
WRITELN (n);
WRITELN ('PRIME: YES(Y) OR NO (N):');
WRITELN (status)
END.
```

See also **Turbo Pascal; Modula-2.**

PASCAL, BLAISE Pascal was a French mathematician who built in 1642 a mechanical adding machine that was one of the early forerunners of calculators and computers.

PASSWORD A password is a secret character string that is required to log onto a computer system, thus preventing unauthorized persons from obtaining access to the computer.

PASTE To "paste" material is to transfer it from a holding area into the document you are editing. (See **cut; copy**.)

PATENT A patent gives legal protection for the design of a machine or mechanical process, preventing others from using the same idea without the inventor's permission. Unlike a copyright, a patent protects an idea itself, not just the expression of the idea. In the U.S., a patent remains in force for 17 years.

Computer programs have not traditionally been considered patentable, but some software patents have been issued in recent years and present law is unclear.

Integrated circuits are often protected by both patents (for the circuit design) and copyrights (for the artwork from which the tiny etch pattern is made, or for data recorded on the chip).

See also **copyright**.

PATH (1) A path specifies how to find a file on a disk that has more than one directory. In MS-DOS (PC-DOS), paths have either of two forms. For example,

\AAA\BBB\CCC

means, "In the root directory there is a directory called AAA. In AAA there is a directory called BBB. In BBB there is a directory or file called CCC."

If the initial backslash is left out, the path starts at the directory currently in use rather than at the root directory. For example, the path

AAA\BBB\CCC

means, "In the current directory there is a directory called AAA. In AAA there is a directory called BBB. In BBB there is a directory or file called CCC."

Paths in UNIX are written the same way but with forward slashes ("/" rather than "\").

(2) The PATH command in MS-DOS (PC-DOS) specifies directories where DOS can search for command files (.BAT, .COM,

and .EXE files) if they are not found in the current directory.
See also **directory**.

PC COMPATIBILITY The original IBM Personal Computer
(PC) was designed quickly by IBM and used little new technology; hence few patents protect it, and it is easy for other companies to make compatible machines (see **clone**).

Clones available today are almost perfect imitations of the
IBM PC, XT, or AT; programs that will run on an IBM but not
on a clone are extremely rare. Earlier MS-DOS machines, such
as the DEC Rainbow or Texas Instruments Professional Computer, were PC-compatible only to a limited extent; they could
read the same disks, but they ran only a subset of IBM software
because they did not emulate the IBM BIOS (see **BIOS**).

If a computer merely needs to exchange data with an IBM
PC, it need not be IBM-compatible at all; all it needs is a suitable communications medium (such as phone lines or a local-area network) with suitable software.

PC-GLOBE See **mapping software**.

PCX PCX is a standard format for graphic image files developed
by ZSoft, manufacturer of a popular paint program called PC
Paintbrush. PCX files use run-length encoding to store bitmaps
compactly. (See **bitmap, data compression**.)

As the name suggests, PCX files are closely tied to the format of IBM PC video memory; this enables them to be displayed on the PC screen very quickly. The PCX format has
been revised several times to support newer video hardware.
See **video modes (IBM PC)**.

In addition to ZSoft products, many other programs also
recognize PCX format. File names usually end in ".PCX." For
comparison, see **TIFF; GIF**.

PDC PROLOG See **Turbo Prolog**.

PEEK PEEK is an instruction or function in BASIC that allows
the programmer to read the contents of a particular memory location, identified by its address. The uses of the PEEK function
depend on the exact type of computer and even the accessories
installed. See also **POKE, BASIC**.

PERIPHERAL A peripheral is a device connected to a computer.
Three examples of a peripheral are *terminals, tape drives*, and
disk drives.

PERSONAL COMPUTER A *personal computer* is designed to be used by only one person, either at home or in a business setting. The term personal computer includes some microcomputers that are too large and expensive to be referred to as home computers. One of the first personal computers was the Digital Equipment Corporation PDP-8, a minicomputer often used in scientific laboratories in the early 1970s. See also **IBM PC; PS1; PS2.**

PERT PERT stands for Program Evaluation and Review Technique, which is a method for project planning by analyzing the time required for each step. See **project management.**

PI The greek letter π (pi) is the symbol for a special number that is approximately equal to 3.14159. If the radius of a circle is r, then the circumference is $2\pi r$, and the area is πr^2.

PICA (1) A pica typewriter prints 10 characters per inch. So do most fixed-pitch computer printers.

(2) In typesetting, a pica is $\frac{1}{6}$ inch, or 12 points.

PICO- The prefix *pico-* means one trillionth (10^{-12}). One picosecond is one trillionth of a second.

PIF In Microsoft Windows, OS/2, and certain other software environments on the IBM PC, a file whose name ends in ".PIF" contains information about how to run an .EXE or .COM file—how much memory it requires, whether it can run in a window, whether it can multitask, and the like. PIF stands for Program Information File.

PILOT PILOT is a programming language especially suited for writing programs for computer-assisted instruction. PILOT makes it easy for teachers to write conversational instructional programs without needing to know much about the details of programming.

PIN The pins in a dot-matrix printer press on the ribbon to make dots on the paper. A 9-pin printer produces readable but inelegant type. Some 9-pin printers have a near-letter-quality mode in which they simulate 18 pins by making two passes across each line; the result resembles the type from a cloth-ribbon typewriter. Printers with 24 pins produce very sharp letter-quality text.

PIPE In UNIX, MS-DOS, and similar operating systems, a pipe is a way of stringing two or more programs together so that the output of one of them is fed to the other as input. For example, the MS-DOS command

```
A> DIR | SORT | MORE
```

invokes DIR (which lists the names of the files on a disk), feeds its output to SORT (which puts the items in alphabetical order), and feeds that output to MORE (which displays it one screenful at a time). The vertical line (|) is the symbol for pipe.

PIRACY Piracy is the unauthorized copying of software, which is forbidden by law. (See **software license; copyright.**)

PITCH The pitch of a printer is the number of characters per inch (most commonly 10). Fixed-pitch type has every character the same width; proportional-pitch type has some characters wider than others (e.g., "M" wider than "I"), and the pitch can only be measured approximately as the average of many different letters.

PIXEL A picture on a CRT screen is made up of tiny elements called pixels. For example, a VGA color screen in high-resolution mode consists of a 640-by-480 pixel array. You can draw pictures on the screen by controlling the color of each pixel. (See **graphics.**)

PL/I (PL/1) PL/I is a very powerful programming language developed by IBM in the early 1960s to accompany its System/360 computer. The name stands for Programming Language One (I) and is also written as PL/1.

PL/I can be described as a combination of ALGOL 60 block structure, FORTRAN arithmetic, and COBOL data structuring. PL/I is the language of choice for writing complex programs on IBM mainframe computers, but it has received little use on other types of machines.

Some of the main features of PL/I are the following:

1. Many data types are available, including floating-point numbers, fixed-point binary numbers, and fixed-point decimal numbers (all of these with any number of significant digits, up to hardware-imposed limits); character strings (of fixed or varying length); bit strings; and several more exotic types such as variables whose values are statement labels.

Undeclared variables are taken to be fixed-point binary numbers if their names begin with I, J, K, L, M, or N, and floating-point numbers otherwise.

2. Values of any type can be assigned to variables of practically any other type: conversions are done automatically. For example, if the fixed-point number 2.45 is assigned to a character string, the result is the string '2.45'. A subroutine can determine, at execution time, the size of an array or character string passed to it as a parameter.

3. Each statement ends with a semicolon. The beginning of a comment is marked with /* and the end of a comment with */.

4. The arithmetic operators are + (addition), − (subtraction), * (multiplication), / (division), and ** (raising to a power). The equals sign, =, is used both in assignment statements and in comparisons.

5. There are many ways of doing input and output. For example,

```
GET LIST (A, B, C);
```

instructs the computer to read A, B, and C from the standard input file; the values of A,B, and C can be written in any reasonable format (as with Pascal's READ and READLN). The corresponding output statement is PUT LIST (A, B, C,);

The statement

```
GET EDIT (A, B, C) ((3)(F(4,2)));
```

tells the computer that A, B, and C are each represented as four digits, two of which are to the right of the decimal point (as in FORTRAN's FORMAT statement; see format). A complete record of a file can be read in one step with the READ INTO statement.

6. There are several types of loops. The equivalent of a FORNEXT loop in BASIC is of the form

```
ALPHA: DO I=10 TO 20 BY 2;
    /* statements in middle go here */
END ALPHA;
```

There are also DO WHILE and DO UNTIL loops, corresponding to Pascal's WHILE and REPEAT constructs.

7. Subroutines and functions are defined by the word PROCEDURE, as in the following:

```
IC: PROCEDURE(A, B, C);
    /* statements */
END IC;
```

Procedures are invoked with a CALL statement, as in FORTRAN:

```
CALL IC (-2, 3, ZZZ);
```

The main program is a procedure with the option MAIN.
Here is a program written in PL/I:

```
PRMCHK: PROCEDURE OPTIONS(MAIN);
   /* THIS PROGRAM READS A SEQUENCE OF
   NUMBERS AND IDENTIFIES WHICH ONES ARE
   PRIME.*/
      DECLARE  (N, I) FLOAT;
               ON ENDFILE GO TO STOP;
      START:   GET LIST(N);
      LOOP:  DO I = 2 TO (TRUNC(SQRT(N))+1);
               IF N/I = TRUNC(N/I) THEN
                  GO TO NPRIME;
             END LOOP;
             PUT SKIP(2) LIST(N, 'IS PRIME');
             GO TO START;
      NPRIME:PUT SKIP(2) LIST(N,'IS NOT PRIME);
             PUT SKIP LIST('IT IS DIVISIBLE BY',I);
             GO TO START;
      STOP:  END PRMCHK;
```

PLANE (1) In geometry, a plane consists of all the points on a flat surface. Thus a plane is a two-dimensional space on which things have length and width but no thickness.

(2) In computer graphics, a plane is one of several images that are superimposed to produce the final image. For example, many video cards have separate planes (internal bitmaps) for red, green, and blue. The complete image is produced by displaying all three planes on the screen simultaneously so the colors mix.

PLASMA See **gas plasma display**.

PLATEN A platen is the roller in a typewriter or printer against which the keys strike. Some printers use the pressure of the platen to pull the paper forward.

PLATFORM A platform is a piece of equipment (or occasionally software) used as a base on which to build something else. For example, a mainframe computer can serve as a platform for a large accounting system.

PLOTTER A plotter is a device that draws pictures on paper by moving pens according to directions from a computer. (See **graphics**.)

POINT In typesetting, a point is $1/72$ inch. The height of type is usually expressed in points. However, this is not a measurement of the size of the letters, but rather of the metal blocks on which the letters were originally cast for printing presses. Therefore, different typefaces of the same point size may be somewhat different sizes.

In a typical book-sized line of type, about 25 picas wide, readability is greatest with 10-point type with 2 points of leading. Greater width calls for larger type, lesser width (as a newspaper column) calls for smaller type. This works out to 6 lines to the inch. (See **leading; typeface; typesetting mistakes**.)

POINT-OF-SALE SYSTEM A point-of-sale system is a computer used in place of a cash register where merchandise is sold. Besides keeping track of cash, the computer can keep track of inventory and print informative invoices and receipts.

POINTER (1) A pointer is a data item consisting of an address that tells where to find a desired item. For examples, see **linked list; tree**.

Pascal provides a specific data type called a pointer variable that can be used to keep track of data structures that vary in size as the program is executed.

(2) The pointer is a symbol that moves around a computer screen under the control of the user. For example, to execute a command on an Apple Macintosh, use the mouse to move the pointer to the icon representing that command, and then press the button on the mouse.

POKE POKE is a BASIC instruction that allows you to put a specific value in a specific memory location. To use the POKE command, you must specify two numbers: an address and the value you want poked into that address. (Fortunately, you may give these values as decimal numbers or expressions.) The effects of the POKE statement depend on the exact type of computer and even the accessories installed. See also **PEEK; BASIC**.

POLISH NOTATION Polish notation is a way of writing algebraic expressions that does not require parentheses to state which operations are done first. It is named in honor of its inventor, Jan Lukasiewicz (1878-1956), whose name most English-speaking mathematicians cannot pronounce.

The ordinary algebraic expression

$$4 + (5 - 3) + 2$$

translates into Polish notation as

$$4\ 5\ 3\ -\ +\ 2\ +$$

To evaluate the expression, work through it from left to right until you encounter an operation (a plus or minus), then perform that operation using an appropriate number of numbers immediately to the left of the operator. Replace the numbers and the operator with the result of the operation, and keep going in the same manner. For the expression above, this works out as follows:

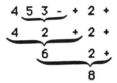

This is technically known as *reverse Polish notation* (*RPN*); the expression can also be written in the other direction and worked through from right to left.

Many calculators and programming language interpreters translate expressions into Polish notation in order to evaluate them. Also, Hewlett-Packard calculators use Polish notation rather than parentheses on the ground that Polish notation is easier to work with once the user becomes accustomed to it.

POLYMORPHISM In object-oriented programming, polymorphism is the use of different procedures, each with the same name, which are associated with different object types. For example, procedures named *draw* could be associated with the types *point*, *circle*, and *square*. Calling *draw* for any particular object then gets the right *draw* procedure for that type. See **object-oriented programming**.

POP See **stack**.

POP-UP MENU See **pull-down menu**.

POP-UP UTILITY See **memory resident**.

PORT (1) To port a program is to adapt it from one kind of computer to another. For example, some IBM PC programs have been ported to the Macintosh.

(2) A serial, parallel, or SCSI port is a connection where a computer can be connected to an external device, such as a modem, printer, or tape drive. See **serial; parallel; SCSI**.

(3) A port address is a unique number used by a microprocessor to identify an input-output device. For example, the hexadecimal number 3F8 is the port address for part of the circuitry that controls the first serial port (COM1) on an IBM PC.

PORTABLE (1) A portable computer is a computer small enough and light enough (under 12 pounds) so that it can be carried around more easily than can a desktop microcomputer. A portable computer is more powerful than a laptop computer, but a laptop computer is easier to carry.

(2) A *portable program* is a program that is machine independent; it can be used on more than one type of machine.

PORTRAIT Portrait orientation refers to paper oriented so that it is higher than it is wide, like a portrait painting. Most printers print with the paper in portrait orientation. If the paper can be turned sideways, the result is called *landscape orientation*. Laser printers typically offer a choice of portrait or landscape orientation.

POSTSCRIPT PostScript, developed by Adobe Systems of Palo Alto, California, is a graphical command language for laser printers (and, potentially, other graphics devices).

A PostScript printer accepts not only characters to be printed but also commands to change the size of type fonts or to draw lines or circles in specific positions.

An application designed to work with PostScript will automatically send PostScript codes to the printer. The user also may write programs in the Postscript language. Here is an example:

```
%! Adobe-PestScript
/Helvetica-Bold findfont 12 scalefont setfont
newpath
72 720 moveto                    %start drawing filled box
142 720 lineto
142 648 lineto
72 648 lineto
closepath
.75 setgray
fill
```

```
0 setgray                    % restore color to black
162 700 moveto
(Filled box) show            % << print text
newpath
100 560 36 0 360 arc stroke  %center (100,560),radius 36,
162 560 moveto               %do complete arc: 0 degrees to 360
(Circle) show                % << print text
/Times-Roman findfont 24 scalefont setfont
100 400 moveto
(Postscript example) show    % << print text
showpage
```

FIGURE 69

The text following the percent signs are comments. Post-Script works with a coordinate system with the origin at the lower left hand corner of the page, with units 1/72 of an inch long. The program demonstrates the use of the *moveto* command, the *lineto* command (which draws a line from the previous point to the indicated point), the *fill* command (which fills an area to a desired shade of gray), and the *arc* command (which can draw portions of circles—in this case, a complete circle). Text is printed by enclosing it in parentheses and then using the command show. Before printing, the appropriate font must be selected; fonts can also be scaled to different point sizes. In more advanced PostScript programs you may use variables and defined procedures. Here is the output of Figure 69:

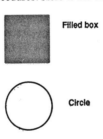

Filled box

Circle

FIGURE 70 PostScript Example

POWER LINE PROTECTION Several things can go wrong with the AC power supplied to a computer from the wall outlet.
1. Brief bursts ("spikes") of excessive voltage can damage the computer. These spikes come from lightning or from large electric motors switching off. They are easily absorbed by a surge protector (see **surge protector**).

2. Power failures cause the computer to shut down or restart suddenly, losing the data that you were working on. A surge protector cannot prevent this; if the problem is frequent, you may want to invest in an uninterruptible power supply (UPS).

3. The computer can emit radio or TV interference through the power line. (See **RFI protection**.)

PPM PPM stands for pages per minute, a measure of the speed of a printer.

PRECEDENCE The precedence rules of a programming language determine in what order the computer will perform the operations if a single expression contains more than one operation. For example, in BASIC, as in many other languages, exponentiations are done first, then multiplications and divisions, and finally additions and subtractions. For example, the BASIC expression

$$2 + 3 * 4 \uparrow 2$$

means $2 + 3 * 16 = 2 + 48 = 50$.

You can use parentheses to change the order of the operations when you need to, since any operation in parentheses will be done first.

Not all languages have the same precedence rules. For example, APL has no precedence rules at all. All APL operations are done in order from right to left.

PRECISION The precision of a quantity refers to how exactly it is specified. For numbers the precision is the number of significant digits that the computer keeps track of when it carries out arithmetic operations. See **rounding error**.

PRESENT VALUE The present value of an amount of money received at a particular time in the future is the equivalent value of that amount if it were available today. In general, amounts further in the future are worth less than amounts closer to the present. The formula for present value is:

$$\text{P.V.} = X/(1 + r)n$$

where X is the amount of money received, r is the interest rate, and n is the number of periods in the future. (If n is the number of years, then r must be the annual interest rate; the same formula works if n is the number of months and r is the monthly interest rate.)

The present value concept is crucial for investment decision-making, since in general an investment project will involve an expenditure of money today with receipts in the future. The present value of each future receipt needs to be calculated. Add these and then subtract the amount of the initial payment to determine the overall present value for the investment project. If the present value is positive, the project is profitable.

Most spreadsheet programs will automatically calculate the present value if you have entered values for the initial payment, the future receipts, and the interest rate. See also **internal rate of return**.

PRESENTATION GRAPHICS A presentation graphics program allows users to create business presentations that integrate drawings, charts, and texts. Examples of software include Persuasion (from Aldus), Hollywood (IBM), Freelance Graphics (Lotus), and PowerPoint (Microsoft). Typically, these programs include drawing tools and the ability to make charts out of data taken from a spreadsheet program. Users can create a complete show by arranging the images in the desired order and standardizing the color scheme for all of the images. By viewing miniature images of the presentation all on the same screen, the user can obtain an overview of the finished product.

PRESENTATION MANAGER In OS/2 1.1 and higher, the Presentation Manager is a user interface similar to Microsoft Windows. It enables the user to control files and software graphically by using a mouse. (See **Windows, Microsoft; OS/2.**)

PRESS To press a mouse button is to depress it and hold it down for about half a second. By contrast, see **click**.

PRIMITIVE A primitive is a basic element or concept in terms of which larger elements or concepts are formed. For example, in programming languages such as FORTH and LISP, it is common for the programmer to create his own statements by defining them in terms of primitives provided by the language.

PRINT SPOOLER A print spooler is a program that stores computer output in memory so that the user's program can finish creating the output without waiting for the printer to print it. The spooler then sends the stored output to the printer at the proper speed. See also **spooling; buffer**.

PRINTER **264**

PRINTER A printer is a device for putting computer output on paper. (See **line printer; daisywheel printer; dot-matrix printer; electrostatic printer; ink-jet printer; laser printer; thermal printer.**)

PRINTF In C, the *printf* statement performs formatted output. For example, the statement

```
printf("The answer is %d\n",i);
```

prints "The answer is," then the value of *i* as a decimal integer, then starts a new line.

The *scanf* statement is very similar, but performs formatted input instead. For example,

```
scanf("%d",&i);
```

reads the value of *i* as a decimal integer from standard input. Its argument is *&i* (the address of *i*), rather than *i* itself, so that it can store a new value in this location. Otherwise it would not be able to change *i*.

The first argument of *printf* or *scanf* is a string with format codes in it. Table 14 gives examples of format codes. There are many others; consult your manual.

TABLE 14 Examples of Format Codes in *printf* and *scanf*

Code	Meaning
%d	Decimal integer
%7d	Decimal integer with 7 digits
%u	Unsigned decimal integer
%x	Hexadecimal integer
%f	Floating-point decimal number
%6.3f	Floating point decimal, occupying a total of 6 characters, with 3 digits to the right of the decimal point
%e	Floating-point number in E format
%c	One character
%s	A character string (*printf* means the entire string; *scanf* reads until a nonblank character is found)
%%	Print '%' (*printf* only)
\n	Start a new line (*printf* only)

PROCEDURE A procedure is a miniature program that is part of a main program. The procedure is executed when the main program calls for it. Here is an example of a Turbo Pascal program with a procedure:

```
PROGRAM divide (INPUT,OUTPUT);
  {This program reads in two integers and then
   performs the division, giving both the
   quotient and the remainder}
VAR a,b:INTEGER;

    PROCEDURE readint(VAR z:INTEGER);
       {This procedure reads in an integer from
        the keyboard.  In case of invalid input,
        it will ask the user to reeneter the data}
       VAR x:STRING; code,z2:INTEGER;
       BEGIN
         WRITE('Enter integer value:');
         READLN(x);
         VAL(x,z2,code);
         WHILE code<>0 DO
            BEGIN
              WRITE('|',x,'|' is invalid; enter integer:');
              READLN(x);
              VAL(x,z2,code)
            END;
         z := z2
       END;

BEGIN {main program block}
  readint(a);  {The procedure is called in each}
  readint(b);  {of these two lines}
  WRITELN('Quotient: ',(a DIV b));
  WRITELN('Remainder:',(a MOD b))
END.
```

FIGURE 71

There are two main advantages to using procedures when writing programs:

1. Often there will be a set of instructions that must be executed at more than one place in a program or in several different programs. Defining those instructions as a procedure saves work and memory space. In the example program, the procedure readint is called twice. This procedure can be included in any program where you need to read in a value that must be an integer.

2. A large program is easier to understand if it consists of procedures. Each procedure should have a well-understood purpose. (See **top-down programming**.)

For another example of a Pascal procedure, see parameter. For an example of the equivalent concept in BASIC, see **subroutine**.

PROCESS In a multitasking computer system, each series of instructions that the computer is executing is called a *process* or *task*. From the user's viewpoint, processes may be programs or parts of programs (such as the editing routine and the printing routine in a word processor that can print while editing). In a multi-user operating system such as UNIX, each user has one or more processes. See **multitasking, UNIX**.

PROCESSOR See **microprocessor; coprocessor; CPU**.

PRODIGY Prodigy is a popular on-line service accessible to computer users with modems. Users can obtain information on news, weather, sports, traveling, shopping, and finance, and they can exchange email.

PROGRAM A program is a set of instructions for a computer to execute. A program can be written in a programming language, such as BASIC or Pascal, or in an assembly language. You may write your own programs if you know a programming language, or you may buy prewritten programs that perform standard tasks, such as word processing or financial calculations. The programs that direct a computer are called *software*.

PROGRAMMABLE FUNCTION KEY A programmable function key is a key on a computer keyboard whose function depends on the software being run. In many cases, programmable function (PF) keys can be defined as equivalent to combinations or sequences of other keys. For example, in IBM PC BASIC, the command

```
KEY 1,"CLS"+CHR$(13)
```

defines function key 1 as equivalent to typing CLS followed by a carriage return [represented by CHR$(13)].

PROGRAMMER A programmer is a person who prepares instructions for computers.

PROGRAMMING Programming is the process of writing instructions for a computer to carry out. A programmer needs to develop a well-defined concept of how to solve a problem. (See **algorithm**.) Then this concept must be translated into a computer language. (See **programming language**.) Finally, the program needs to be turned into machine-readable form and fed into the computer through an input device.

PROGRAMMING LANGUAGE The following is a classification of commonly used programming languages according to their main applications. Several languages fit into more than one category; most are dealt with in separate articles in this book. See also **machine language and assembly language**.

1. General purpose for large, complex programs: PL/I, C, C++, Pascal, Modula-2, Ada.
2. General purpose for smaller programs, especially on microcomputers: BASIC, Pascal.
3. Computer-based education: BASIC, PILOT, LOGO.
4. Mathematical calculation, science, and engineering: FORTRAN, APL, and the general-purpose languages named above.
5. Business data processing: COBOL, RPG. Where microcomputers are involved, BASIC, Pascal, and C are coming into use.
6. Artificial intelligence and programs of extreme logical complexity: LISP and Prolog.

   Another useful classification is based on the way the program is organized.

1. Sequential languages treat the program as a series of steps, with an occasional GOTO statement as a way of breaking out of the sequence. In this category are FORTRAN, BASIC, and COBOL (though COBOL also allows programs to be written in a style more like a block-structured language).
2. Block-structured languages encourage structured programming by allowing the programmer to group statements into functional units. (See **structured programming**.) In this category are ALGOL 60 and 68, PL/I, C, Pascal, Modula, and Ada.
3. Extensible languages build up complex programs by allowing the programmer to define her statements in terms of pre-

viously defined statements. This category includes FORTH, LISP, and LOGO.

PROJECT In Turbo Pascal, Visual Basic, and the UNIX "make" command, a project consists of all the files needed to produce the ready-to-use version of a program. Typically, the compiler accepts procedures from several different files and combines them into one executable (.EXE) file. See **link; make.**

PROJECT MANAGER A project-manager program is a program designed to help plan the scheduling of a complex project involving many different tasks. A typical task requires some resources and a certain amount of time; it also requires that certain other tasks have already been finished. You may sometimes schedule two tasks to be performed simultaneously if they don't overtax the supply of available resources, but when the tasks are sequential, you must schedule them in the proper order. For example, the engines on the wings of an airplane cannot be installed until the wings have been built. A project-manager program takes the information the user enters for each task and then determines how to schedule the tasks. The results are often presented in the form of a diagram called a Gantt chart (see Figure 72).

Task	Weeks						
	1	2	3	4	5	6	7
visit houses	█						
make decision		█					
loan application			█				
shop for furniture				█			
send notices of address change					█		
sign closing papers						█	
order phone						█	
move							█

FIGURE 72 Gantt Chart. This sample shows the scheduling of activities that need to be done when a family moves to a new home. The blocked-out sections show when each task is scheduled.

PROLOG The programming language Prolog (Programming in Logic) was developed in the early 1970s by Alain Colmerauer at the University of Marseilles. Prolog is used for writing computer programs that model human thinking. It exemplifies logic programming, a kind of programming developed by Robert Kowalski of the University of London.

In ordinary programming, a program describes the steps that a computer is to work through in order to solve a problem. In *logic programming*, the program gives the computer facts about the problem, plus rules by means of which other facts can be inferred. The computer then applies a fixed procedure to solve the problem automatically.

Suppose, for example, we want to know whether Atlanta is in North America. We have the following information to work from:

1. X is in North America if X is in the United States.
2. X is in North America if X is in Canada.
3. X is in the United States if X is in Georgia.
4. X is in the United States if X is in Florida.
5. Atlanta is in Georgia.

As Kowalski has pointed out, this can be described equally well in terms of reasoning procedures as follows:

1. To show that X is in North America, show that X is in the United States.
2. To show that X is in North America, show that X is in Canada.
3. To show that X is in the United States, show that X is in Georgia.
4. To show that X is in the United States, show that X is in Florida.
5. To show that Atlanta is in Georgia, do nothing.

It is then obvious that our problem can be solved by chaining statements 1, 3, and 5 together.

We would express the available information in Prolog as follows:

```
/* Rule 1 */ north_america(X) :- united_states(X).
/* Rule 2 */ north_america(X) :- canada(X).
/* Rule 3 */ united_states(X) :- georgia(X).
/* Rule 4 */ united_states(X) :- florida(X).
/* Rule 5 */ georgia(atlanta).
```

The symbol /* indicates the beginning of a comment, and */ indicates the end of the comment. All of these statements are rules, X is a variable that can be matched with any constant, and : – means "if." Rule 1 means "If X is in the United States, then X is in North America." Rule 5 is a special kind of rule called a *fact* because it does not contain an "if."

To find out whether Atlanta is in North America, we then give Prolog the following query:

```
?- north_america(atlanta).
```

To solve the query, Prolog looks for a rule the first part of which will match the query. Rule 1 will work, provided that variable X is given the value "atlanta." Then the second part of the rule becomes the new query:

```
?- united_states(atlanta).
```

Again, we look for a rule that will match the query. Rule 3 will work, and the new query becomes

```
?- georgia(atlanta).
```

When we look for a rule that matches this query, we find that rule 5 matches it exactly and does not contain an "if"— hence it does not introduce a new query, the process is complete, and the question can be answered "yes." If the process had ended with a query that no rule would match, the question would be answered "no."

One of the most important properties of Prolog is its ability to *backtrack*, that is, to back up and try alternative solutions. This is necessary whenever the search starts pursuing a chain of rules that do not lead to a solution. For example, rules 2 and 4 do not lead to a solution in our example; if the computer tried either of them, it would need to back up and try alternatives.

The Prolog example shown above uses the syntax implemented by W.F. Clocksin and C.S. Mellish at the University of Edinburgh. Some implementations use a more LISP-like syntax in which the preceeding example would look like this:

```
((NORTH_AMERICA X) (UNITED_STATES X))
((NORTH_AMERICA X) (CANADA X))
((UNITED _STATES X) (GEORGIA X))
((GEORGIA ATLANTA))
```

For an example of **Prolog programming**, see **expert system**.

PROM PROM is an acronym for Programmable Read-Only Memory, which is a computer memory that can be programmed once, but not reprogrammed.

PROMPT The prompt is a symbol that appears on a computer terminal screen to signal to the user that the computer is ready to receive input. Different programs use different prompts. For example, under CP/M and IBM PC DOS, the prompt looks like A> or B>, depending on whether A or B is the default drive. The PROMPT command can be used to change the appearance of the prompt in MS-DOS. For an example, see **hard-disk management**.

PROPORTIONAL PITCH In proportional-pitch type, different letters are of different widths (e.g., "M" is wider than "I"). Compared to an ordinary typewriter or printer, this improves the appearance of the type and makes it more readable. Most books and newspapers are set in proportional type. (See **type; typeface**.)

Because the letters are of different widths, it is not possible to count letter spaces in proportional-pitch type the way one does on a typewriter. (See **typesetting mistakes**.)

PROPRIETARY "Proprietary to" means "owned by." A feature of a computer is proprietary if one company has exclusive rights to it.

PROPRINTER The IBM Proprinter is a dot-matrix printer that recognizes Epson control codes and supports Epson-compatible graphics modes. (See **Epson**.)

PROTECT(ED) MODE Protected mode (also called protect mode) is the mode in which an 80286, 80386, or 80486 microprocessor can access the largest possible amount of memory. In this mode, these processors can only run programs designed for protected mode, not programs designed for earlier processors such as the 8088. In Microsoft Windows and OS/2, the user can switch between protected mode (for running Windows or OS/2 programs) and real mode or virtual 8086 mode (for running DOS programs).

In protected mode, different parts of memory are allocated to different programs, and memory is protected in the sense that a program can only write to the memory allocated to it. By contrast, see **real mode; multiple virtual mode**.

PROTOCOL A protocol is a standard way of regulating data transmission between computers. (See **handshaking; X-OFF; X-ON; XMODEM; Kermit.**)

PS/1 See **IBM PC.**

PS/2 See **IBM PC.**

PSEUDOCODE One of the best ways to plan a computer program is to make an outline of it, using a mixture of a programming language and a human language. This mixed language is called pseudocode.

For example, here is a pseudocode outline of a Pascal program to find the largest of a set of 10 numbers:

```
begin
   repeat
      read a number;
      test whether it is the largest found so far
   until 10 numbers have been read;
   print the largest
end.
```

Here is the program that results from translating all of the pseudocode into genuine Pascal:

```
PROGRAM findthelargest (INPUT, OUTPUT);
VAR
   num, largest, count : INTEGER;
BEGIN
   count := 0;
   largest := 0;
   REPEAT
      count := count + 1;
      READ(num);
      IF num> largest THEN largest := num
   UNTIL count = 10;
   WRITELN('The largest number was',largest)
END.
```

(This program assumes that the largest number will be greater than zero.)

The advantage of pseudocode is that it allows the programmer to concentrate on how the program works while ignoring the details of the language. By reducing the number of things the programmer must think about at once, this technique effectively amplifies the programmer's intelligence.

PUBLIC DOMAIN A computer program is in the public domain if it is not covered by any kind of copyright. Few substantial public-domain programs exist, but the term "public domain" is often used incorrectly to describe other kinds of freely copyable software (see **free software**).

PULL-DOWN MENU A pull-down menu (also called a *drop-down menu* or a *pop-up menu*) is a menu that appears when a particular item in a menu bar is selected. For picture, see **window**. See also **menu bar**.

PUNCHED CARD A punched card is a stiff paper card on which holes can be punched according to a particular pattern that can be read by a computer. Standard punched cards are $7\,^3/_8$ inches long and $3\,^1/_4$ inches high. Each card contains 80 columns and 12 rows. Each column represents one letter, number, or other symbol, depending on the pattern of holes in that column. Figure 73 shows a standard way for coding symbols on the card.

The holes are usually punched on the cards by a keypunch machine, which has a keyboard like a typewriter. Since most people have trouble reading punched-card hole language, most keypunch machines print the symbol stored in each column at the top of the column.

The computer reads the cards when they are passed through a card reader, which can flip through cards at a rate of up to 1,000 cards per minute. Each card passes between a light source and a row of solar cells, which detect the location of the holes in the card. The pattern of holes is thus transformed into a pattern of electric signals. The card reader sends these signals to the computer, where they are translated into machine instructions.

The use of punched cards for data processing actually preceded the invention of the computer by more than 50 years. Herman Hollerith realized that it took several years to process data from the 1880 census. He figured that, unless a faster method was found, the U.S. Census Bureau would still be working on the results from the 1890 census when it came time to start the 1900 census. Hollerith developed a system in which census data were punched on cards, and machines were used to sort and tabulate the cards. Even earlier, in 1801, a system of punched cards was used to direct the weaving pattern on the automatic Jacquard loom in France.

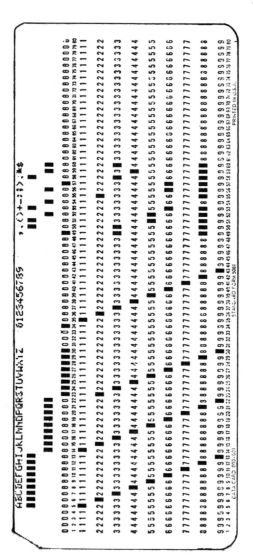

FIGURE 73

In the 1960s, punched cards were the dominant way of feeding programs into computers, but they have now been replaced by interactive terminals.

PUSH See **stack**.

PUSHDOWN STACK See **stack**.

PUSHDOWN STORE See **stack**.

q

QUERY LANGUAGE When you are communicating with a database system, you type commands to the computer using the query language that is part of that system. See **SQL**.

QUEUE A queue is a data structure from which items are removed in the same order in which they were entered. By way of contrast, see **stack**.

QUICK C Microsoft Quick C is an easy-to-use C compiler with built-in editor, similar in design to Turbo Pascal and Turbo C. See **C; Turbo C++; Turbo Pascal**.

QUICKBASIC Microsoft QuickBASIC is a high performance compiler for BASIC. It accepts programs written for BASICA or GWBASIC, but it also adds many new kinds of statements and allows the programmer to leave out line numbers. Beginning with version 4.0, QuickBASIC has two unusual technical features. First, it is an incremental compiler, meaning that lines are compiled as soon as they are typed in. Second, it compiles into threaded code, a special kind of machine language that corresponds line-by-line to the original program. Thus, compilation is very fast and can be undone to reconstruct the BASIC program that was compiled.

QUICK PASCAL Microsoft Quick Pascal is an easy-to-use Pascal complier with built-in editor, similar in design to Turbo Pascal. It accepts Turbo Pascal syntax rather than the dialect of Pascal used by other Microsoft Pascal compilers. See **Turbo Pascal**.

QUICKSORT Quicksort is a sorting algorithm invented by C.A.R. Hoare and first published in 1962. Quicksort is faster than any other sorting algorithm available unless the items are already in nearly the correct order, in which case it is relatively inefficient.

Quicksort is a recursive procedure (See recursion.) On each iteration, it rearranges the list of items so that one item (the "pivot") is in its final position, all the items that should come before it are before it, and all the items that should come after it are after it. Then the lists of items preceding and following the pivot are treated as sublists and sorted in the same way. Figure 74 shows how this works.

(a) Choose the last item in the list, 41, as the pivot. It is excluded from the searching and swapping that follow.

(b), (c) Identify the leftmost item greater than 41 and the rightmost item less than 41. Swap them.

(d), (e), (f), (g) Repeat steps (b) and (c) until the leftmost and rightmost markers meet in the middle.

(h), (i) Now that the markers have met and crossed, swap the pivot with the item pointed to by the leftmost marker.

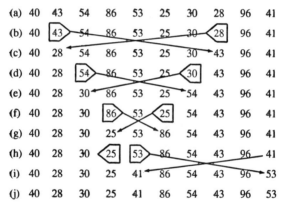

FIGURE 74 Quicksort in Action

(j) Now that the pivot is in its final position, sort each of the two sublists to the left and in right of it.

Quicksort is difficult to express in languages, such as BASIC, that do not allow recursion. The amount of memory required by Quicksort increases exponentially with the depth of the recursion. One way to limit memory requirements is to switch to another type of sort, such as selection sort, after a certain depth is reached. (See **selection sort**.) The following program shows the Quicksort algorithm expressed in Pascal.

```
{ Quicksort in Pascal - M. Covington 1991 }
{ To sort a[1..n], an array of integers. }

PROCEDURE swap(VAR x,y: INTEGER);
VAR
  t: INTEGER;
BEGIN
  t:=x; x:=y; y:=t
END;

PROCEDURE partition(first,last:INTEGER; VAR p:INTEGER);
  { Partitions a[first]...a[last] into 2 sub-arrays using }
  { a[first] as pivot.  p is position where pivot ends up. }
VAR
  i, j: INTEGER;
  pivot: INTEGER;
BEGIN
  pivot := a[first];
  i:=first;
  j:=last+1;
  REPEAT
    REPEAT i:=i+1 UNTIL a[i]>=pivot;
    REPEAT j:=j-1 UNTIL a[j]<=pivot;
    IF i<j THEN swap(a[i],a[j])
  UNTIL j<=i;
  swap(a[j],a[first]);
  p := j
END;

PROCEDURE quicksort(first,last:INTEGER);
  { Sorts the sub-array from a[first] to a[last]. }
  { To sort the whole array, call quicksort(1,n).}
VAR p: INTEGER;
BEGIN
  IF first < last THEN
    BEGIN
      partition(first,last,p);
      quicksort(first,p-1);
      quicksort(p+1,last)
    END
END;
```

FIGURE 75

r _____

RACAL-VADIC Racal-Vadic is a company that manufactures modems and other electronic equipment. The Racal-Vadic 3400 format is a method of sending 1200-baud serial data over phone lines; it is similar but not identical to the Bell 212A format. (See **Bell 212A.**)

RADIAN MEASURE Radian measure is a way of measuring the size of angles in which a complete rotation measures 2π radians. (See **angle.**)

Zeof trigonometric functions in most computer languages expect their arguments to be expressed in radians. To convert degrees to radians, multiply by $\pi/180$ (approximately $1/57.296$).

RADIO BUTTON See **option button.**

RADIO SHACK Radio Shack is a division of Tandy Corporation, of Fort Worth, Texas, which makes Tandy computers. Radio Shack operates one of the most widespread chains of retail computer stores. The TRS-80 line of computers was one of the earliest lines of home computers in the late 1970s and early '80s.

RADIX The radix of a number system is the same as the base of the number system. Binary numbers have a radix of 2, and decimal numbers have a radix of 10.

RADIX SORT The radix sort algorithm puts data in order by classifying each item immediately rather than comparing it to other items. For example, you might sort cards with names on them by putting all the A's in one bin, all the B's in another bin, and so on. You could then sort the contents of each bin the same way using the second letter of each name, and so on. For other sorting methods, see **sort.**

The radix sort method can be used effectively with binary numbers, since there are only two possible bins for the items to be placed.

Figure 76 is a Pascal program to perform a radix sort on a list of numbers. The program actually starts by sorting the items according to the last digit, then the second to the last digit, and so on. The last step is to sort according to the first digit. This program assumes that the values have been read into memory, but it could work just as well if the data items were in a random access file.

This program sorts the items in place—that is, they are not actually moved. Two index arrays are used to keep track of the location: ind1 and ind2. For example, if ind1[1] is 6, then the first element in the ordered list is in position 6 of the actual list. ind2 gives the opposite; in this case ind2[6] would be 1.

If sorting a long list of names, it would take too long to start with the last character. Instead, the program could be redesigned so that it would sort on only the first 4 or 5 characters. Then the program could complete the sort by switching to another method that is efficient with an almost-sorted list, such as insertion sort.

```
PROGRAM radixsort(INPUT,OUTPUT);
  {This Turbo Pascal program performs a radix sort on a list
   of 4-digit integers}
CONST maxbins=9; maxitems=500; maxlength=4;
VAR a,ind1,ind2:ARRAY[1..maxitems] OF INTEGER;
    i,digitnum,n:INTEGER;
    pwr10:ARRAY[0..maxlength] OF INTEGER;


PROCEDURE binplace(digitnum:INTEGER);
VAR i,j,k,binnumber:INTEGER;
  bincount,binstartloc: ARRAY[0..maxbins] OF INTEGER;
  binlist:ARRAY[1..maxitems] OF INTEGER;

    FUNCTION digit(x,dnum:INTEGER):INTEGER;
      {This function returns the digit in position dnum
       of the integer x.}
      BEGIN digit := (x MOD pwr10[dnum]) DIV pwr10[dnum-1]
      END;

BEGIN
  FOR k := 0 TO maxbins DO bincount[k] := 0;
  FOR i := 1 TO n DO
    BEGIN {this loop counts how many items
           go in each bin}
      j := ind1[i];
      binnumber := digit(a[j],digitnum);
      binlist[j] := binnumber;
      bincount[binnumber] := bincount[binnumber]+1
    END;
```

```
    binstartloc[0] := 1;
    FOR k := 1 TO maxbins DO
        binstartloc[k] := binstartloc[k-1]+bincount[k-1];
  FOR i := 1 TO n DO
    BEGIN {this loop determines the new position
           after an item has been placed in its bin}
      j := ind1[i];
      binnumber := binlist[j];
      ind2[j] := binstartloc[binnumber];
      binstartloc[binnumber] := binstartloc[binnumber]+1
    END
END;

BEGIN {main program block}
  pwr10[0]:=1; pwr10[1]:=10; pwr10[2]:=100;
  pwr10[3]:=1000; pwr10[4]:=10000;
  WRITE('How many items? '); READLN(n);
  FOR i := 1 TO n DO
    BEGIN READLN(a[i]); ind1[i] := i END;
  digitnum := 1;
  REPEAT {now perform the sort}
    binplace(digitnum);
    FOR i := 1 TO n DO ind1[ind2[i]] := i;
    digitnum := digitnum+1;
  UNTIL digitnum>maxlength;
  {Output:}
  FOR i := 1 TO n DO WRITELN(i:3,' ',a[ind1[i]])
END.
```

FIGURE 76

RAGGED A ragged margin is one that has not been evened out by
   justification. For an example, see **flush left**.

RAM RAM is an acronym for <u>R</u>andom-<u>A</u>ccess <u>M</u>emory, which is
   a memory device whereby any location in memory can be
   found, on average, as quickly as any other location. A computer's RAM is its main memory where it can store data, so the
   size of the RAM (measured in kilobytes) is an important indicator of the capacity of the computer. (See **memory**.)

RAM DISK A RAM disk, also called a *virtual disk*, is an area of RAM (random-access memory) that is used to simulate an additional disk drive (see **disk**). Data can be written and read much more quickly on a RAM disk than on a real disk. Naturally, a RAM disk goes blank whenever the computer is turned off; its contents must be copied onto it from a real disk whenever the computer is turned on. RAM disks are ordinarily employed to store frequently used programs or temporary working files.

RAM disks are especially popular under the MS-DOS operating system (see **MS-DOS**). A RAM disk is created by modifying the operating system so that an area of RAM is treated in a special way; no modification to the machine is required.

RANDOM-ACCESS DEVICE A random-access device is a memory device in which it is possible to find any particular record as quickly, on average, as any other record. The computer's internal RAM and disk storage devices are examples of random-access devices. For contrast, see **sequential-access device**.

RANDOM-ACCESS MEMORY See **RAM**.

RANDOM-NUMBER GENERATOR A random-number generator is a computer program that calculates numbers that seem to have been chosen randomly. In reality, a computer cannot generate numbers that are truly random, since it always generates the numbers according to a deterministic rule. However, certain generating rules produce numbers whose behavior is unpredictable enough that they can be treated as random numbers for practical purposes. The RND function in BASIC is an example of a random-number generator contained in a computer programming language. Random-number generators are useful in writing programs involving games of chance, and they are also used in an important simulation technique called Monte Carlo simulation.

RASTER A raster is a scan pattern that fills the screen of a CRT. Like television sets, present-day computers scan the entire screen continuously with an electron beam. Earlier graphics terminals worked more like oscilloscopes—they directed the electron beam only at places where lines were to be drawn. (See **bit-mapped graphics; vector graphics**.)

RAY TRACING In computer graphics, ray tracing is the generation of very realistic images of three-dimensional objects by computing the exact amount of light that would be reflected toward the viewer from each point on the object. This requires very large amounts of arithmetical calculation.

RBBS RBBS is a popular program for implementing bulletin-board systems. (See **BBS**.)

READ-ONLY MEMORY See **ROM**.

READ A computer is said to read information when it transfers it from an external medium, such as a diskette, to its memory.

REAL MODE Real mode is the operating mode in which an 80286, 80386, or 80486 microprocessor acts like an 8086 or 8088, with a maximum of one megabyte of memory of which only 640K is available to user programs. The PC AT and PS/2 run DOS in real mode. By contrast, they run OS/2 in protected mode, allowing access to much larger amounts of memory. In OS/2, the user can switch between protected mode and real mode.

In real mode, the segment and offset registers contain the true addresses of memory locations, while in protected mode, segment registers point to entries in a lookup table. (See **protected mode; multiple virtual mode**.)

REAL NUMBER The set of real numbers consists of all of the numbers that can be represented either as integers, decimal fractions with a finite number of digits, decimal fractions with an infinite number of digits that endlessly repeat the same pattern, or decimal fractions with an infinite number of digits that do not repeat a pattern. Each real number can be represented by a point on a number line and vice versa.

Examples are 0, 2.5, 345, -2134, 0.00003, $\frac{1}{3}$, $\sqrt{2}$, and π. But $\sqrt{-1}$ is not a real number (it does not exist anywhere among the positive or negative numbers).

On computers, real numbers are represented with a finite number of digits, thus limiting their accuracy. See **rounding error**.

REAL TIME The term *real time* refers to the actual amount of time consumed by an operation, rather than just the amount of computer time. (On a timesharing computer, programs do not consume computer time when the computer is working on something else. See **timesharing**.)

Real-time programming is programming in which the proper functioning of the program depends on the amount of real time consumed. For instance, computers that control automatic machinery must often both detect and introduce time delays of accurately determined lengths.

REBOOT To reboot is to restart a computer, that is, turn it off and then on again. (See **boot**.)

RECOGNIZER A recognizer for a particular programming language is a program that reads in a program written in that language and then determines whether the program is valid according to the rules of the language.

RECORD A record is a collection of related data items. For example, a company may store information about each employee in a single record. Each record consists of several fields—a field for the name, a field for Social Security number, and so on.

Here is an illustration of the Pascal record data type. Suppose information for each customer at a store will be kept in a record with three fields: name, address, and account balance. Create the record type "customer" as follows:

```
TYPE
   customer = RECORD
      name : STRING;
      Address : STRING;
      class : INTEGER;
      balance : REAL
   END;
```

Then we can create the array clist, which will be an array of items of type customer:

```
VAR
   clist : ARRAY[1..number] OF customer;
```

Now the expression clist[7].name will refer to the name for customer 7, clist[8].balance will refer to the balance for customer 8, and so on.

RECOVERING ERASED FILES When you erase a file on a computer disk, the space that the file occupied is marked as free, but it is not actually overwritten until the space is needed for something else. If you erase a file accidentally, you can often get it back by using programs such as the Norton Utilities (on the IBM PC) or analogous programs on other machines. As soon as you realize you want to recover a file, remove the disk from the machine so that nothing else will be written in the space that the file occupied.

RECURSION Recursion occurs when a procedure calls itself while being executed. To allow recursion, a programming language must allow for local variables (thus, recursion is not easy to accomplish in most versions of BASIC). Each time the procedure is called, it needs to keep track of values for the variables that may be different from the values they had the last time the procedure was called. Therefore, a recursive procedure that calls itself many times can consume a lot of memory.

Recursion is the natural way to solve problems that contain smaller problems of the same kind. Examples include drawing some kinds of fractals (see **fractal**); parsing structures that can have similar structures inside them (see **parsing**); sorting (see **Quicksort**); and calculating the determinant of a matrix by breaking it up into smaller matrices.

A recursive procedure can be used to calculate the factorial of an integer. (See **factorial**.) Here is a Pascal program to do so:

```
PROGRAM factcal(INPUT,OUTPUT);
   VAR x:INTEGER;
FUNCTION fact(x:INTEGER) :INTEGER;
   VAR z:INTEGER;
   BEGIN
     WRITELN('Now looking for factorial of',x);
     IF x > 0 THEN z :=x * fact(x-1)
              { Here is the recursion }
     ELSE z := 1;
     WRITELN('The factorial of ',x,'is',z);
     fact :=z
   END;
BEGIN   { main program block }
   READLN(x);
   WRITELN(fact(x))
END.
```

The recursion occurs when the function "fact" calls itself. Note that the ELSE clause is crucial. That clause gives a nonrecursive definition for the factorial of zero. If it was not there, the program would end up in an endless loop as the function fact kept calling itself until the computer ran out of memory. Any time recursion is used, it is necessary to make sure that there is some condition that will cause the recursion to halt. Following is an example of the output from this program when the number 4 is given as the input. In practice, you would want to remove the two WRITELN statements from the function, but they are included here to make it possible to see the order of execution.

```
Now looking for factorial of 4
Now looking for factorial of 3
Now looking for factorial of 2
Now looking for factorial of 1
Now looking for factorial of 0
The factorial of 0 is 1
The factorial of 1 is 1
The factorial of 2 is 2
The factorial of 3 is 6
The factorial of 4 is 24
```

Recursion can also be used to construct iterative programs, and it is often used for that purpose in LISP and Prolog.

RE-ENTRANT A program or procedure is said to be re-entrant if more than one copy of it can be executed at the same time without conflict. See **multitasking.**

REGISTER A register is a row of flip-flops used to store a group of binary digits while the computer is processing them. (See **flip-flop.**) A group of binary digits (bits) is called a *word.* A flip-flop can be in either of two states, so one flip-flop can store 1 bit. A register consisting of 16 flip-flops can store words that are 16 bits long. The accumulator is an example of a register.

REGULAR EXPRESSION A regular expression is a way of defining a possible series of characters. Table 15 gives some examples. In UNIX, the "grep" command searches a file for character strings that match a regular expression; regular expressions are also used in the programming language AWK and in some editors. See **grep; AWK.**

Regular expressions are efficient to process because the computer can always tell whether a string matches a regular expression by working through the string and the expression from left to right, one item at a time. This is simpler than the methods used to parse Backus-Naur form or other kinds of syntactic description. See **parsing; Backus-Naur form.**

Table 15 Examples of Regular Expressions

Expression	Matches
abc	The string "abc"
a.c	Like "abc" but with any character in place of b
a*bc	Zero or more a's, followed by "bc"
a*b+c	Zero or more a's, one or more b's, and c
*	An asterisk
\\	A backslash
[BbCx]	The character B, b, C, or x
[A-E2-3]	The character A, B, C, D, E, 2, 3, or 4
[^A-E2-3]	Any character except A, B, C, D, E, 2, 3, or 4
[Ff]ill	"Fill" or "fill"
^abc	"abc" at beginning of line
abc$	"abc" at end of line

RELATIONAL DATABASE A relational database consists of tables made up of rows and columns. For example:

Name	City	State
Downing, D.	Seattle	Washington
Covington, M.	Athens	Georgia

The table defines a *relation* between the things in each row; it says that Seattle is the city for Downing, Athens is the city for Covington, and so on.

One important operation in a relational database is to *join* two tables, i.e., cross-reference information between them. For example, the names in the table above could be cross-referenced to another table containing names and salaries; the result would be a table relating name, city, state, and salary.

A database with only one table is called a *flat-file database*.

Every relational database has a query language for expressing commands to retrieve data. See **query language; SQL.**

RELATIVE ADDRESS (1) A relative address is a computer address where it is necessary to add a base address in order to obtain the actual absolute address in the machine memory.

(2) In a spreadsheet program, a relative address is a cell address that indicates the position of a cell relative to another cell. If this formula is copied to another location, the address will be changed so that it refers to the cell in the same position relative to the new cell. In Lotus 1-2-3, a cell address is treated as a relative address unless it contains dollar signs. (See **absolute address.**) For example, if the formula 2*D7 is entered into the

cell E9, the D7 really means, "the cell that is one column to the left and two rows above." If this formula is now copied to cell H15, the formula will now become 2*G13, since G13 is the cell that is one column to the left and two rows above the cell H15.

RELOCATABLE A relocatable machine-language program can execute correctly regardless of the location where it is loaded into the computer's memory. The loader changes the addresses referred to within the program to reflect the program's actual position. (See **COM file; EXE file**.)

REPEAT The keyword REPEAT is used to define one kind of loop in Pascal. The word REPEAT marks the beginning of the loop, and the word UNTIL marks the end. Here is an example:

```
x := 1;
REPEAT
   WRITELN(x);
   x := 2*x;
   WRITELN ('Type S if you want to stop.');
   READLN(query);   {Query is of type CHAR.}
UNTIL query = 'S';
```

The computer always executes the loop at least once, because it does not check to see whether the stopping condition is true until after it has executed the loop. See also **WHILE**.

REQUIRED HYPHEN In word processing, a required hyphen is a hyphen that does not indicate a place where a word can be broken apart. For instance, if the hyphenated word "flip-flop" falls at the end of the line, then "flip-" may appear on one line, with "flop" at the beginning of the next. But if you type "flip-flop" with a required hyphen, it will not be split up.

In Word Perfect, a required hyphen is typed by hitting the Home key and then the hyphen key.

REQUIRED SPACE In word processing, a required space is a blank space that does not denote a place where words can be split apart at the end of a line. For example, if you type two words with an ordinary space between them, and the first word falls at the end of a line, the second word will be at the beginning of the next line. But if you put a required space between them, they will always stay together on the same line.

In Word Perfect, a required space is typed by hitting the Home key and then the space bar.

RESEDIT <u>Res</u>ource <u>Edit</u>or, or ResEdit, is a program distributed by Apple Computer for configuring the operating system of the Macintosh and for editing resources of all types. See **resource**.

RESERVED WORD A reserved word is a word that has a special meaning in a particular programming language and cannot be used as a variable name. For example, in BASIC and Pascal, IF is a reserved word. COBOL has dozens of reserved words; FORTRAN and PL/I have none, since in these languages it is always possible to tell from the context whether or not a word is a variable name.

RESISTANCE The resistance of an electronic component is a measure of how difficult it is for electric current to flow through the component. Resistance is measured in a unit called the *ohm*. (See **Ohm's law; resistor**.)

RESOLUTION The resolution of a printer or screen is a measure of the sharpness of the images it can produce. For instance, many laser printers have a resolution of 300 dots per inch (DPI), meaning that they print characters using a grid of black or white squares each 1/300 of an inch across. This is equivalent to 150 lines per inch (LPI), because in order to distinguish two lines, the row of dots between them must be left blank.

The human eye normally resolves about 150 lines per inch at normal reading distance, but a person examining a page critically can distinguish two or three times this much detail.

The resolution of a screen is given as the total number of pixels in each direction (e.g., 640 x 480 pixels across the whole screen). The equivalent number of dots per inch depends on the size of the screen. Present-day video screens resolve about 80 dots per inch; they are not nearly as sharp as ink on paper.

A big advantage of draw programs, as opposed to paint programs, is that they can use the full resolution of the printer; they are not limited to printing what they display on the screen. But some paint programs can handle very detailed images by displaying only part of the image at a time. See **draw program; paint program; vector graphics**.

RESOURCE On the Macintosh and under Microsoft Windows, a resource is a modifiable part of an application program or of the operating system. Resources include menus, icons, and fonts.

RESTORE To restore a window is to make it go back to its previous size after being either minimized or maximized. To restore a window, choose "restore" on its control menu. To see the control menu, click once on the control-menu box (if the window has been maximized) or on the icon (if the window has been reduced to an icon). See also **window; minimize; maximize.**

RETURN KEY The return key on a computer terminal is the key that tells the computer that the end of a line has been reached. On some terminals this key is called the **enter key.** On IBM 3270 terminals, the return and enter keys are distinct.

REXX The REXX programming language is often used to write command procedures (the equivalent of MS-DOS.BAT files) under VM/CMS and TSO. It is also a convenient language for testing algorithms and writing sample utility programs when execution speed is not important.

Figure 77 shows a simple REXX program. Each statement ends with a semicolon or end of line. Communication with the user and with the operating system is particularly easy: *arg* retrieves command-line arguments, *pull* breaks up a line of input into arguments separated by spaces, and any string or string expression, when used by itself as a statement, is passed to the operating system as a command.

```
/* CHKDSK -- Sample program in REXX -- M. Covington 1991 */
/* Displays free space on a virtual disk under VM/CMS */

/* Tell REXX not to display statements being executed */

trace off;

/* Obtain diskletter from command line. If none, use 'A'. */

arg diskletter;
if diskletter='' then diskletter='A';

/* Pass a QUERY DISK command to the operating
   system, then retrieve and parse its output. */

'QUERY DISK ' diskletter ' (STACK FIFO)';
pull;
pull x1 x2 x3 x4 x5 x6 x7 x8 x9 x10 . ;

/* Process the information in variables x7, x9, x10 */

pos = index(x9,'-')+1;
percent = substr(x9,pos,2);
freesp = x7 * x10;
say 'Disk' diskletter 'is' percent '% full (' freesp 'bytes free).'
```

FIGURE 77

In some implementations REXX programs are required to begin with '/*' or with a line containing 'REX,' so they can be distinguished from command procedures written in other languages. Under VM/CMS, you can get more information about REXX by typing HELP REXX. REXX stands for Restructured Extended Executor.

RFI PROTECTION Computers use the same kind of high-frequency electrical energy as radio transmitters. This often causes RFI (radio-frequency interference), also called EMI (electromagnetic interference). All computers interfere with nearby radio and TV reception to some extent, and sometimes the problem is severe. On rare occasions, the opposite happens—a strong signal from a nearby radio transmitter disrupts the computer, or two computers interfere with each other.

Here are some suggestions for reducing RFI:

1. If possible, move the radio or TV receiver away from the computer, and plug it into an outlet on a different circuit.
2. Supply power to the computer through a surge protector that includes an RFI filter (see **surge protector**).
3. Ground the computer properly (again, see **surge protector**).
4. Use high-quality shielded cables to connect the parts of the computer system together. Make sure all cable shields and ground wires are connected properly. This is especially important for the monitor cable and the printer cable. If possible, wind the cable into a coil to increase its inductance.
5. Check that the computer has the appropriate approval from the FCC (Federal Communications Commission). Some computers are not approved for use in residential areas.

See **FCC**.

RGB MONITOR An RGB monitor is a color monitor that uses separate signals for the three additive primary colors (red, green, and blue). Each primary color is either on or off at any moment. For example, yellow is displayed by turning red and green on and blue off. Only eight colors can be displayed using this system.

Most RGB monitors have an additional signal, called *intensify*, that makes the color brighter. For instance, light red is the same as dark red except that the intensify signal is also on. This gives a total of 16 colors that can be displayed. An RGB monitor with an intensify signal is sometimes called an RGBI

monitor; RGBI monitors are used with the IBM C̲olor/G̲raphics
A̲dapter (see **CGA**).

The monitors used with the IBM E̲nhanced G̲raphics
A̲dapter (EGA) have two level signals for each color, giving a
total of 64 combinations. (See **EGA.**)

See also **analog monitor**.

RGBI MONITOR See **RGB monitor**.

RISC RISC stands for r̲educed i̲nstruction s̲et c̲omputer; it refers
to a computer with a small number of machine language instructions, each of which can be executed very quickly. The
Sun Sparcstation is an example of a RISC computer. The opposite of RISC is CISC (see **CISC**).

RISC architecture was developed for speed. The RISC computer can execute each instruction faster because there are
fewer instructions to choose between, and thus less time is
taken up identifying each instruction.

RISC and CISC computers can run the same kinds of software; the only difference is in what the software looks like in
machine code. CISC is faster than RISC if memory access is
relatively slow; the RISC machine has to fetch more instructions from memory than the CISC machine to do the same
work. RISC is faster than CISC if memory access is very fast.

RIVER A river is a series of white spaces between words that appear to flow from line to line in a printed document. Rivers result from trying to justify type when the columns are too
narrow or the available software or printer are not versatile
enough. (See **justification.**)

RLL An RLL (run-length-limited) hard-disk controller gets about
50 percent more data on the same disk as a conventional hard-
disk controller by using data compression technology. Thus,
the Shugart ST-225 hard disk has 20 megabytes of capacity
with a conventional controller, or 30 megabytes with an RLL
controller. For contrast, see **MFM**.

When a hard disk is converted from conventional to RLL
usage, it must be reformatted; this operation erases all the data
on it. Also, disks designed for conventional (MFM) use may
not be reliable when used in RLL format. See **ST-506.**

RLOGIN On UNIX networks, the "rlogin" command (short for
"r̲emote l̲ogi̲n") allows you to use your computer as a terminal

on another computer. Unlike telnet, rlogin does more than just establish a communication path; it also tells the other computer what kind of terminal you are using and sends it your user name.

ROLL OUT See **timesharing**.

ROM ROM is an acronym for <u>r</u>ead-<u>o</u>nly <u>m</u>emory. A ROM contains computer instructions that do not need to be changed, such as permanent parts of the operating system. The computer can read instructions out of ROM, but no data can be stored in ROM. See also **CD-ROM; PROM; EPROM**.

ROMAN See **typeface**.

ROOT DIRECTORY The root directory is the main directory of a disk, containing files and/or subdirectories. (See **directory**.)

ROUNDING ERROR A rounding error occurs because the computer cannot store the true value of most real numbers; instead, it can only store an approximation of a finite number of digits. If you wish to write $1/3$ as a decimal fraction, you may approximate it as 0.333333333, but it would require an infinite number of digits to express it exactly. The computer faces the same problem except that internally it stores the numbers in binary, and it can lose accuracy in converting between binary and decimal. For example, 0.1 has no exact representation on a computer; if you add 0.1 to 0 ten times, you will not get exactly 1.

   To avoid rounding error, some computer programs represent numbers as decimal digits. See **binary-coded decimal**.

RPG RPG (<u>R</u>eport <u>P</u>rogram <u>G</u>enerator) is a programming language developed by IBM in the 1960s in an attempt to simplify programming for business applications. RPG is based on the principle that most business computer programs have the same structure: a large file is read one record at a time, some actions are performed for each record (e.g., adding numbers to running totals, or perhaps writing an altered form of the record onto another file), and other actions are performed only at the end (e.g., printing out the totals). The RPG programmer specifies only the details of these actions, not the overall structure of the program.

   Because RPG programming can be reduced to a fixed procedure for filling out forms, RPG is often the first programming language taught to trainees. However, RPG programs are markedly less readable than programs in other languages, and complex algorithms are difficult to express in RPG.

Figure 78 shows a fragment of an RPG program that subtracts EXPENSE from GROSS, giving NET, and then adds NET to PROFIT if NET is positive, or to LOSS if NET is negative. The subtraction in the first line sets indicator 27 if the result is negative and indicator 28 if it is zero. The second line executes only if neither indicator 27 nor indicator 28 is set; the third line executes only if indicator 27 is set.

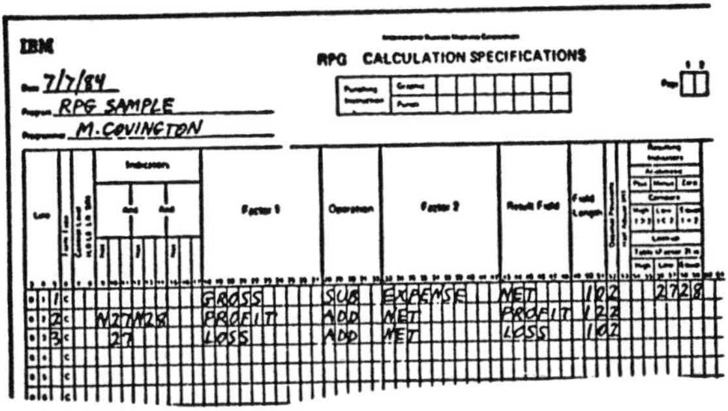

FIGURE 78 Part of an RPG Program

RPN See **Polish notation.**

RS-232 The Electronics Industries Association's (EIA) recommended standard 232-C (RS-232C, or RS-232 for short) defines a standard way of transmitting serial data by wire. This standard is now officially known as EIA-232D. Almost all modems, asynchronous computer terminals, and serial printers follow, at least to some degree, the RS-232C standard.

The connection includes lines for sending and receiving data, ground connections, and, usually, one or more control lines such as Carrier Detect or Data Terminal Ready (see below). The data are sent as a stream of bits at a constant speed. Each character is preceded by a start bit and followed by one or two stop bits.

The signal voltages are +5 to +15 volts (binary 0 on the data lines, "high" or "true" on the control lines) and -5 to -15 volts (binary 1 on the data lines, "low" or "false" on the control lines). A disconnected wire can be recognized because it is neither positive nor negative, but few RS-232 ports do this.

RS-232 ports usually have 25-pin connectors, but the connector is not part of the standard and its usage varies somewhat.

Table 16 shows the usual pin assignments. Table 17 shows the 9-pin connector used on the IBM PC AT. (The Macintosh follows the RS-422 standard; see **RS-422**.) Figure 79 shows the solutions to some common cabling problems.

See also **serial; parallel; baud; RS-422; RS-423.**

Normal terminal-to-modem or computer-to-modem connection
(All 25 pins may be connected straight through. Minimally, pins 1-8 and 20 should be connected in order to pass all commonly used control signals.)

```
GND ——— GND
TD  ——— TD
RD  ——— RD
RTS ——— RTS
CTS ——— CTS
DSR ——— DSR
CD  ——— CD
DTR ——— DTR
SG  ——— SG
```

Simplest terminal-to-modem or computer-to-modem connection
(Some control signals are ignored; "fake" control signals are generated by looping back outputs to inputs.)

```
TD  ——— TD
RD  ——— RD
RTS ⅃ ⌐ RTS
CTS ⅃ ⌐ CTS
DSR ⅃ ⌐ DSR
CD  ⅃ ⌐ CD
DTR ⅃ ⌐ DTR
SG  ——— SG
```

Full-featured "modem eliminator" for connecting computer to computer or terminal to terminal

```
GND ——— GND
TD  ⤬ TD
RD  ⤬ RD
RTS ⤬ RTS
CTS ⤬ CTS
DSR ⌐ ⌐ DSR
CD  ⌐⤬⌐ CD
DTR ——— DTR
SG  ——— SG
```

Simplest modem eliminator, sacrificing some control signals

```
TD  ⤬ TD
RD  ⤬ RD
RTS ⅃ ⌐ RTS
CTS ⅃ ⌐ CTS
DSR ⅃ ⌐ DSR
CD  ⅃ ⌐ CD
DTR ⅃ ⌐ DTR
SG  ——— SG
```

FIGURE 79 Solutions to Some RS-232 Cabling Problems

**Table 16 RS-232 Pin Assignments on Commonly Used
25-Pin Connectors (Pin numbers are embossed on the connector.)**

Pin	Signal	Direction	Explanation
1	GND	Both	Frame ground—ties together chassis of terminal and modem often omitted
2	TxD	To modem	Transmitted data
3	RxD	To terminal	Received data
4	RTS	To modem	Request to send—high when terminal is on and able to communicate
5	CTS	To terminal	Clear to send—high when computer on other end is able to receive
6	DSR	To terminal	Data set ready—high when modem is on and functioning
7	SG	Both	Signal ground—reference point for all signal voltages
8	CD	To terminal	Carrier detect—high when a connection to another computer has been established
12	CD	To terminal	On Hayes modems this is high when high speed (1200 baud) is being used. Other usage varies.
20	DTR	To modem	Data terminal ready—high when terminal is on and functioning. Most modems hand up phone when DTR goes low.
22	RI	To terminal	Ring indicator—high when telephone is ringing.

TABLE 17 Pin Connections for IBM PC AT Serial Port

Pin	Signal
1	Carrier detect
2	Receive data
3	Transmit data
4	Data terminal ready
5	Signal ground
6	Data set ready
7	Request to send
8	Clear to send
9	Ring indicator

RS-422, RS-423A These two standards, recommended by the Electronics Industries Association (EIA), define a format for transmitting serial data by wire, intended to replace the older RS-232 format. The new format offers faster data rates and greater immunity to electrical noise.

The format exists in two versions. RS-422 uses balanced (differential) signaling with two wires for each signal. The computer responds only to the difference between the two wires and ignores any noise that is picked up by both. RS-423A is a simpler format using only one signal per wire; at suitable data rates, it is compatible with older RS-232 equipment.

The Apple Macintosh has an RS-422/RS-423A port; Table 18 shows the pin connections. For RS-232 compatibility, use only the "-" line in each pair.

Table 18 Pin connections for Macintosh RS-422 Port
(Pin numbers are embossed on the connector.)

Original Macintosh (9-pin D-connector):

Pin	Signal
1	Frame ground
2	+5V power to external device
3	Signal ground
4	Transmit +
5	Transmit –
6	+12V power to external device
7	Clear to send
8	Receive +
9	Receive –

Macintosh SE, Macintosh II (8-pin mini-DIN connector):

Pin	Signal
1	Data terminal ready
2	Clear to send
3	Transmit –
4	Signal ground
5	Receive –
6	Transmit +
7	Carrier detect or clock input (Not used on Macintosh Plus)
8	Receive +

RS/6000 See **workstation.**

RUN To run a program is to make the computer execute it. A distinction is often made between "compile time" (the time when the program is compiled; see **compiler**) and "run time" (the time when the program is run.)

RUN-LENGTH ENCODING See **data compression**.

RUN-TIME ERROR A run-time error is an error that occurs when a program is being executed. For example, a run-time error might occur if division by 0 is attempted, or if the subscript for an array is outside the allowable bounds for that array. A run-time error may cause the program to stop execution, or it may be handled by an error-trapping routine (see **trapping**). For contrast, see **compile-time error**.

S

SAA Systems Application Architecture (SAA) is a set of guidelines promoted by IBM for standardizing the design of large pieces of software. It includes a set of user interface guidelines called Common User Access (CUA), as well as guidelines for data communication, programming languages, and procedure libraries.

See also **CUA; user interface**.

SANS-SERIF Sans-serif type does not have serifs; for example, the letter "I" is a vertical line with no ornaments at the top or bottom. For illustration, see **serif; typeface**.

Use sans-serif type with caution. It is not as readable as type with serifs.

SAVE To save information is to transfer it from the computer's memory to a storage device, such as a disk drive. Saving data is vital because the contents of the computer's memory are lost at the time the power is turned off. The opposite process is known as loading.

SCALABLE FONT A scalable font is a font that can be used to print characters of any size. Many newer laser printers include scalable fonts. To be fully scalable, the shapes of the characters must be stored in the form of vector graphics. See **font; vector graphics**.

SCANF See **printf**.

SCANNER A scanner is a device that enables a computer to electronically read a printed or handwritten page. The simplest scanners give the contents of the page to the computer as a graphic image—a handy way of putting pictures into the computer (see **desktop publishing**). More advanced scanners can also read the letters of typewritten text, transmitting them into the computer as if they were typed on the keyboard. This process, however, is seldom 100 percent accurate.

Several other kinds of electronic devices are called scanners, including bar code readers (see **bar code**) and devices for scanning the radio spectrum.

SCROLL To scroll information is to move it across the screen as if the screen were a window or porthole through which you are looking. For example, all word processing programs can scroll vertically, and some can also scroll horizontally.

SCROLL BAR The scroll bar on a window enables you to scroll the window, i.e., look at different areas of the data that the window is displaying. To scroll, click on the arrows at the ends of the scroll bar or use the mouse to move the scroll box along the bar. For pictures, see **window**.

SCSI The small computer systems interface (SCSI) is a standard way of interfacing a computer to disk drives, tape drives, and other devices that require high-speed data transfer. Up to seven SCSI devices can be linked to a single SCSI port. Thus, a single SCSI adapter can interface a computer to one or more hard disks, an optical disk, a tape drive, and a scanner.

SCSI is especially popular with Macintoshes and UNIX workstations but is also used on some IBM-PC-compatible computers. By way of contrast, see **ST-506; ESDI; IDE.**

SEARCH AND REPLACE To search and replace is to work through a file, changing every occurrence of a particular sequence of characters into some other sequence of characters. (See **editor**.)

SEARCHWARE Searchware refers to the software used to search through a database. For example, an encyclopedia available on CD-ROM must come with searchware to allow the user to find specific entries. See **full text search; hypertext.**

SECOND-GENERATION COMPUTERS The term *second-generation computers* refers to computers made with transistors in the 1950s and 1960s.

SECTOR A sector is a part of track on a disk. For example, a typical diskette system partitions the disk into 40 circular tracks with each track having 10 sectors. (See **track; disk**.)

SEGMENT On a microprocessor such as the 8088, the segment address is one of two numbers that define a memory location. (See **offset**.)

On the 80286, 80386, and 80486, in protected mode, the segment address itself is not added to the offset; rather, it serves as a pointer to a table of segment descriptors that define the locations to which offsets are added.

SELECTION SORT Selection sort is an algorithm for sorting the elements of an array by first selecting the lowest-valued item, then the next lowest, and so on. In practice, the lowest valued item is exchanged with the first item in the part of the array being searched, and the search is confined to the remainder of the array from then on.

Selection sort is probably the easiest to remember of the many general-purpose sorting algorithms. The following program implements selection sort in BASIC:

```
10    REM Selection sort in BASIC
20    REM Assume X has been dimensioned
30    REM and contains N values
40    FOR I = 1 TO N
50       M = I
60       FOR J = I + 1 TO N
70          IF X(J)>= X(M) THEN 90
80          M = J
90       NEXT J
100      Y = X(M)
110      X(M) = X(I)
120      X(I) = Y
130   NEXT I
```

SEMICONDUCTOR A semiconductor is a material that is neither a good conductor nor a good insulator. Semiconductor devices, such as diodes, transistors, and integrated circuits, are the essential parts that make it possible to build small, inexpensive electronic machines.

The most common semiconductor material is silicon. Each atom in a silicon crystal contains four outer-level (or valence) electrons. A pure silicon crystal is not a very good conductor, because these electrons will normally stay bound to their atoms. An N-type semiconductor region is formed by adding a bit of impurity to the pure silicon. This process is known as *doping*. The impurity added is a material such as phosphorus, where each atom has five valence electrons. The result is a crystal very much like the original one, except that there are now a few extra electrons floating around (one for each atom of phosphorus that was added). The whole crystal is called an *N-type* region, because it contains free negative charges. If an impurity with only three valence electrons, such as boron, is added to the silicon crystal, gaps are left in the crystal structure because there are not enough electrons to fill all the spaces in the crystal. Each gap is called a *hole*. Even though a hole is nothing but the absence of an electron, it can be thought of as carrying a mobile positive charge. A semiconductor region with an excess of holes is called a *P-type* semiconductor region.

Electric current can flow in an N-type region in much the same way that it flows in a regular conductor. In a conductor, the current is made up of outer-level valence electrons that are not too tightly bound to their atoms. When a negative voltage is applied to one end of the N-region and a positive voltage is applied to the other, the loose electrons will be repelled by the negative voltage and attracted by the positive voltage.

Current can flow in the P-type region, but the process is quite different. If a negative voltage is applied to one end of the P-type region, the electrons will be repelled. However, the P-type region does not contain any mobile electrons. What an electron can do is jump into one of the holes. This process creates a new hole where the original electron used to be. We can think of the hole itself as moving toward the negative voltage, carrying a positive charge with it.

A semiconductor diode is formed by joining a P-type region and an N-type region. A transistor consists of a thin layer of one type of semiconductor between two layers of the opposite type. A semiconductor integrated circuit is made by placing many P and N regions on a single chip, so as to form a complex circuit containing many miniature transistors and other circuit elements.

SEND TO BACK In some graphical editing environments, the Send to Back command puts an object or window "at the back," so that other objects or windows are allowed to overlap it. See also **overlaid windows; bring to front.**

SEQUENTIAL-ACCESS DEVICE A sequential-access (or serial-access) device is a memory device in which it is necessary to read through all preceding records before the computer finds the record it is looking for. Tape storage devices are examples of sequential-access devices. For contrast, see **random-access device.**

SERIAL To transmit data serially is to transmit it one bit at a time over a single wire. Serial transmission is the normal way of linking computers to terminals and is often used to link microcomputers to printers, especially relatively slow ones. (See **baud; parallel; RS-232.**)

SERIAL-ACCESS DEVICES See **sequential-access device.**

SERIAL MOUSE See **mouse.**

SERIAL PORT A serial port is a connection by which a computer can transmit data to another device using serial transmission— that is, one bit at a time. It is common for a microcomputer to have a serial port that is connected to a modem or printer. Most serial ports follow the EIA-232D (RS-232) standard. See **RS-232.** For contrast, see **parallel port.**

SERIAL PRINTER A serial printer is a printer that connects to a computer's serial port. See **serial port; parallel port.**

SERIES Two electronic components are connected in series if they are joined one right after the other (see Figure 80).

FIGURE 80 Series

SERIF Serifs are small ornaments at the ends of the lines that constitute a letter or digit, such as the flat parts on the top and bottom of the letter "I" (see Figure 81). Serifs originated as the points at which Roman stonecutters inserted their chisels into the stone. Today, serifs make type more readable by helping the reader's eye stay on the line.

FIGURE 81 Serifs on "T" at left. There are no serifs on "T" at right.

SERVER A server is a computer that provides services to another computer (called the *client*). On multitasking machines, a process that provides services to another process is sometimes called a server.

For specific examples see **file server; X server; DDE.**

SET (1) Pascal provides for a data type known as a set, which consists of a group of objects of a specified type. For example, a set can be declared with a statement such as

VAR smallnum : SET OF INTEGER;

and then it can be assigned a set of values with an assignment statement such as:

smallnum := [1,2,3,4];

Now you can test to see whether a given integer x is contained in this set. The expression x **IN smallnum** will be true if x has the value 1, 2, 3, or 4; otherwise, it will be false. Pascal also provides for standard set operations, such as union (symbolized by +), intersection (*), and set difference (−).

(2) The set input of a flip-flop causes the state of the flip-flop to become 1. (See **flip-flop.**)

(3) In MS-DOS (PC-DOS) and OS/2, the SET command stores information in the operating system's *environment area* (see **environment**). In UNIX, it has a similar effect. In other operating systems (e.g., VM/CMS and VAX/VMS), the SET command allows the user to customize many aspects of the operating system.

SEVEN LAYERS See **data communication.**

SHAREWARE Shareware is software that is copyrighted but can be distributed free of charge to anyone. Users are asked or required to make a payment directly to the author if they use the program regularly. Shareware is often misleadingly described as "free" (see **free software**).

Shareware has been criticized for relying on the unpaid work of users to do much of the advertising and distribution while the income goes only to the author. On the other hand, shareware products can be much less expensive than comparable commercial products.

SHELL In MS-DOS (PC-DOS), a shell is a second copy of DOS, loaded into unused memory on top of an application program (such as a word processor or spreadsheet). By using a shell, the application program can pass commands to DOS or allow the user to use DOS without leaving the application program, provided enough memory is available.

The SHELL statement in IBM PC BASIC (GW-BASIC) creates a shell. To leave a shell, type the DOS command EXIT.

SHELL SORT The Shell sort algorithm is a variation of the insertion sort algorithm (see **insertion sort**). A Shell sort is a series of insertion sorts in which each item, instead of being compared with the items next to it, is compared with items a certain number of elements away. On each pass, this number (the "skip count") becomes smaller until it reaches 1; thus, the last pass is an ordinary insertion sort. The earlier passes take care of large moves that would be time-consuming in a pure insertion sort.

Here is a Pascal program that reads 10 numbers and performs a Shell sort:

```
PROGRAM shellsort;
  { Based on R. Sedgewick, ALGORITHMS (1983) }

LABEL 1;
CONST n = 10;
VAR
  a: ARRAY[1..n] OF INTEGER;
  i, value, position, skip: INTEGER;

BEGIN
  { Read in the data }
    FOR i := 1 TO n DO
      BEGIN
        write('Enter item ',i:2,': ');
        readln(a[i])
      END;
```

```
      { Choose initial skip count }
        skip := 1;
        REPEAT
          skip := 3*skip + 1
        UNTIL skip > n;

      { Perform the Shell sort }
        REPEAT
          skip := skip DIV 3;
          FOR i:=skip+1 TO n DO
            BEGIN
              value := a[i];
              position := i;
              WHILE a[position-skip]>value DO
                BEGIN
                  a[position] := a[position-skip];
                  position := position - skip;
                  IF position <= skip THEN GOTO 1
                END;
1:          a[position] := value
            END
        UNTIL skip = 1;

      { Print the results }
        FOR i:=1 TO n DO write(a[i]:5);
        writeln
    END.
```

FIGURE 82

SHIFT REGISTER A shift register is a register in which all the bits can be moved one place to the left (or the right) when a particular control signal is pulsed. For example, the register containing 0 0 0 0 1 1 0 1 when shifted left once is 0 0 0 1 1 0 1 0, and when shifted twice is 0 0 1 1 0 1 0 0. For an application, see binary multiplication.

SIDE EFFECT A side effect occurs when the execution of a program or subprogram causes unanticipated effects on the computer system. For example, this Pascal procedure

```
PROCEDURE swap (VAR a,b : INTEGER);
  BEGIN
    t := a;
    a := b;
    b := t
  END;
```

will swap two values. For example, if it is called by the statement swap(x, y), it will cause the variables x and y to swap values. However, in addition to this intended effect, the procedure will also have the unintended effect of changing the value of the global variable t, if there is one, which may cause errors to arise elsewhere in the program. This problem could be avoided by declaring t to be a local variable within the procedure. Then there would be no side effect because the value of the global variable t would not be affected. (See **local variable.**)

SIDELIT A liquid crystal display (LCD), as on a laptop computer, requires built-in illumination to be easily read; if the illumination comes from the side of the display panel it is said to be sidelit.

SILICON Silicon is the primary material used to make semiconductor devices. Each atom in a silicon crystal contains 14 protons and 14 electrons. Ten of the electrons are tightly bound to the nucleus, while the outer four valence electrons can be dislodged relatively easily. (See **semiconductor.**)

SIMM A single in-line memory module (SIMM) is a tiny printed circuit board to which several memory chips are attached. It plugs into a slot on a larger printed circuit board and is handled as if it were a single integrated circuit.

SIMULATION Simulation is the process of representing one system by another. In computer science, simulation means representation of the real world by a mathematical model solved by a computer. A mathematical model of population growth can simulate a real population. A *deterministic* simulation occurs when the future path of the system is exactly determined by the parameters of the system. A *Monte Carlo* simulation occurs when probabilities are known and a selection of random numbers is used to guide the system.

SIN If A is an angle in a right triangle, then the sine of A (written as sin A) is given by

$$\sin A = \frac{\text{length of opposite side}}{\text{length of hypotenuse}}$$

The function SIN(A) on most computers calculates the value of sin A. Many computers require that the value of A be expressed in radians. (See **radian measure.**)

SITE LICENSE A site license is a software license that allows unlimited copying of a computer program for use by a single organization at a specified site. A site license is often much cheaper than the purchase of multiple copies. See also **software license**.

SLOT A slot is a socket in a microcomputer designed to accept a plug-in circuit board. (See **card**.)

SMALLTALK Smalltalk was one of the first object-oriented programming languages. It was developed at Xerox Palo Alto Research Center (PARC) in the late 1970s and included a powerful graphical user interface that influenced the design of the Macintosh and on Microsoft Windows. See **object-oriented programming; graphical user interface**.

SMTP SMTP (**S**imple **M**ail **T**ransfer **P**rotocol) is a protocol used to transfer electronic mail between computers on the Internet and other TCP/IP networks. See **Internet; TCP/IP**.

SNOBOL SNOBOL is a language for processing character-string data, developed at Bell Telephone Laboratories in 1962. It is based on the theory of finite-state Markov processes, and surprisingly concise and powerful programs can be written in it. However, since nearly every SNOBOL statement contains at least one conditional jump, structured programming in SNOBOL is impossible and nowadays the language is little used.

SNOW Small flickering white spots on a computer screen are called snow. The IBM **C**olor/**G**raphics **A**dapter (CGA) produces snow when the contents of video memory are changed rapidly. Compatible video adapters from other manufacturers can run the same software without producing snow. (See **CGA; video modes [IBM PC]**.)

SNOWFLAKE See **fractal**.

SOFT FONT A soft font is a description of a kind of type to be printed on a laser printer. Unlike a font cartridge or an internal font, a soft font consists of data transmitted to the printer by the computer before the text is printed. The soft font will vanish from the printer's memory when the power to the printer is turned off, so it will be necessary to reload it each time the printer is powered on. The availability of a wide variety of soft fonts provides users with great flexibility. For contrast, see **font cartridge; internal font**.

SOFT-SECTORED DISK When a soft-sectored disk is formatted, the computer writes a magnetic pattern onto the disk to mark the boundaries of each sector. (See **disk**.)

SOFTWARE The software of a computer system is the set of programs that tell the computer what to do. The term *software* is contrasted with *hardware*, which refers to the actual physical machines that make up a computer system. The hardware by itself is of little value without the instructions that tell it what to do.

Software can be classified into systems software (see **operating system**) and applications software. For examples of common types of application software, see **entries for word processing, spreadsheet, database management**. For information on creating software, see **programming** and **programming language**.

SOFTWARE INTERRUPT See **interrupt**.

SOFTWARE LICENSE A software license is an agreement between the publisher of a computer program and the person who buys a copy of it. Some licenses specify that when you buy a copy of a program, you do not really own the copy but have merely bought the right to use it in certain ways. Other licenses allow you to make a working copy of the program, which would otherwise be forbidden by copyright law (see **copyright**).

Most licenses allow a single copy of the program to be used on only one machine at a time. It can be copied for backup purposes, and it can be moved from one machine to another, but it cannot be actually in use in two places at once. Thus you are forbidden to load the same program into more than one machine through a network (see **local-area network**). However, it is usually permissible for several people to use the same program on a multiuser machine with a single CPU.

A *site license* allows unlimited copying of a program for use by a single organization at a specified site. A site license is often much cheaper than the purchase of multiple copies. Another alternative for schools and colleges is the use of *student editions* of software; these are less powerful than the commercial version and are sold at much lower prices.

Many aspects of software licenses have not yet been tested in court. In particular, the license document is often packed where the user cannot see it until after buying and opening the software package. In such cases, it can hardly be described as a valid contract. When dealing with unclear or unreasonable licenses, users should make a good-faith effort to obey copyright law and to avoid depriving the publisher of income.

See also **free software**.

SORT To sort a group of items, such as the elements in an array or the records in a file, is to arrange them in numerical or alphabetical order. There are many different algorithms that can be used to sort a group of items. If the number of items is small, it is probably best to use an algorithm that can be represented by a short program. If the number of data items is large, then it is more important to use a more complicated algorithm that executes more quickly. Some algorithms assume that the data items have been read into the memory of the computer. However, if there is a very large number of items, it will be necessary to use an algorithm that works when the data are stored on an auxiliary storage device. Since sorting is such a common operation, many operating systems include built-in sorting algorithms. For examples of specific sorting algorithms, see **bubble sort; insertion sort; merge sort; Quicksort; radix sort; selection sort; and Shell sort**.

SOURCE (1) In a copy operation, the source refers to the place where the information is coming from. (See **target**.)

(2) The source is one of the three parts of a field-effect transistor (see **field-effect transistor**).

SOURCE PROGRAM A source program is a program written in a programming language (such as FORTRAN) and fed into a computer. The computer translates the program into a machine language object program.

SPARC The SPARC (Scalable Processor Architecture) microprocessor was developed by Sun Microsystems and is used in Sun Sparcstations as well as computers made by other manufacturers. It uses RISC architecture to achieve very high speed. See **workstation; Sparcstation; Sun workstations; RISC**.

SPARCSTATION The Sun Sparcstation is a high-performance workstation that uses the SPARC microprocessor. See **SPARC; Sun workstations**.

SPELL CHECKER A spell checker is a program that checks the spelling of every word in a document by looking up each word in a dictionary. If the word does not appear in the dictionary, the user is alerted to a possible misspelling.

Many word processing programs include spell checkers. An effective spell checker needs to store a large number of words using efficient data compression techniques, and it must be able to search the list quickly with a binary search. See data compression; binary search.

A spell checker will not recognize unusual proper names or specialized terms, but it will often allow you to create your own personal dictionary of specialized words you will often use.

Spell checkers are valuable aids to proofreading, but they cannot catch the substitution of one correctly spelled word for another (such as *form* for *from* or *to* for *too*). Thus they do not guarantee that a document is free of spelling errors.

SPLINE A spline is a curve calculated from a mathematical function to smoothly connect a series of points. For example, suppose you need to represent the points shown in Figure 83. It would require a large amount of memory to represent a complex curve if it was necessary to store the coordinates of thousands of points along the curve. If a simple formula, such as a polynomial, can be found to represent the curve, it requires much less memory. Also, if a curve is represented as a formula, it can be easily rescaled. (See **vector graphics.**) Unfortunately, it is seldom possible to represent a complex curve by a single formula, but often a sequence of formulas will work.

One possibility is to represent each segment of the curve as a cubic (third degree) polynomial, of the form $y = ax^3 + bx^2 + cx + d$. Suppose x_1 and x_2 represent the two end points of an interval, and suppose you know the value of y at the two end points (y_1 and y_2) and the slope of the curve at each of the end points: y_1' and y_2'. Then you have this four equation system:

$$y_1 = ax_1^3 + bx_1^2 + cx_1 + d$$
$$y_2 = ax_2^3 + bx_2^2 + cx_2 + d$$
$$y_1' = 3ax_1^2 + 2bx_1 + c$$
$$y_2' = 3ax_2^2 + 2bx_2 + c$$

This equation can be solved for the four unknowns: a, b, c, and d, and then you will know the equation of the curve.

In reality, you will need a separate equation for each segment of your curve, and you will not know the slope at the end point of each interval. Instead, you need to impose the condition that the curve for each segment smoothly joins the curve for the next segment. It is then necessary to solve a large linear equation system, but this is the type of task that can easily be accomplished on the computer.

FIGURE 83

SPOOLING Spooling is the process of storing the computer output before sending it to the printer.

SPREADSHEET A spreadsheet is a table of numbers arranged in rows and columns. Spreadsheets have long been used for business calculations. However, spreadsheet calculations can be very tedious; changing a single number can affect the results in many different rows and columns. Therefore, it helps greatly to have a computer perform spreadsheet calculations. Several software packages are available that turn the computer into an electronic spreadsheet. Some of the popular spreadsheet packages are Lotus 1-2-3, Excel, and Quattro.

When you first start working with a spreadsheet program, your screen will be filled with an array of blanks. You will probably want to define a label for each row and each column. Then you will want to enter some numbers into the table. Each location in the spreadsheet is called a cell. By using the appropriate cursor movement keys, you can enter values in whichever cells you choose. Suppose you would like one column to consist of values that grow at 5 percent per year. You can use a command that causes the values in the column to increase automatically by 5 percent.

To do calculations, you must use the commands that define formulas for all the rows and columns. For example, you might want one row to consist of the totals of the values in all of the rows above it, or you might want a column labeled "profit" to be equal to the difference between the column labeled "revenue" and the column labeled "cost." The important feature about spreadsheets is that the computer can remember the formulas associated with a particular row or column even when the numerical values change. For example, suppose you calculate a revenue forecast based on the assumption that sales grew by 5 percent per year. If you now change the sales column so that it grows by

8 percent per year, you can execute the "recompute" command and the computer will automatically fix all of the other values in the table to correspond to the new value for sales.

Here is a very simple example of a spreadsheet calculation. Let's keep track of the statistics for the players on a basketball team. We will label the columns "FG," "FGA," "FT," "FTA," "PTS," "FG PCT," and "FT PCT." The rows will be labeled with the names of the players. The bottom row will calculate the totals for the team. Column 5 (points) is defined by the formula

(column 5) = 2 * (column 1) + (column 3)

Columns 6 and 7 are defined by the formula

(column 6) = (column 1)/(column 2)
(field goal percent)
(column 7) = (column 3)/(column 4)
(free throw percent)

Here is an example of how the spreadsheet looks on the screen:

	FG	FGA	FT	FTA	PTS	FG PCT	FT PCT
	—1—	—2—	—3—	—4—	—5—	—6—	—7—
1 JONES	7	14	0	4	14	0.500	0.000
2 SMITH	9	20	5	5	23	0.450	1.000
3 JOHNSON	11	24	1	4	23	0.458	0.250
4 HERNANDEZ	18	25	1	4	37	0.720	0.250
5 RUSSELL	8	17	1	2	17	0.471	0.500
6 TOTAL	53	100	8	19	114	0.530	0.421

After we have printed the report we can erase all of the current data (but not the formulas) and then enter the statistics for the next game. The computer will automatically calculate the totals and the last three columns.

More elaborate spreadsheet packages can also fulfill other functions. For example, Lotus 1-2-3 provides graphic capabilities that make it possible to create graphs based on the spreadsheet data. See **Lotus 1-2-3.**

SPRITE A sprite is a moving element in a graphical display. Most video games use sprites.

SQL Structured Query Language (SQL, formerly Sequel) is a standard query language used by many programs that manipulate large databases. Here is an example of an SQL query:

```
SELECT NAME, SALARY FROM TABLE1
WHERE SALARY > 35000
```

This means "Give me the name and salary from each row in TABLE1 where the salary is more than 35,000." See **relational database; query language**.

ST-506 The Shugart ST-506 standard denotes the electrical interface between hard disk and controller in most IBM PC-compatible computers. The ST-506 interface is used for both MFM and RLL data encoding. ST-506-compatible disks and controllers are made by many different companies. (See **MFM; RLL**.)

Instead of ST-506, newer PC-compatible computers use the IDE, ESDI, or SCSI interfaces. (See **IDE; ESDI; SCSI**.)

STACK (1) A stack, also called a *pushdown stack* or *pushdown store*, is a data structure from which items are removed in the reverse order from which they were inserted. For example, when a program calls a subroutine, information about how to return to the main program is usually placed on the stack. If the subroutine then calls another subroutine, information about how to return to the first subroutine is placed on the stack. Since this information is retrieved from the stack in the opposite order from which it was placed there, each subroutine returns control to the right place. Stacks are very useful for dealing with one operation nested inside another.

To *push* a data item is to place it on a stack; to pop the stack is to remove an item from it.

(2) A stack is a collection of information used by Hyper-Card. (See **HyperCard**.)

START BIT The start bit indicates the beginning of an asynchronous RS-232 character. (See **RS-232**.)

STATEMENT A statement is a set of instructions that make up one unit of a computer program. (See **programming language**.)

STATISTICS PROGRAM A statistics program is a software package designed especially for performing statistical calculations. A statistics program works with lists of numbers instead of single values. It should have built-in commands for calculating the average and standard deviation of the elements of a list, for testing hypotheses about the relationships between variables through methods such as multiple regression, for performing transformations (such as taking the logarithm of the elements in a list), and for drawing graphs of the data. Examples of statistics programs include SAS (Statistical Analysis System) and SPSS (Statistical Program for the Social Sciences).

STOP BIT The stop bit indicates the end of an asynchronous RS-232 character. (See **RS-232**.) Normal practice is to use two stop bits at 110 baud and one stop bit at higher baud rates.

STORE To store an item of data is to transmit the data from the computer to a memory device.

STORED PROGRAM COMPUTER A stored program computer is a computer that can store its own instructions as well as data. In current usage the term *computer* usually refers to a stored program computer. The concept was originated by Babbage in the nineteenth century and was developed by von Neumann. The ability of a computer to store instructions allows it to perform many tasks without human intervention. The instructions are usually written in a programming language. (See **computer**.)

STRING A string (or *character string*) is a group of characters stored in a computer.
    See **string operations**.

STRING OPERATIONS There are several operations that are typically performed on character string data. A programming language that is capable of working on string data will normally include built-in commands to perform the functions listed below. Here are some examples from Microsoft BASIC, where A$ represents the string "GEORGE" and B$ represents "WASHINGTON".

1. Compare two strings to see if they are the same (often symbolized by an equal sign) or if one string comes before the other in alphabetical order (often symbolized by a less than sign). Alphabetical order is determined on the basis of ASCII codes, so lower-case letters come after upper-case letters (see ASCII).
2. Join two strings together (concatenation). This is often symbolized by a plus sign. For example, A$ + " " + B$ is "GEORGE" + " " + "WASHINGTON".
3. Calculate the length of a string. In BASIC, this is symbolized by LEN. For example, LEN (B$) is 10.
4. Select specified characters from the middle of the string. In BASIC, this is symbolized by MID$. For example, MID$(A$,3,2) is "OR", which means select two characters starting at position 3. BASIC also provides LEFT$ and RIGHT$ to automatically select a specified number of characters from the left or right end of the string, respectively.

5. Determine if one string is contained in another string, and if so, at what position it starts. In BASIC, this is written INSTR. For example, INSTR("OR",A$) is 3; INSTR("AND",A$) is 0.

6. Determine the ASCII code of an individual character. In BASIC, this is written ASC. For example, ASC("A") is 65.

7. Determine the character associated with a given ASCII code. In BASIC, this is written CHR$. For example, CHR$(65) is "A".

8. Determine the numerical value of a string that represents a number. In BASIC, this is written VAL. For example, VAL("86") is the number 86. If the string does not represent a number, then the result is 0 (for example, VAL(A$) is 0.)

9. Convert a numeric value into a string. In BASIC, this is written STR$. For example, STR$(86) is the string "86".

STRUCTURED PROGRAMMING One of the most important barriers to the development of better computer software is the limited ability of human beings to understand the programs that they write. Structured programming is a style of programming designed to make programs more comprehensible and programming errors less frequent. Because it is more a popular movement than a precise theory, structured programming can be defined in several ways, but it usually includes the following:

1. Block structure. The statements in the program must be organized into functional groups. For example, of the following two Pascal program fragments, the first is structured, while the second is not:

```
Structured:              Unstructured:
IF x<=y THEN             IF x>y THEN GOTO 2;
  BEGIN                  z := y-x;
    z := y-x;            q := SQRT(z);
    q := SQRT(z)         GOTO 1;
  END                  2:z := x-y;
ELSE                     q := -SQRT(z);
  BEGIN                1:WRITELN(z,q);
    z := x-y;
    q := -SQRT(z)
  END;
WRITELN(z,q);
```

FIGURE 84

Note that it is much easier to tell what the first example does.

2. The avoidance of jumps ("GOTO-less programming"). It can be proved mathematically that, if a language has structures equivalent to the (block-structured) IF-THEN and WHILE statements in Pascal, it does not need a GOTO statement. Moreover, GOTO statements are often involved in programming errors; the programmer becomes confused as to the exact conditions under which a particular group of statements will execute. Advocates of structured programming allow GOTO statements only under very restricted circumstances (e.g., to deal with error conditions) or not at all.

3. Modularity. If a sequence of statements continues uninterrupted for more than about 50 lines, human beings have a hard time understanding it because there is too much information for them to keep track of. As an alternative, programs should be broken up into subroutines, even if some of the subroutines are called only once. Then the main program will read like an outline, and the programmer will never need to understand more than about one page of code at a time. (He must know what the subroutines do, but not how they do it.) This principle is sometimes called *information hiding*—irrelevant information should be kept out of the programmer's way.

STUFFIT StuffIt, by Raymond Lau, is a popular data compression program for the Macintosh. Like ARC and ZIP on the IBM PC, StuffIt allows several files to be combined into one. StuffIt can also encode and decode BinHex files. See **data compression; ARC; ZIP; BinHex.**

STYLE A style of type is a particular size, either plain, boldface, or italic. (See **font; typeface.**)

SUBDIRECTORY A subdirectory is a disk directory that is stored in another directory. (See **directory.**)

SUBROUTINE A subroutine is a set of instructions, given a particular name, that will be executed when the main program calls for it. In BASIC, a subroutine is labeled by the statement number of its first line and is executed when a GOSUB command is reached. For example, suppose that X is a real number between 0 and 24 that tells the number of hours after midnight that a particular event occurs. Here is a BASIC program that uses a subroutine to convert X into hours:minutes:seconds and tell whether it is A.M. or P.M.:

```
10    INPUT "NUMBER OF HOURS AFTER MIDNIGHT:";X
20    GOSUB 100
30    PRINT H;":";S;D$
40    END                    :REM END OF MAIN PROGRAM
100   REM START OF SUBROUTINE
110   H = INT(X)             :REM NUMBER OF HOURS
120   F = 60*(X - H)
130   M = INT(F)             :REM NUMBER OF MINUTES
140   S = 60*(F - M)    :REM NUMBER OF SECONDS
150   IF X>=12 THEN D$ = "P.M."
160   IF X<12 THEN D$ = "A.M."
170   IF H>12 THEN H = H - 12
180   IF H = 0 THEN H = 12
190   RETURN                 :REM END OF SUBROUTINE
```

The command RETURN marks the end of the subroutine and tells the computer to return to the main program.

There are two main advantages to using subroutines when writing programs. If a complicated set of instructions is needed at different locations in the program, then making the instructions into a subroutine can save considerable work since it will be unnecessary to type the instructions more than once. Also, a complicated program is best written as a collection of smaller parts, each with a well-understood purpose. (See **top-down programming; procedure**.)

SUBSCRIPT A subscript is a number or letter used to identify a particular element in an array. In mathematics, subscripts are written below the main line, as in x_1 or a_{23}. In most computer languages, however, subscripts are surrounded by parentheses, as in X(1) or A(J). (See **array**.)

SUBSCRIPTED VARIABLE A subscripted variable is another name for an array, since it is necessary to use subscripts to identify a particular element. (See **array**.)

SUN MICROSYSTEMS Sun Microsystems of Mountain View, California, is a leading manufacturer of workstations. See **Sun workstations**.

SUN WORKSTATIONS Sun workstations are high-performance desktop computers manufactured by Sun Microsystems of Mountain View, California. Most are marketed as single-user systems although each will support more than one user. All run SunOS, a proprietary version of UNIX based on System V and incorporating some BSD features.

Important Sun models and their CPUs are, respectively, the Sun-3 (Motorola 68000 series), Sun-4 and Sparcstation (SPARC), and Sun 386i (Intel 80386). See **UNIX; System V; BSD; workstations; SPARC.**

SUN OS See **Sun workstations.**

SUPER VGA A super VGA is a video card for PC-compatible computers that provides all the functions of the VGA plus one or more higher-resolution modes. Many different manufacturers have made super VGAs with various features.

Under DOS, the special modes of a super VGA are available only with software designed to exploit them. Under Microsoft Windows, if a super VGA software driver is installed, all Windows software can then use the super VGA at its full resolution because graphics resolution is controlled by Windows, not by individual pieces of software.

See **VGA; video modes (IBM PC); Windows.**

SUPERCOMPUTER A supercomputer is designed to be markedly larger and/or faster than ordinary mainframe computers. Examples are the Cray vector processors and the Intel iPSC parallel processor.

SUPERTWIST A liquid crystal display (LCD) works by twisting light waves and using polarizing filters to allow the twisted light to pass. A supertwist display provides increased twist and higher contrast

SURGE PROTECTOR A surge protector absorbs brief bursts of excessive voltage coming in from the AC power line. These surges are created by lightning or by electric motors switching off. Early microcomputers were easily damaged by surges, but present-day personal computers usually have adequate surge protection built in.

Surge protectors do little good unless the power line is properly grounded. Always plug the computer into a three-wire outlet that meets modern wiring standards. Never try to use a two-wire outlet with an adapter.

Many surge protectors also incorporate RFI protectors to help reduce radio and TV interference emitted by the computer into the power line. (See **RFI protection.**)

A surge protector cannot do anything about momentary power failures. See also **power line protection; uninterruptible power supply.**

SWAPPING Swapping is the temporary copying of data from RAM to disk so that the RAM can be used for something else. Swapping is practiced by operating systems such as OS/2 and VAX/VMS, but not MS-DOS or CP/M.

SX The 80386 SX is a microprocessor like the 80386 except that it has a 16-bit rather than 32-bit bus, and is therefore slower. The 80486 SX is like the 80486 except that it lacks the 80486's built-in math coprocessor. See **microprocessor.**

SYMBOLIC ALGEBRA A symbolic algebra program on a computer is a program that is capable of performing operations on symbols representing variable names (for example, calculating that (A+B) times (C+D) is equal to the expression $AC + AD + BC + BD$). In this type of program, a variable can represent an expression as well as a value. For example, the variable Y could represent the expression $AX^2 + BX + C$. Then there are three possible ways in which a user might wish to use Y: (1) use it as a literal, for example, having 2Y appear as 2Y; (2) replace it with the expression it represents, for example, having 2Y appear as $2AX^2 + 2BX + 2C$; or (3) replace it with the numerical value of the expression it represents, for example, if X has the value 3, A = 2, B = 7, and C = 10, then 2Y would appear as 98. The programming language LISP is suited for symbolic computation such as this. By contrast, a language such as BASIC is designed only to work with the numeric value of mathematical variables.

SYMBOLIC DEBUGGER A symbolic debugger allows you to step through a compiled program, interrupting it at any point and examining or changing the values of variables. A symbolic debugger analyzes the source code and the object code together, so that even though the program has been compiled, you can work with it as if you were editing the source program.

SYNTAX The syntax of a programming language is the set of rules that specify how the language symbols can be put together to form meaningful statements. Syntax rules are like grammar rules. If a program violates the language syntax rules, a syntax error has occurred.

SYS REQ KEY On IBM mainframe terminals, the Sys Req (system request) key enables the user to communicate with the communications system itself rather than the application program. The IBM PC AT and PS/2 have a Sys Req key, but little or no software has been written to make use of it.

SYSOP The SYSOP (system operator) is the person who manages a bulletin-board system. (See **BBS**.)

SYSTEM V AT&T System V is one of the most widely used versions of the UNIX operating system. See **UNIX; SunOS; BSD**.

SYSTEM 7 Introduced in 1991, System 7 is a major new version of the Apple Macintosh operating system. See **Macintosh**.

SYSTEMS APPLICATION ARCHITECTURE See **SAA**.

SYSTEMS PROGRAMMER A systems programmer is a person who writes the programs needed for a computer system to function. Some of the programs that systems programmers write include operating systems, language processors and compilers, and data file management programs. Systems programming, which is usually done in an assembly language, requires considerable knowledge of the particular computer system being used. By way of contrast, see **application programmer**.

t _____

TAN If A is an angle in a right triangle, then the tangent of A (written as tan A) is defined to be

$$\tan A = \frac{\text{length of opposite side}}{\text{length of adjacent side}}$$

The function TAN (A) on many computers calculates the value of tan A. Many computers require that the value of A be expressed in radians. (See **radian measure**.)

TAPE Magnetic tape can be used to store information in a form that can be easily read by a computer. It is much cheaper to store information on tape than in the computer main memory or on a disk memory device, but a longer time is required to locate a particular data item if it is stored on tape. (See **memory**.)

In the late 1970s, it was common for microcomputers to store data on ordinary audiocassette tapes. Now, reel-to-reel tape systems are often used for data storage on mainframe systems.

TAPE DRIVE A tape drive is a device that converts information stored on magnetic tape into signals that can be sent to a computer.

TARGET (1) The target is the place to which information is supposed to be copied (e.g., the "target disk" when copying disks) (See **source**.)

(2) A target is something that is being searched for (as when searching for a word in a document).

TASK See **process**.

TBBS TBBS is a popular program for implementing bulletin-board systems. (See **BBS**.)

TCP/IP TCP/IP (Transport Control Protocol/Internet Protocol) is a standard format for transmitting data in packets from one computer to another. It is used on the Internet and various other networks. The two parts of TCP/IP are TCP, which deals with construction of data packets, and IP, which routes them from machine to machine. See **Internet; wide area network**.

TELEX TELEX (teletypewriter exchange) is an international system similar to the telephone system, but linking teletypewriters. TELEX messages can be sent and received by computer using carriers such as MCI Mail (MCI Communications, Inc.).

TELNET On the Internet and other TCP/IP networks, the "telnet" command (sometimes called "tn") lets you use your computer as a terminal on another computer. Normally, the telnet program provides a direct path so that the remote computer communicates directly with the terminal you are actually using. But if you are connecting to an IBM mainframe, you should use "tn3270," which emulates an IBM 3270 full-screen terminal even though your real terminal is something else. See **TCP/IP; Internet; rlogin.**

TEMPLATE (1) A template is a plastic card with flowchart symbols cut out of it. A programmer using a template card can easily trace out the symbols that are needed in drawing a flowchart.

(2) A template is a particular pattern for a spreadsheet program or a database program that is frequently used. Therefore storing the template will save you from having to retype the specifications each time.

TERMINAL A computer terminal is an input-output device whereby a user is able to communicate directly with a computer. A terminal must have a keyboard, so that the user can type in instructions and input data, and a means of displaying output, such as a CRT (television) screen or a typewriter. The earliest terminals were teletype machines. Today, personal computers are often used as terminals on larger computers. (See **data communication; modem; upload; download.**)

TERMINAL-NODE CONTROLLER See **packet radio.**

TERMINATE-AND-STAY-RESIDENT See **memory resident.**

TEX TeX (pronounced "tek"), by D. E. Knuth, is a computer typesetting program used by the American Mathematical Society and many book publishers and educational institutions. Unlike most desktop publishing systems, TeX does not attempt to show you the appearance of the finished document on the screen as you edit it (though screen previews can be generated). Instead, you type a document with codes in it that indicate boldface, italics, special characters (e.g., "\integral" for an integral sign), and the like.

The rationale is that correct typesetting relies on distinctions that are too subtle to see on a computer screen. A user who wants an em dash rather than an en dash should say so with explicit codes, rather than trying to make a mark that appears the right length on the screen. Likewise, large-scale aspects of design should be automated; you should be able just to give the title of a chapter, and let the computer take care of numbering the chapter and putting the title in the right place on the page.

TeX is generally considered the most sophisticated computer typesetting system, as well as (for an experienced user) one of the easiest to use. It sets a standard that other desktop publishing systems try to emulate.

TEXAS INSTRUMENTS (TI) A manufacturer of semiconductors and computers, TI is headquartered in Dallas, Texas. Jack S. Kilby developed the first working integrated circuit ("silicon chip") at TI in 1958, making it possible to miniaturize electronic equipment to a degree far beyond earlier expectations. Currently, TI produces parts for practically all makes of computers, as well as a number of micro- and minicomputers of its own. Recent products include the TravelMate notebook computers.

TEXT BOX In a dialog box, a text box is an area in which the user can type or edit characters. For picture, see **dialog box.**

TEXT EDITOR A text editor is an editor designed primarily or exclusively for handling textual material (letters, manuscripts, etc.) rather than programs. (See **editor.**)

TEXT FILE A text file is a file that contains lines of written information that can be sent directly to the screen or printer by using ordinary operating system commands.

The files produced by word processors are usually not text files. Although they contain text, they also contain special codes (for margins, underlining, etc.) whose meaning is known only to the word processing software. Many word processors can, however, produce text files ("nondocument mode" in WordStar, "DOS text files" in Word Perfect).

On machines that use the ASCII character set, text files are often called ASCII files.

To create a text file on the Macintosh, save a document as "text only."

THERMAL PRINTER A thermal printer prints by heating spots on the paper with an array of tiny, fast-acting heating elements. Thermal printers are among the least expensive printers and are often used on calculators and very low-priced computers. However, they require special paper that may discolor with age.

THIRD-GENERATION COMPUTERS The term *third-genera-tion computers* refers to computers made with integrated cir-cuits. Current computers built with circuits that have large-scale integrations are often called *fourth-generation computers.*

THREADED INTERPRETIVE LANGUAGE See **FORTH.**

THREE-DIMENSIONAL GRAPHICS In CAD/CAM systems, it is frequently helpful to be able to see representations of three-dimensional objects that can be viewed from different angles. Suppose that you wish to build a cube. Figure 85 is a BASIC program that keeps track of the coordinates of the vertices of the cube (in three dimensions) and then figures out how to dis-play the appearance of the cube in two dimensions. In this pro-gram the user can choose which direction to rotate the cube, and then a coordinate rotation formula from trigonometry is used to shift the coordinates of the vertices to their new locations.

```
1  REM  THIS GW BASIC PROGRAM DRAWS A CUBE ON THE
2  REM  SCREEN AND THEN MAKES IT POSSIBLE FOR THE USER TO
3  REM  ROTATE THE CUBE TO SEE HOW ITS APPEARANCE CHANGES
100 DIM A(8,3) ' THE ARRAY A CONTAINS THE X,Y,Z COORDINATES
101              ' OF THE 8 VERTICES OF THE CUBE
110 REM -- READ IN INITIAL COORDINATES
120 FOR I=1 TO 8:FOR J=1 TO 3:READ A(I,J):NEXT J:NEXT I
130 DATA  1,1,1,  -1,1,1,  -1,-1,1,  1,-1,1
140 DATA  1,1,-1, -1,1,-1, -1,-1,-1, 1,-1,-1
210  H=120 : SCALE=40  'THE VALUE OF SCALE CAN BE ADJUSTED TO
211                     'CHANGE THE SIZE OF THE CUBE
220 FOR I=1 TO 8:FOR J=1 TO 3:A(I,J)=A(I,J)*SCALE:NEXT J:NEXT I
230  GOSUB 300  'DRAW CUBE
240  GOSUB 400  'INPUT COMMAND
250  GOSUB 500  'PERFORM ROTATION
260  GOTO 230
299 '
300 REM -- DRAW CUBE
305 SCREEN 1:CLS
306 REM  IT TAKES 12 LINES TO DRAW THE CUBE
310  FOR I=1 TO 4
315    V1 = I : V2 = I+1 : IF V2=5 THEN V2=1
```

FIGURE 85

FIGURE 85 Continued

```
320    GOSUB 380  'DRAW LINE
325    V1 = I+4 : V2 = I+5 : IF V2=9 THEN V2=5
330    GOSUB 380
335    V1 = I : V2 = I + 4
340    GOSUB 380
345  NEXT I
350  RETURN
379  '
380 REM DRAW LINE
385 LINE(H+A(V1,1),H+A(V1,3))-(H+A(V2,1),H+A(V2,3))
390 RETURN
399  '
400 REM INPUT COMMAND
401 LOCATE 24,1
410 REM THESE ARE THE ALLOWABLE COMMANDS:
411 'R : ROTATE RIGHT BY A CERTAIN ANGLE     EXAMPLE: R 10
412 'D : ROTATE DOWN BY A CERTAIN ANGLE      EXAMPLE: D -20
420 INPUT X$
430 IF X$="S" THEN END  'S MEANS TO STOP
440 DIRECTION$=LEFT$(X$,1)  'DIRECTION OF ROTATION, R OR D
450 ANGLE = (3.14159/180)*VAL(MID$(X$,2,LEN(X$)-1))
451 REM  NOTE - THE ANGLE IS READ IN DEGREES AND
452 REM          THEN CONVERTED TO RADIANS
460 RETURN
499  '
500 REM PERFORM ROTATION
510 IF DIRECTION$="R" THEN GOTO 520 ELSE GOTO 600
520    REM - ROTATE TO THE RIGHT
530    FOR I=1 TO 8
540      X=A(I,1):Y=A(I,2)  'Z COORDINATE IS UNCHANGED
550      X2=X*COS(ANGLE)+Y*SIN(ANGLE)
560      Y2=Y*COS(ANGLE)-X*SIN(ANGLE)
570      A(I,1)=X2:A(I,2)=Y2
575    NEXT I
580    RETURN
600    REM - ROTATE DOWN
610    FOR I=1 TO 8
620      Y=A(I,2):Z=A(I,3)  'X COORDINATE IS UNCHANGED
630      Y2=Y*COS(ANGLE)+Z*SIN(ANGLE)
```

FIGURE 85 Continued

```
640    Z2=Z*COS(ANGLE)-Y*SIN(ANGLE)
650    A(I,2)=Y2:A(I,3)=Z2
660  NEXT I
670  RETURN
```

THREE-DIMENSIONAL SPREADSHEET In a three-dimensional spreadsheet, each cell is identified by three coordinates—row, column, and page—which makes it possible to organize work into separate pages. This makes it much easier to manage large spreadsheets.

Imagine you were organizing a large paper spreadsheet with several hundred rows and columns arranged on one giant two-dimensional page. That would be very awkward; it is easier to organize paper in the form of pages in a book. In the early 1990s, most spreadsheet programs acquired three-dimensional capability; Lotus 1-2-3, Excel, and Quattro Pro are examples.

In Lotus 1-2-3 release 3, a cell address looks like this: C:E4. The first letter (C) identifies the page. The remainder is the same as a two-dimensional spreadsheet: the second letter (E) identifies the column and the number (4) identifies the row.

Pages can be *grouped*, i.e., given the same format. This makes it possible, for example, to put the budgets for several divisions on different pages of the same spreadsheet. It is also possible to work on pages independently.

TIFF Tag Image File Format (TIFF) was developed by Microsoft, Aldus, and several other companies as a standard format for recording bit-mapped images on disk. TIFF files can store images of any size with any number of colors, using several kinds of data compression. For comparison, see **PCX; GIF**. See also **bitmap**.

TILDE The tilde is the mark "~" written above the letter N in Spanish (e.g., ñ). The ASCII character "~" is also called a tilde.

TILED WINDOWS Tiled windows divide the screen into sections without overlapping one another. By contrast, see **overlaid windows; cascaded windows**.

TIMES ROMAN See **typeface**.

TIMESHARING Timesharing is a way of running more than one program on the same computer at the same time, so that, for example, the computer can serve many users at different terminals simultaneously.

Timesharing is based on the idea that a computer spends most of its time waiting for things to happen. Almost all input-output devices (printers, card readers, disks, etc.) operate much more slowly than the CPU itself; the extreme case is a terminal or console, where the computer may spend minutes or hours waiting for someone to type something. In a timesharing system, more than one program is loaded into memory at once, and when the computer is unable to proceed with one program, it jumps to another.

In practice, the computer does not stay on one program more than a fraction of a second even if there is nothing to wait for; to do so would prevent other, possibly shorter, programs from being executed. Also, programs that are not executed are frequently "rolled out" of memory (i.e., copied to disk) to make memory space available to programs that are actually running.

TITLE BAR The title bar is the label at the top of a window, usually identifying the program or file to which it belongs. (See **window**.)

TN See **telnet**.

TN3270 See **telnet**.

TNC See **packet radio**.

TOGGLE To toggle something is to switch it back and forth from one state to another. For instance, in some editors, the Ins key "toggles" insert mode; that is, it turns insert mode on if it is off, or off if it is on.

TOKEN RING A token-ring network is one in which the computers are connected together in a ring. A special message, called the *token*, is passed from one machine to another around the ring, and each machine can transmit only while it is holding the token. IBM markets a token-ring network for the PC family of computers. (See **local-area network**; **ARCNET**.)

TONER CARTRIDGE The toner cartridge of a laser printer contains the toner (ink) that will be used to make marks on the paper.

TOP-DOWN PROGRAMMING The top-down approach to programming means to first look at the broad outline of a programming problem; then to divide the problem into a collection of separate tasks, each with a well-defined purpose; and finally to write the separate parts and put them all together into one program. The top-down approach is usually the best way to write complicated programs. Detailed decisions are postponed until the requirements of the large program are known; this is better than making the detailed decisions early and then forcing the major program strategy to conform to them. Each part of the program (called a *module*) can be written and tested independently.

TOPOLOGY Topology is the mathematical study of how points are connected together. If an object is stretched or bent, then its geometric shape changes but its topological properties remain unchanged.

The topology of a computer network is the pattern of connections between the machines in the network. Figure 86 illustrates some common topologies: a ring network, a star network, and a bus network. See **local area network**.

TRACK Data that are recorded on a disk are arranged in many concentric circles, each of which is called a track. (See **disk**.)

TRACKBALL A trackball is a computer pointing device similar in function to a mouse. Instead of rolling the mouse around the desktop, the user rotates the ball on the trackball in the direction desired. The trackball unit itself does not move, which is

328

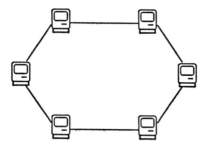

Ring network

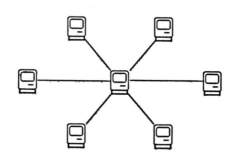

Star network

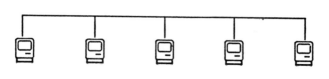

Bus network

FIGURE 86

an advantage if there is not enough desktop space to conveniently operate a mouse.

TRACTOR FEED A tractor feed is a mechanism that uses toothed gears to pull the paper forward in a computer printer. The teeth fit into the feed holes in the side of the paper.

TRANSISTOR A transistor is an electronic device that allows a small current in one place to control a larger current in another place; thus, transistors can be used as amplifiers in radio and audio circuits, and as switches in logic gates (see **NOT gate; NOR gate; OR gate; NAND gate; AND gate.**)

This article deals with *bipolar* transistors, the most common kind. For contrast, see field-effect transistor.

A bipolar transistor is made by sandwiching a thin layer of one kind of semiconductor material (P-type or N-type) between two layers of the opposite type (N-type or P-type, respectively). Thus an NPN transistor is a P layer between two N layers; a PNP transistor is the opposite. (See **semiconductor.**) The circuit diagram symbols for NPN and PNP transistors are shown in Figure 87. The middle section of a transistor is called the *base* and the other two are the *emitter* and *collector*.

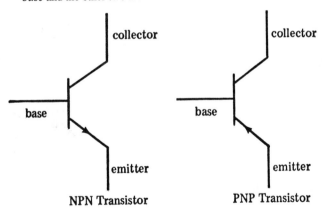

NPN Transistor   PNP Transistor

FIGURE 87

Figure 88 shows how an NPN transistor works. (A PNP transistor works the same way with all polarities reversed.) The emitter is connected to ground (0 volts) and the collector is connected to +5 volts through some type of load. Electrons try to flow from emitter to collector, but with 0 volts on the base, they can't get through because the base-collector junction is like a reverse-biased diode (see **diode**).

But if the base were to become full of electrons, it would no longer behave like P-type material, and the base-collector junction would no longer block electron flow. We can get electrons into the base by pulling them in from the emitter. Thus if we forward-bias the base-emitter junction by applying a positive voltage to the base, the base-collector junction will act as if it were forward-biased too. A small flow of electrons through the base controls a much larger flow of electrons through the collector.

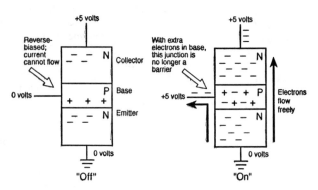

FIGURE 88

In computers, transistors act as switches (see Figure 89). If a positive voltage is applied to the base, current will flow from the emitter to the collector, and the transistor acts like a switch that is on (or closed). If a negative voltage is applied to the base, the base-emitter junction is reverse biased, causing the flow of electrons from the emitter to the base to stop. Since no more electrons are being driven into the base, there are no electrons to sneak across the base into the collector. This means that the current from the emitter to the collector stops, so the transistor acts like a switch that is off (or open).

TRANSPARENT In computing, something is transparent if it has no visible effect. For instance, if a print-spooling program is

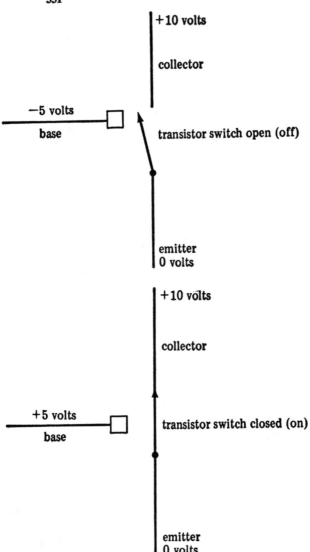

FIGURE 89 NPN Transistor

transparent, all other software works exactly as if the print-spooling program were not installed. This is a desirable feature.

TRAPPING To trap an event is to perform a special action when something happens that would ordinarily interrupt the operation of the computer. For instance, some programming languages provide "error trapping," which means that when the program attempts to do something impossible (such as divide by zero or read a file that doesn't exist), control will be transferred to an error-handling routine supplied by the programmer. If no error trapping were provided, the program would simply end with an error message that might puzzle the user. In BASIC, trapping is activated by statements such as ON ERROR.

Trapping also refers to special actions activated by the system clock or by events such as data arriving through a serial port.

TRAVELING SALESMAN PROBLEM See **limits of computer power.**

TREE A tree is a data structure similar to a linked list, except that each element carries with it the addresses of two or more other elements, rather than just one. (See **linked list.**)

Trees are a very efficient way of storing items that must be searched for and retrieved quickly. Suppose, for example, that you want to store the following names in a computer:

Jones	Voss
Steinfeld	Marino
Alexander	Williams
Bateman	Rodriguez

The names can be arranged into a tree by using the following two-step procedure:

1. Use the first name on the list as the root of the tree.
2. To find where to put each subsequent name, start at the root of the tree. If the name you are dealing with precedes the root name alphabetically, follow the left pointer; otherwise follow the right pointer. Proceed in this way until you come to an empty pointer; attach the new name to it.

The result is the tree shown in Figure 90. Step 2 in the procedure above can be used to locate names already in the tree in a minimum of steps (in this case, no more than four steps even though there are eight names in the list). The search sequence that results is not quite as good as a binary search, but it is much better than having to work through the whole list. Furthermore, as with linked lists, new nodes can be added at any time without requiring that existing nodes be moved.

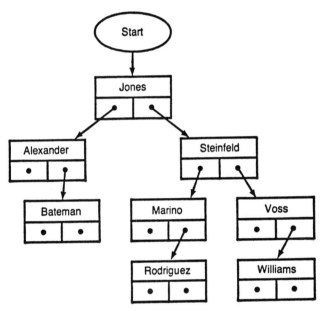

FIGURE 90 A Search Tree

TROJAN HORSE A Trojan horse is a computer program with a hidden destructive function, such as erasing the disks on a specified date. Trojan horses are often distributed as counterfeit "new" versions of shareware products.

Knowingly distributing a destructive computer program is a crime under common law and under specific laws of various states. See also **virus**.

TRUNCATION In truncation, all the digits of a number that are to the right of the decimal point are dropped. For example, the truncation of 6.45 is 6, and the truncation of 737.984 is 737. In Pascal this operation is symbolized by TRUNC; in BASIC, by INT.

TSO TSO (<u>ti</u>me<u>sh</u>aring <u>op</u>tion) is the part of OS/360 and related IBM operating systems that supports timesharing terminals.

TSO data set names consist of one or more fields joined by periods, such as

JONES.MATRIX.MULT345.PLI

where each field consists of one to eight alphanumeric characters, beginning with a letter, and the overall length of the name does not exceed 40 characters. Under TSO, the first field is normally the user ID and the last field indicates the type of file: PLI for a PL/I source program, OBJ for an object program, DATA for all-upper-case, fixed-record-length data, or TEXT for data with variable record length and both upper- and lowercase letters. (Only a few commands are sensitive to the last field; changing the name of a file does not automatically change its type.)

Some commonly used TSO commands are as follows:

HELP	Display information about other commands.
EDIT	Edit a data set. (Within EDIT, type HELP for more information.)
LISTCAT	Display the names of a user's data sets.
LIST	Display the contents of a data set.
DELETE	Get rid of a data set.
ALLOCATE	Assign a file name or other attributes to a data set (like the JCL DD card).
FREE	Cancel a previous ALLOCATE command
SUBMIT	Submit a data set to OS as a batch job.
LOGOFF	End the session. Data sets are permanent, but they may be erased after a few hours, depending on local policy

The details of TSO vary considerably from installation to installation; for more information, consult local manuals.

TSR See **memory resident**.

TTL TTL (<u>T</u>ransistor-<u>T</u>ransistor <u>L</u>ogic) is a type of integrated circuit that operates at very high speeds and requires relatively large amounts of power at an accurately regulated voltage (5 volts). Most microcomputers use TTL devices for input-output and control functions. TTL integrated circuits are recognizable because their type numbers contain "74" or "74LS" followed by two or three digits (e.g., SN7402N).

TTL MONOCHROME MONITOR See **monitor.**

TURBO BASIC Borland International's Turbo BASIC is a high-performance compiler for essentially the same language as Microsoft QuickBASIC, with minor differences in the syntax of a few of the newest features. Turbo BASIC is a conventional compiler similar in spirit to Turbo Pascal.

TURBO C++ Turbo C++ is a compiler for the C and C++ languages similar in design to Turbo Pascal and produced by the same company, Borland International. It supersedes an earlier product, Turbo C, and is accompanied by a more elaborate compiler package, Borland C++, which is marketed mainly to professional programmers. See **Turbo Pascal; Borland International; C; C++.**

TURBO PASCAL The Turbo Pascal compiler, the first major product of Borland International, is one of the most popular compilers ever written (see **Borland International**). Turbo Pascal compiles Pascal programs 50-100 times faster than conventional compilers, and it includes a built-in full-screen editor for writing programs. If the compiler finds a syntax error, it immediately calls up the editor and places the cursor on the offending character so that the programmer can correct the error. This makes it possible to develop and refine programs very quickly.

The Turbo Pascal language is close to the ISO standard (see ISO) but does not include the predefined procedures GET and PUT, nor is the behavior of READ, EOF, and EOLN entirely standard. Many extensions to the language have been added, including "typed constants" (actually variables initialized at compile time), additional ways of using pointers, and predefined procedures for screen control, graphics, and operating system services.

Turbo Pascal obtains its remarkable compilation speed partly because it is extremely well designed, and partly because it takes a number of shortcuts. The compiler does not produce object listings nor does it have to recover from syntax errors, since it calls up the editor as soon as the first error is found.

The first versions of Turbo Pascal were released in 1984 for computers running the CP/M and MS-DOS operating systems. Priced at $49.95, and outperforming compilers in the $300 to $800 range, Turbo Pascal almost drove its competitors off the market. Turbo Pascal is also available for Windows and the

Macintosh. Current versions include a symbolic debugger and support object-oriented programming. See **object-oriented programming**.

TURBO PROLOG Turbo Prolog is a Prolog-like language originally introduced by Borland International (the maker of Turbo Pascal) but now marketed by Prolog Development Center, Copenhagen, Denmark, under the name PDC Prolog.

Compared to Prolog, Turbo Prolog sacrifices some power in order to get programs to run faster. The ability of the program to modify itself—a key requirement for advanced artificial intelligence work—is severely limited, and the types of all arguments have to be declared. However, Turbo Prolog provides an excellent development environment and a powerful set of screen input-output routines, and it is often used to develop commercial expert systems. See **Prolog; expert system; Borland International**.

TURING MACHINE A Turing machine is an imaginary machine conceived by A.M. Turing in the 1930s to help identify the kinds of problems that are potentially solvable by machines. The machine is a kind of simple computer. It consists of a long string of paper tape and a machine through which the tape can be fed. The machine can do four things; it can move the tape one space, it can place a mark on a space, it can erase a mark, or it can halt. Turing's thesis states that this simple machine can solve any problem that can be expressed as an algorithm (if it has an unlimited supply of paper tape). As you might imagine, in practice it would be difficult to give instructions to a Turing machine so that it could solve a particular problem. The Turing machine is important theoretically, however, because it provides an indication of what kinds of problems computers can solve, and what kinds they can never solve.

TURNKEY SYSTEM A turnkey system is a computer system that is ready to perform a particular task with no further preparation. A turnkey system is sold as a complete package from a single vendor. By contrast, most computer systems are assembled step-by-step by users who obtain hardware and software from various suppliers.

TURTLE In LOGO and related computer languages, a turtle is a pointer that moves around the screen, leaving a trail as it goes.

Originally, the turtle was a small robot that rolled around on a large piece of paper, drawing a line.

Turtle graphics is a form of vector graphics. The turtle cannot be told to go to a particular position; it can only be told to turn through a particular angle and go a particular distance. See **vector graphics**. For an example of turtle graphics programming, see **LOGO**.

TWISTED PAIR A twisted pair of wires provides a cheap and relatively noise-free way to transmit signals. The two wires carry equal and opposite signals. Any electrical noise that they pick up will be the same (rather than the opposite) in the two wires, and the circuitry on the receiving end can be designed to ignore it. By contrast, see **coaxial cable**.

TYPE Under CP/M, MS-DOS (PC-DOS), OS/2, VAX/VMS, or VM/CMS, the command TYPE causes the contents of a text file to be displayed. For example:

```
TYPE LETTER.DOC
```

causes the file LETTER.DOC to be displayed on the screen. The equivalent UNIX command is CAT.

TYPEFACE Most of the typefaces used on computer printers today fall into the following categories (see Figure 91):

1. *Roman type, proportionally spaced, with serifs.* This kind of type originated with the stone engravers of ancient Rome. "Proportionally spaced" means that different letters are different widths (e.g., "M" is wider than "I"); serifs are the marks at the ends of the strokes (e.g., the horizontal marks at the top and bottom of "I"). Times Roman is a popular Roman typeface.

   Roman type is the most readable kind of type and is used for the text of most books. *Blocks of Roman type should never be underlined;* use italics instead (or boldface in some situations). Underlining on typewriters was originally a substitute for italics.

   Roman type usually includes some characters that are not on a typewriter, such as the dash (—) and distinct opening and closing quotation marks (" "). Be sure to use these where appropriate. (See **typesetting mistakes**.)

2. *Sans-serif type, proportionally spaced.* Two popular typefaces of this kind are Geneva and Helvetica. This kind of

Times Roman

Proportional pitch, with serifs

24 point 18 point

14 point 12 point 10 point 9 point
ABCDEFGHIJKLMNOPQRSTUVWXYZ
abcdefghijklmnopqrstuvwxyz 1234567890
Plain **Boldface** *Italic*

Helvetica

Proportional pitch, without serifs

24 point 18 point

14 point 12 point 10 point 9 point
ABCDEFGHIJKLMNOPQRSTUVWXYZ
abcdefghijklmnopqrstuvwxyz 1234567
Plain **Boldface** *Italic*

Courier

Fixed pitch (all letters same width)

24 point 18 point

14 point 12 point 10 point 9 pt
ABCDEFGHIJKLMNOPQRSTUVWXYZ
abcdefghijklmnopqrstuvwxyz 123
Plain **Boldface** *Italic*

FIGURE 91 Samples of Various Typefaces on an Apple Laserwriter

type is better for short captions, posters, or labels, but can be tiring to read for long periods.

3. *Fixed-pitch, typewriter-like typefaces.* Courier and similar fixed-pitch typefaces are used when all characters must be

the same width in order to line up properly, such as in computer program listings (see **COBOL** in this book for an example), or when presenting financial tables, or when printing documents that were laid out for a simpler kind of printer.

4. *Novelty typefaces* such as Old English (not shown in the figure, but often used in ecclesiastic settings). These should be used very sparingly to make dramatic-looking titles or mastheads.

See also **font; serif; pitch; point; leading; desktop publishing**.

TYPESETTING MISTAKES The following pointers will help you avoid common mistakes in designing documents with desktop publishing software.

1. Notice the differences between typesetting and the typewriter: (a) left and right quotation marks are different characters ("like this"); (b) a dash is not the same as two hyphens; (c) underlining is rarely used—where you would underline on a typewriter, use italics (or possibly boldface) in type.

2. Your type is proportionally spaced; letters are not all the same width. You can't count letter spaces the way you do on a typewriter; but must use other means of aligning.

3. Always align columns with the tab key, not the space bar.

4. Type carefully. Be sure not to hit the space bar more than once between words. It's hard to tell the difference between one space and two spaces by just looking at the screen.

5. Don't justify everything. Justified type looks good only when the columns are rather wide. Flush-left type with a ragged right margin is easier to read if the columns are narrow; with narrow columns, justification puts excessive space between words. (See **justification**.)

6. Don't use more than one or at most two fonts in a document. (Italics, boldface, and different sizes count as a single font.) Multiple-font documents are almost always ugly. Odd typefaces (such as Old English) are very hard to read.

7. Make sure your document is not missing any essential features such as adequate margins or page numbers. If in doubt, find a well-designed document or book and imitate it.

8. Use appropriate features of your software. When you type a footnote, use the footnote instruction if there is one, rather than just moving the cursor to the foot of the page. That

way, if you change the layout later, the software will probably still handle the footnote correctly.

9. *Standardize.* Don't face each document as an original design problem. Develop a standard format that you like, and
stick with it.

u

ULTRIX ULTRIX is a proprietary version of UNIX for Digital
Equipment Corporation computers. See **UNIX.**

UCSD P-SYSTEM The UCSD P-system is an operating system
that was developed at the University of California at San Diego
(UCSD) and implemented on many different microcomputers.
The P-system itself and the object code produced by its compilers are written, not in machine language, but in a language
called P-code. Implementing the P-system on a computer consists of little more than writing a P-code interpreter in the computer's machine language.

UNDOCUMENTED A feature of a computer or of a program is
undocumented if it is not described in the literature (documentation) provided by the manufacturer.

Some computer programs rely on undocumented features of
the machine on which they run. The risk of using undocumented features is that they may not be the same in future versions
of the program or machine.

Undocumented features exist for several reasons. Some are
accidental omissions from the documentation. Others represent
incompletely tested features that will be made reliable and documented in future versions. Still others may be kept secret in
order to give the vendor a competitive advantage in making
add-on products.

See also **documentation.**

UNERASE See **recovering erased files.**

UNINTERRUPTIBLE POWER SUPPLY An uninterruptible
power supply uses batteries to continue providing electricity to
a computer for a few minutes in the event of a power failure.
This makes it possible to shut down the computer in an orderly
way without losing data.

UNIX UNIX is an operating system, or family of operating systems, developed at Bell Laboratories in the early 1970s as a replacement for an earlier system called *Multics*. UNIX is noteworthy because, although developed by a small team of about four people, it is in many ways superior to operating systems developed by large teams at tremendous expense (e.g., OS/360).

The main features of UNIX include the following:

1. Highly modular, structured design. The entire system is defined in terms of a relatively small number of subroutines; UNIX can be implemented on any machine by implementing those routines. Furthermore, the operation of the whole system is based on a relatively small number of principles carried through very consistently; there is little arbitrary detail for the user to learn.

2. Extensibility. In many operating systems, a user can create commands of his own that execute sequences of ordinary commands stored on files. UNIX, however, provides a full-fledged programming language for this purpose (the "shell"), with IF, WHILE, and CASE statements similar to those of Pascal, as well as extensive facilities for string handling.

3. Input-output redirection. Any program invoked by a command can be told to take its input from, and/or write its output onto, a file rather than the user's terminal. For example:

```
SORT <ALPHA >BETA
```

tells the SORT program to take its input from ALPHA and write its output onto BETA. UNIX also supports pipelines, which allow one program to transmit its output directly into the input of another program. (See **MS-DOS**.)

Many UNIX commands, called *filters*, read a file and output a copy of it that has undergone some simple transformation, such as removing repeated lines. Powerful operations can be accomplished by stringing filters together through pipelines.

4. Tree-structured directories. In all earlier operating systems, a user's files were kept in a single list called a *directory*. In UNIX, however, directories are handled like files and a user can have an unlimited number of them, each of which must be listed in a higher directory until the main ("root") directory is reached. This makes it possible to arrange files into

logical groups—for example, to put all files related to a particular project into a single directory. Tree-structured directories are a virtual necessity if one user is to keep track of more than a few dozen files, as is required, for example, on a microcomputer with a hard disk.

The following are some common AT&T UNIX commands. They may be different in other versions of UNIX.

cc	Compile a C Program. (See C.)
cp	Copy a file onto a file or into a directory.
diff	Display the differences between two files.
ed	Edit a file.
grep	Search a file for lines matching a pattern.
ls	List contents of a directory.
mkdir	Create a directory.
pr	Print a file.
rm	Remove a directory entry. (This is the normal way to delete a file.)
rmdir	Delete a directory (which must be empty).

UPLOAD To upload is to transmit a file to a central computer from a smaller computer or a computer at a remote location. See **Kermit; XMODEM; FTP.** For contrast, see **download.**

UPS See **uninterruptible power supply.**

UPWARD COMPATIBILITY Upward compatibility is the situation in which a computer program or accessory works not only on the machine for which it was designed but also on newer models. For instance, programs written for the IBM PC in 1981 will still run (considerably faster) on the IBM PS/2 Model 70, introduced in 1988. Thus we say that the PS/2-70 is upward compatible with the PC. By contrast, see downward **compatibility.**

USENET Usenet is a wide-area network for UNIX machines exchanging files through the UUCP ("UNIX-to-UNIX copy") command. Usenet addresses contain extensive information about the route by which a message is to be delivered. For example, psuvax!ugacc!aisun1!mcovingt means "user MCOVINGT on machine AISUN1, which can be reached through UGACC, which can be reached through PSUVAX."

Today, the main function of Usenet is to maintain a large set of newsgroups (public forums), which are transmitted mainly through the Internet. See **newsgroup; Internet.**

USER-FRIENDLY A user-friendly computer program is designed to be easy for people to use. In the days when computers were operated only by specialists, little attention was paid to making programs user-friendly. However, when computers became more popular, it became very important to write programs that could be easily understood by the people who use them. The most important requirement for making a program user-friendly is a clear, understandable manual that explains how the program works. Other features that can help make a program user-friendly are menus that clearly list the available choices and command names that are easy to remember. However, a program should not contain so many on-screen explanatory messages that it becomes cumbersome to use for people who have already learned how the program works.

USER INTERFACE The user interface of a program or operating system is the way it communicates with the person who is using it. There are three important types of user interfaces:

1. *Command languages.* This is a common way to giving intructions to operating systems; for instance, in CP/M, MS-DOS (PC-DOS), OS/2, or VAX/VMS, the user can obtain a list of files by typing the command *dir*. Command languages work well only if they are used constantly so that the user never forgets the commands.
2. *Menus.* The user chooses an item from a displayed list. Menus are ideal for software that is seldom used, but experienced users may find them too slow.
3. *Graphical environments.* The user performs operations by selecting icons (pictures) with a mouse. Environments of this type can be highly productive. For examples, see **Macintosh; Windows; Microsoft.** A drawback is that there is no simple way to describe how something is done; you almost have to see someone else do it. By contrast, commands in a command language can be written down on paper and even embedded in computer programs.

UTILITIES Utilities are programs that assist in the operation of a computer but do not do the main work for which the computer was bought. For instance, programs that compress data or defragment disks are utilities (see **data compression; fragmentation; Norton Utilities**). By contrast, word processors, financial programs, engineering programs, and other programs that do actual work for the user are called *application programs.*

UUCP On UNIX networks, the "uucp" (<u>UNIX</u>-to-<u>UNIX</u> <u>c</u>opy) command transfers files from one computer to another. It has largely been superseded by FTP. See **FTP**.

The Usenet network is sometimes called the UUCP network. See **Usenet**.

UUDECODE See **uuencode**.

UUENCODE In UNIX, the "uuencode" program provides a way of sending binary files through electronic mail services that only accept text files. An encoded file consists of printable characters arranged in lines of reasonable length. The "uudecode" program regenerates the original binary file from it. See **BinHex; binary file; text file**.

V

V.21 CCITT standard V.21 defines a format used for 300-baud data communication over phone lines in Europe and Japan. By contrast, the Bell 103 format is used in the United States for the same purpose. (See **Bell 103A; CCITT**.)

V.22 CCITT standard V.22 defines a format for sending 1200-baud data over phone lines designed to carry voice signals. A different format, Bell 212A, is more commonly used in the United States. (See **Bell 212A; CCITT**.)

V.22 BIS CCITT standard V.22 bis defines the worldwide standard format for sending 2400-baud data over telephone lines designed to carry voice signals. (*Bis* is Latin for "a second time" and indicates that this is an extension of standard V.22.) The standard specifies that if the phone line is of low quality, the modem will drop back to 1200-baud in V.22 format. Some 2400-baud modems either do not do this or drop back to Bell 212A format instead. (See **V.22; Bell 212A; CCITT**.)

V.24 This CCITT standard for data communication is essentially identical to the American RS-232C standard. (See **RS-232; CCITT**.)

V.29 CCITT standard V.29 defines a format for sending 4800-baud and 9600-baud serial data over telephone lines. This format is half-duplex only. (See **CCITT**.)

V.32 CCITT standard V.32 defines a standard format for sending 4800- or 9600-baud data over telephone lines designed to carry voice signals. The modem automatically analyzes the sound quality of the line and adjusts its output as needed. In general, V.32 modems will drop back to 2400 baud (V.22 bis format) or 1200 baud (V.22 or Bell 212A format) when line conditions are poor. (See **CCITT**.)

V SERIES The V series of CCITT standards defines ways of sending high-speed digital data over telephone lines. (See **CCITT; V.22; V.29; V.32**.)

VACCINE A vaccine is a computer program that offers protection from viruses (see **virus**) by making additional checks of the integrity of the operating system. No vaccine can offer complete protection against all viruses.

VACUUM TUBE A vacuum tube is an electronic component consisting of electrodes placed inside an evacuated glass tube. Vacuum tubes work by using electric and magnetic fields to control the movements of electrons that have been emitted by one of the electrodes.

A CRT (cathode ray tube) television screen is one example of a vacuum tube. The vacuum tubes originally used in computers performed the same type of functions that semiconductor diodes and transistors perform now. A vacuum tube diode consists of two electrodes; a cathode, which emits electrons, and an anode, or plate, which collects electrons. The diode will conduct electricity only when a positive voltage is applied to the cathode. A vacuum tube triode contains an electrode called the *grid*, located between the cathode and the plate. The flow of electrons from the cathode to the plate is controlled by the electric field of the grid. (Similarly, the current flow from the emitter to the collector in a transistor is controlled by the voltage applied to the base.) Vacuum tube triodes can be used for amplifications and logic functions.

The first electronic digital computer, the ENIAC (see **computer**), consisted of 18,000 vacuum tubes. The disadvantages of vacuum tube computers are that they are very big, they consume a great deal of power, and they generate a lot of heat. Also, it is necessary to constantly replace burned-out tubes.

VARIABLE A variable is a symbol that represents a data item, such as a numerical value or a character string, that can change its value during the execution of a program. Programming languages typically require that variable names start with letters. It is generally good practice when writing a program to include variables instead of constants, even if the value of the variable is not intended to change during the execution of the program. The value may need to change at some future date when you are running that same program, and it would be much easier to change one assignment statement for that variable than to change the value of a constant everywhere it occurs in the program.

See also **data types; data structures.**

VAX Digital Equipment Corporation produces the popular VAX line of minicomputers. (See **Digital Equipment Corporation; VAX/VMS.**)

VAX/VMS VAX/VMS is the most widely used operating system of Digital Equipment Corporation VAX computers. The command language is similar to MS-DOS. Some important commands are:

`dir`	Display a list of files.
`type xxx`	Show what is file xxx (a text file).
`help`	Invoke the help system.
`@xxxxx`	Execute the commands on file xxxxx.com.
`run xxxxx`	Execute the machine language program on file xxxxx.exe.

An unusual feature of VAX/VMS is the way it keeps previous versions of files. If you create a file called XXXX.YYY, it will be known as XXXX.YYY;1. If you then edit it, you will create XXX.YYY;2, and XXXX.YYY;1 will still exist. Whenever you do not specify a version number, you will get the latest version of the file. To delete all versions, you must use an asterisk in place of the version number, thus:

```
del xxxx.yyy;*
```

The command

```
purge xxxx.yyy
```

will delete all but the latest version of xxxx.yyy.

VDT VDT is an acronym for video display terminal, that is, a computer monitor. See **monitor.**

VECTOR GRAPHICS Vector graphics is a method of creating pictures on a computer telling it to draw lines in particular positions. The lines may be displayed on a screen or plotted on paper by a motor-driven pen. An advantage of vector graphics is that a picture can easily be moved from one output device to another, since it makes no assumptions about the exact way the lines are drawn. For the same reason, a vector graphics picture can be enlarged or reduced without loss of sharpness. By contrast, see bit-mapped graphics. See also **draw program; paint program.**

VECTOR PROCESSOR A vector processor (also known as an *array processor*) is a computer that can perform an operation on an entire array in a single step. Most presently available array processors are large mainframes, such as the Cray supercomputers.

Consider, for example, the problem of adding the corresponding members of two 100-element arrays A and B to produce a third array C (that is, $C(1) = A(1) + B(1)$, $C(2) = A(2) + B(2)$, and so forth). On an ordinary computer, this is done with instructions such as the following BASIC statements:

```
10   FOR I = 1 TO 100
20   LET C(I) = A(I) + B(I)
30   NEXT I
```

On a vector processor, however, the entire operation is done in a single machine instruction. The additions need not be done simultaneously; the important thing is that time is saved because the CPU need not fetch another instruction each time or calculate values for the variable I.

VENTURA Xerox Ventura Publisher is a desktop publishing program for the IBM PC family of computers. It was developed by Xerox Corporation using the software technology of the Xerox Star typesetting and layout workstation. (See **desktop publishing.**)

VGA The IBM video gate array (VGA) is the video circuit built into most models of the PS/2. VGA cards are also available for conventional PC's. The VGA provides high-resolution graphics modes and crisp text as well as emulation of the CGA, EGA, and MDA. (See **video modes [IBM PC].**)

VIDEO ADAPTER See **video card.**

VIDEO CARD A video card (video adapter) is a plug-in circuit board that enables a computer to display information on a particular type of monitor (screen).

VIDEO MEMORY Video memory is where a computer keeps track of the present contents of the screen. On the IBM PC, video memory occupies various locations above 640K, which is why only 640K of memory is available for programs even though the processor can address a full megabyte (1024K).

A fast way to change what is on the screen is to store new values directly into video memory.

See also **snow.**

VIDEO MODES (IBM PC) The ability of an IBM PC or PS/2 computer to display graphics depends on the video adapter (video card) that is installed in the machine and on the type of monitor connected. Regardless of which video adapter is installed, all of these machines can display text, including special box-drawing characters. (See **IBM PC.**)

Table 19 lists all the video modes of the IBM PC and PS/2 (not counting the Hercules Graphics Card or special products such as the IBM 8514 video adapter). Table 20 lists which modes are available with each video adapter and monitor.

Software will not use a particular video mode unless it is designed to do so. If you change video adapters and/or monitors, you can easily get sharper text, but you will not get increased graphics capability unless you use software designed for your new equipment.

TABLE 19 Video Modes of the IBM PC and PS/2 Family of Computers

Mode	Description
0	Text, 40 columns, black and white
1	Text, 40 columns, 16 colors
2	Text, 80 columns, black and white
3	Text, 80 columns, 16 colors (most popular text mode)
4	Graphics, 320 × 200, 4 colors (widely used graphics mode)
5	Graphics, 320 × 200, black and white
6	Graphics, 640 × 200, 1 color (widely used graphics mode)

7	Text, 80 columns, monochrome, with ability to underline (ideal for word processing)
8, 9, 10	Used only on PCjr
11, 12	Not used
13	Graphics, 320×200, 16 colors
14	Graphics, 640×200, 16 colors
15	Graphics, 640×350, monochrome
16	Graphics, 640×350, 16 colors
17	Graphics, 640×480, 2 colors
18	Graphics, 640×480, 16 colors
19	Graphics, 320×200, 256 colors (good for digitized photographs)

TABLE 20 Video Modes Available with Particular Video Adapters and Monitors

IBM Monochrome Display Adapter (MDA)
    Mode 7 only
IBM Color Graphics Adapter (CGA) with RGB color monitor
    0, 1, 2, 3, 4, 5, 6
IBM Color Graphics Adapter (CGA) with composite video monitor
    0, 1, 2, 3, 4, 5, 6
    (If the monitor is monochrome, colors are rendered as shades of gray or striped patterns.)
IBM Enhanced Graphics Adapter (EGA) with EGA-type color monitor
    0, 1, 2, 3, 4, 5, 6, 13, 14, 16
IBM Enhanced Graphics Adapter (EGA) with CGA-type color monitor
    0, 1, 2, 3, 4, 5, 6, 13, 14
    (but not 16, which is the most widely used EGA graphics mode)
IBM Enhanced Graphics Adapter (EGA) with TTL monochrome monitor
    7, 15
    (not the same as any of the modes available on a color monitor)
IBM Monochrome/Color Graphics Adapter (built into PS/2 25 and 30)
    All except 13, 14, 15, 16, and 18
IBM Video Gate Array (VGA) and *Extended Graphics Array (XGA)* (built into higher PS/2 models)
    All modes are available.

Video modes are becoming less important as more and more software accesses the video screen through device drivers. This makes it possible to upgrade a piece of software to use a new video adapter by supplying only a device driver. Under Microsoft Windows and OS/2, all graphics are performed through device drivers and any software will run on any video adapter.

See also **XGA; VGA; super VGA; Hercules Graphics Card.**

VIRTUAL 8086 MODE In virtual 8086 mode, an 80386 or 80486 microprocessor simulates one or more 8086 (IBM PC-type) microprocessors. This enables it to run the same kinds of programs as in real mode, but with multitasking. This gives the 80386 a big advantage over the 80286, which can only run 8086-type programs in real mode, without multitasking. See **real mode; protected mode, microprocessor; IBM PC; OS/2; Windows.**

VIRTUAL DISK See **RAM disk.**

VIRTUAL MACHINE A virtual machine is a computer that does not physically exist, but rather is simulated by another computer. In IBM's VM/SP operating system, the computer simulates multiple copies of itself. See also **virtual 8086 mode.**

VIRTUAL STORAGE The term *virtual storage* refers to a way of extending the effective size of a computer's memory by using a disk file to simulate additional memory space. Typically, the operating system keeps track of which memory addresses actually reside in memory and which ones must be brought in from disk when they are referred to. Virtual storage is divided into units called *pages*, and the operation of bringing in a page from disk is called a *page fault*.

VIRUS A virus is a computer program that automatically copies itself, thereby "infecting" other disks or programs without the user knowing it, and then plays some kind of trick or disrupts the operation of the computer.

Viruses have existed as academic pranks since the 1960s, but 1987 saw the first malicious viruses, apparently the work of disgruntled programmers trying to sabotage their competition.

The best protection against viruses, is to obtain all your software from reliable sources, make regular backup copies of your work, write-protect disks that you boot from and other disks that do not need to be written to, and reboot by turning the computer off and then on again.

Knowingly spreading a computer virus is a crime under common law and under specific laws in various states.

See also **vaccine; Trojan horse.**

VISICALC VisiCalc, developed for the Apple II in the late 1970s, was the first electronic spreadsheet program. (See **spreadsheet**.)

VISION Computer displays rely on many special properties of human vision, among them the following:

1. The eye blends together images that are less than $1/30$ second apart. Most computers redisplay the screen image every $1/50$ second or so, and the human viewer does not see any flicker.

2. Movements that are made in steps lasting $1/30$ second or less appear to be continuous. A moving image is actually a series of still images presented in very rapid succession.

3. Colors can be simulated by mixing other colors. For example, yellow on a computer screen does not contain any yellow light; instead, it is a mixture of red and green light. See **RGB monitor; plane**.

Working with a computer screen can be tiring to the eyes, especially if the display is blurry or glare is a problem, but no permanent harm results. Eyeglasses designed for the proper working distance can make computer work much easier. See **eyeglasses for computer users**.

VISUAL BASIC Microsoft Visual Basic is a programming environment marketed by Microsoft for Microsoft Windows and OS/2. The programmer designs various windows (forms) graphically, then writes procedures to respond to all the menu choices and other actions that are possible on each form. These procedures are written in a very modern dialect of BASIC that looks much like Pascal. Visual Basic makes it possible to develop practical programs very quickly. Figure 92 shows what the screen looks like during a development session.

Visual Basic implements event-driven programming. There is no "main program" that calls procedures; instead, procedures are called automatically when the appropriate events occur, such as menu choices and mouse movements. In effect, the end user himself calls the procedures. See **event-driven programming**.

Visual Basic is only partly object-oriented. Windows, menus, and other input-output mechanisms are objects and have procedures and instance variables associated with them, but the user is not free to define new objects. See **object-oriented programming**.

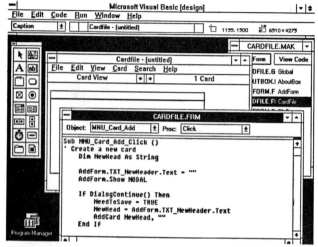

FIGURE 92

VLSI VSLI is an acronym for <u>v</u>ery <u>l</u>arge <u>s</u>cale <u>i</u>ntegration, which refers to chips containing 10,000 or more logic gates.

VM/CMS See **CMS; VM/SP.**

VM/SP VM/SP (<u>v</u>irtual <u>m</u>achine/<u>s</u>ystem <u>p</u>roduct), an operating system for large IBM mainframe computers, such as the 370, 3081, and 390, is based on the idea of one computer simulating multiple copies of itself.

There is a straightforward way to make one computer simulate another; simply program the first (real) computer to recognize the second (virtual) computer's instructions and respond appropriately. If the real computer is capable of interleaving several tasks, it can even simulate several virtual computers at once.

Under VM/SP, one IBM 370 (or the equivalent) simulates many separate IBM 370s at once. The user of each virtual 370 can then program it as if he had an entire 370 to himself; the effect is very much like using a large, fast personal computer that runs IBM 370 software. VM/SP creates and deletes virtual machines as users log on and off, keeps the virtual machines from interfering with each other, and allows them to communicate in controlled ways.

Most VM/SP virtual machines run CMS and serve only one user at a time. (See **CMS**.) However, within a VM/SP system it is quite possible to create a virtual machine that runs MVS (with TSO) and serves dozens of users at once, just as a real 370 does. This is particularly convenient for installations that are converting from MVS to CMS and want to support both at once. (See **MVS; TSO**.)

VOICE RECOGNITION See **natural language processing**.

VOLT The volt is the unit of measure of electronic potential. If a potential of 1 volt is applied to a resistor with a resistance of 1 ohm, then a current of 1 ampere will flow through the resistor. (See **Ohm's law**.) One volt can also be defined as 1 joule/coulomb, where a joule is a measure of energy: 1 joule = 1 (kilogram) (meter)^2/(second)^2.

VON NEUMANN, JOHN John von Neumann was a twentieth century mathematician who worked on one of the earliest computers and developed the stored program concept.

VT-100 The Digital Equipment Corporation VT-100 computer terminal has had a major impact on the computer industry because it provides convenient control codes for positioning the cursor, clearing the screen, and selecting normal, bold, or underlined type. (See **ANSI screen control**.) This makes it possible to implement full-screen, personal-computer-like software on an asynchronous terminal. Most present-day asynchronous terminals are VT-100 compatible, and most personal computers can emulate the VT-100.

VT-101, VT-102, VT-220, VT-320 The VT-101, VT-102, VT-220, and VT-320 are computer terminals made by Digital Equipment Corporation. They are upward compatible with the VT-100. (See **VT-100**.)

W

WAIT STATE A wait state is a brief delay introduced when a microprocessor reads data from memory, to allow extra time for the memory chips to respond. Wait states are used when a fast microprocessor is used with relatively slow memory chips.

A processor with one wait state on each memory access will typically be 10 percent to 20 percent slower than the same processor with no (zero) wait states.

WARM BOOT, WARM START See **boot.**

WATCH ICON On the Macintosh, the pointer turns into a watch face when the user needs to wait until the computer has completed an operation.

WATFIV WATFIV (<u>Wat</u>erloo <u>F</u>ORTRAN <u>IV</u>) is a FORTRAN compiler developed for teaching purposes at the University of Waterloo, Ontario. The WATFIV compiler is used on mainframe computers such as the IBM 370; it requires less CPU time and memory than a conventional FORTRAN compiler, making it cheaper to run large numbers of student programs.

The WATFIV language is based on FORTAN IV but contains a number of Pascal-like extensions, including a WHILE loop, a block-structured IF-THEN-ELSE statement, and a new type of subroutine, called a *remote block*, that is internal to the main program rather than being compiled as a separate unit.

WATT The watt is a unit for measuring the rate at which electrical power is being consumed. One watt is equivalent to one joule per second.

Wattage depends on both voltage and current, as follows:

$$Watts = Volts \times Amperes$$

For example, a 5-volt, 10-ampere power supply delivers 50 watts. The amount of AC power going into the power supply is considerably greater, depending on the inefficiency of the supply. See also **watt-hour.**

WATT-HOUR A watt-hour is the amount of energy consumed by using energy at the rate of one watt for one hour. One watt-hour equals 3600 joules. In the United States, electricity costs about 10 cents for 1000 watt-hours (one kilowatt-hour).

WEIGHT The weight of a typeface is its boldness; that is, **this is heavy-weight type** and this is ordinary-weight type. Some fonts provide several different weights (light, medium, demibold, bold, and extra bold).

WHETSTONE See **MIPS.**

WHILE The keyword WHILE defines one kind of loop in Pascal and related programming languages. The loop is executed over and over as long as the condition is true. Here is an example:

```
writeln('How many times?  (0 or more): ');
readln(n);
i := 1;
WHILE i <= n DO
  BEGIN
    writeln(i);
    i := i + 1
  END;
```

The condition is tested *before* each pass through the loop; if it is false at the beginning, the loop will never be executed. For contrast, see **REPEAT**.

WIDE-AREA NETWORK A wide-area network is a set of widely separated computers connected together. For example, the worldwide airline reservation system is a wide-area network. By contrast, see **local-area network**. See also **Internet**.

WIDOW The first line of a paragraph is called a widow if it appears by itself as the last line of a page. Some word processors automatically adjust page breaks so that there are no widows. (See also **orphan**.)

WILD CARD A wild card symbol is a symbol that matches any other symbol. For instance, the MS-DOS (PC-DOS) command

```
dir ab*.exe
```

means "Show me the files whose names begin with 'ab' and end with '.exe'." The symbol '*' is a wild card and stands for the middle part of the file name, whatever it may be.

WINCHESTER DISK See **hard disk**.

WINDOW A window is an area of the screen set aside for a special purpose. On the Macintosh and in Microsoft Windows, the screen is divided into windows for different pieces of software. The user can control the size, shape, and positioning of the windows. The *active window* is the one in which you are currently typing.

Figure 93 shows the main parts of a window in Microsoft Windows. To move the window, place the mouse pointer on the title bar, hold down the left button, and move the mouse. To change the size of the window, do the same thing but with the pointer on the left, right, or bottom border of the window. To close the window, double-click on the control menu box.

See also **icon; scroll bar; menu bar; pull-down menu; title bar; minimize; maximize.**

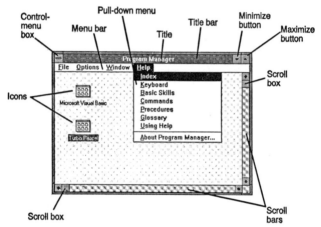

FIGURE 93

WINDOWS, MICROSOFT Microsoft Windows is an extension to the MS-DOS operating system that provides a graphical user interface, extended memory, and multitasking. The screen is divided into windows, and the user uses a mouse to start programs and make menu choices. (See **window.**) Windows can run not only Windows software (which use the graphical user interface) but also ordinary DOS software. Several pieces of Windows software are included with Windows, including a text file editor, a paint program, and a terminal emulator.

Windows runs in three modes. *Real mode* works on any IBM PC-compatible computer but is used mainly for running older Windows software. Most newer software will not run in real mode.

Standard mode requires an 80286 or higher microprocessor and runs virtually all Windows and DOS application software. The CPU runs in protected mode to give Windows applications access to larger memory area.

Enhanced mode requires an 80386 or 80486 and can multi-task; it can run several Windows and/or DOS application programs concurrently, each in its own window. The CPU runs protected mode and virtual 8086 mode. Many experts regard enhanced mode as a transition to OS/2.

Under Windows, screen and printer output is handled by device drivers. Thus, all Windows applications run correctly on whatever screen and printer Windows is configured for. To use a new printer or video card, it is only necessary to reconfigure Windows, not the application software. Like OS/2, Windows can use a disk file as *swap space* to substitute for extra memory.

See also **multitasking; OS/2; real mode; protected mode; virtual 8086 mode; device driver; PIF.**

WIRELESS LAN A wireless LAN is a local-area network (LAN) in which computers communicate by radio signals. See **LAN; Part 15 device.**

WORD A word is a group of bits stored in a computer memory. The number of bits in a word depends on the type of computer being used. A minicomputer typically may use words that are 16 bits long. Large computers may use words that are up to 64 bits long.

WORDPERFECT WordPerfect is the most popular word processing program for the IBM PC family of computers. There are also versions available for the Macintosh and several other computers.

WordPerfect is noted for its ability to handle a wide variety of document formats, including footnotes, legal citations, and foreign language characters. The user need not memorize many special keys because most functions are available through the F keys, which are labeled on a plastic template that attaches to the keyboard. Beginning with version 5.1, virtually all functions are also available through CUA-compliant menus. See **CUA.**

WordPerfect versions 5.1 and higher have a huge repertoire of special characters, which are printed by switching the printer into graphics mode when necessary. These include full character sets for mathematics, Greek, Russian, Hebrew, and Japanese kana. Special characters are typed by hitting Ctrl-V followed by the code, which may consist of two characters (such as a' for á) or two numbers joined by a comma (such as 6,15 for ∈).

Table 21 Some Common WordPerfect Special Characters with Their Codes.

a '	= á	8,1	= α	/ 2	= ½	5,9	= ♪
a '	= à	8,3	= β	/ 4	= ¼	5,10	= ♫
a ^	= â	8,7	= γ	4,66	= ⅛	5,27	= ♯
a "	= ä	8,9	= δ	4,67	= ⅜	5,28	= ♭
a @	= å	8,11	= ε	4,68	= ⅝		
e '	= é	8,13	= ζ	4,69	= ⅞	5,34	= ␣
(etc.)		(etc.)		4,64	= ⅓	- -	= —
				4,65	= ⅔	+ -	= ±
n ~	= ñ	c /	= ¢			> =	= ≥
s s	= ß	L -	= £	5,0	= ♥	< =	= ≤
! !	= ¡	Y =	= ¥	5,1	= ♦	~ ~	= ≈
? ?	= ¿	c o	= ©	5,2	= ♣	6,8	= +
< <	= «	r o	= ®	5,3	= ♠	6,39	= ×
> >	= »	t m	= ™	5,7	= ☺	6,19	= ∞
P		= ¶	o *	= °	5,24	= □	6,45	= '
4,6	= §	* *	= ●	5,30	= ☎	6,46	= "

WordPerfect is a product of WordPerfect Corporation, Orem, Utah.

WORD PROCESSING Word processing is the act of using a computer to prepare a letter, manuscript, or other document. There are several advantages to using a computer word processing system for writing. Without a word processor, revision of a document is a lot of work because the entire document must be retyped. With a word processor you can make your revision and then have the computer print out the entire final document.

You need three parts of a word processing system. First, you need a computer. Second, you need a word processing program. Several word processing programs are available for microcomputers; some popular programs are Word Perfect,

WordStar, and Microsoft Word. These programs have different characteristics, and the decision as to which program will work best for you depends on what type of writing you do. It is also possible to obtain dedicated word processor systems that do nothing but word process. Once you obtain a suitable program, you will need to learn how it works. That is the hardest part about word processing. Finally, you need a printer. Dot-matrix printers are fast and inexpensive. Laser printers provide the best results.

The process of initially typing a document on a computer is similar to typing a document on a typewriter. You type at the keyboard, and the results appear on the screen. The advantage of word processing becomes clear when you make a mistake. You can move the cursor back over something you have typed and either delete the character that is there, add a new character, or replace the existing character with a different one. The word processor will automatically realign the rest of the text.

Other special features that word processors often include are the following:

- the ability to delete an entire block of text, or else move the block to a new location
- the ability to search through the entire text and change a specified word to another word every time it occurs
- the ability to automatically number the pages and put headings at the tops of the pages
- the ability to include footnotes
- the ability to print specified words in boldface or to underline them

You may also be able to obtain a spelling checker program that reads through each word in your file and identifies the words that are not included in its dictionary, allowing you to type a correction if a word has been misspelled.

When you have finished working on a document, you must make sure that it is saved on a disk so that it will be available for you to use the next time you need it. Once you have completed a rough draft of your document, you can print it and then review it further. After marking revisions on the printed copy, you can then use the word processor to make the same revisions on the text stored on the disk.

See also **desktop publishing**.

WORD WRAP Word wrap occurs when, as you reach the end of a line, the cursor automatically jumps to the next line, rearranging the placement of words as necessary to avoid breaking a word. This is a useful feature when you are using a computer as a word processor because it means that you do not need to hit the return key at the end of each line. It also makes it possible to "even up" the lengths of the lines when material has been added or deleted or margins have been changed.

WORDSTAR WordStar is a popular word processing program. To give commands to WordStar, you type the control key simultaneously with the appropriate letter or letters. For example, typing "control-Y" deletes a line of text and typing "control-K-D" saves your document file on the disk. To help you in case you can't remember all the commands, WordStar contains several menus that appear on the screen to display some of the command options.

WORKSTATION A workstation is a powerful microcomputer typically used for scientific and engineering calculations. A workstation typically has more than four megabytes of RAM, more than 100 megabytes of disk capacity, and a screen with graphics resolution of at least 800×1000. Examples are the Sun Sparcstation and IBM RS/6000. Some 80386 and 80486-based PC's and some of the most powerful Macintoshes fall into the category of workstations. See **IBM PC; Macintosh; Sun workstations; RISC**.

WORM WORM is an acronym for write once, read many storage, which refers to a type of optical disk where a computer can save information once, can then read that information, but cannot change it. By contrast, with CD ROM (compact disk read only memory), the computer cannot save any information on the disk and can only read the information provided by the supplier of the disk. (See **CD ROM**.)

WRITE-PROTECT To write-protect a disk or tape is to set it so that the computer will not write or erase the data on it. Table 22 shows how to write-protect various kinds of diskettes.

Write-protecting a diskette can keep a computer virus from being copied onto it. However, write-protecting will also block the operation of any software that normally writes on the diskette. See also **file-protect ring**.

TABLE 22 Write Protection for Disks

Kind of diskette	How to write-protect
8" diskette	Uncover the notch on the side
5¼" diskette	Place an opaque cover on the notch on the side
3½" diskette	Slide the movable tab so that the hole is uncovered

WYSIWYG WYSIWYG is an acronym for "What you see is what you get." With a word processing program, this means that the appearance of the screen exactly matches the appearance that the document will have when it is printed.

X

X.21 This CCITT standard defines a format for transmitting serial data by wire. It includes signals that enable computers to dial their own calls when connected to an all-digital telephone line. By contrast, present-day auto-dial modems are used on voice telephone lines. (See **CCITT**.)

X.21 BIS This CCITT standard is virtually equivalent to RS-232C (see **RS-232**). It is a temporary substitute for X.21. (*Bis*, which is Latin for "a second time," denotes an alternative or substitute (see **CCITT**).

X.25 CCITT protocol X.25 defines a standard way of arranging data in packets. Each packet contains information indicating which computer sent it and which computer should receive it. See **packet.** X.25 has been adapted for amateur packet radio and the adapted version is called AX.25.

X-HEIGHT The x-height of a typeface is the height of the smallest letters (such as "x") which have no ascenders or descenders, compared to the height of the larger letters. For example, some typefaces make "x" half as high as "X"; some make it 40% as high; and some make it 60% as high.

A typeface with a large x-height looks larger than a typeface of the same overall size with a small x-height.

X-OFF, X-ON X-OFF and X-ON are codes that respectively turn off and on the transmission of data from a computer to a terminal. Many computers are programmed so that, if the person at the terminal types CTRL S (X-OFF), the computer will stop transmitting until the person types CTRL Q (X-ON). This is convenient when the computer is transmitting information too fast for the user to read it. Moreover, when the terminal is actually another computer, X-OFF and X-On signals can be used to keep information from being transmitted faster than it can be processed.

X SERVER In X Windows, the X server is the process that manages the screen, keyboard, and mouse. See **X Windows**.

X TERMINAL An X terminal is a terminal that is actually a small computer capable of running X Windows. The terminal functions as an X server, managing the screen, keyboard, and mouse, while all other computation is done on the remote computer. See **X Windows**.

X WINDOWS The X Window System ("X Windows" for short) is a software package for UNIX systems that allows programs to display text and graphics in windows and respond to a mouse (see **window**). X Windows software was developed at MIT and is distributed free.

X Windows relies on multitasking. A process called an *X server* manages the screen, keyboard, and mouse; other processes call on the X server when they want to use these devices.

XGA IBM's Extended Graphics Array (XGA) is an integrated circuit that is built into the PS/2 model 90 and up. The XGA is a video adapter that emulates the VGA, EGA, and CGA, as well as providing additional graphics modes with resolution as high as 1024×768. These additional modes are normally accessed through device drivers. See **video modes (IBM PC); device driver**.

XMODEM XMODEM is a protocol for transmitting files from one microcomputer to another and detecting transmission errors if they occur. XMODEM was developed by Ward Christensen and is used extensively by microcomputer hobbyists.

A computer using XMODEM transmits 128-byte blocks of data, each of which is followed by a checksum (a number derived mathematically from the ASCII codes of all the characters in the block). (See ASCII; checksum.) The receiving computer computes a checksum from the characters that it receives; depending on whether or not this checksum agrees with the checksum transmitted with the data, the receiving computer then either asks for the next block or asks for the same block to be retransmitted.

The technical specifications for XMODEM are as follows:

1. Both computers must be set to transmit and receive 8 data bits per character (instead of the usual 7).
2. The receiving computer starts by transmitting ASCII code 21 once every 10 seconds until transmission begins.
3. Each block transmitted by the transmitting computer consists of the following, in the order named: ASCII code 01; an ASCII character indicating the block (01 for the first block, 02 for the second, etc.); an ASCII character whose code is 255 minus the block number; 128 bytes of data; and, finally, a checksum obtained by adding the ASCII codes for all the characters and taking the sum modulo 256.
4. The receiving computer indicates successful reception by transmitting ASCII 06, or asks for retransmission by transmitting ASCII 21.

A number of similar protocols such as YMODEM and ZMODEM have been developed. They provide faster data transfers by using longer packets and allowing transmission of a packet to begin before acknowledgment of the previous packet has been received.

See also **Kermit**.

XT XT (e**X**tended **T**echnology) refers to the second model of IBM PC, introduced in 1983. The PC XT had eight expansion slots instead of the original five and it included a 10-megabyte hard disk. The microprocessor was a 4.77-MHz 8088 with an 8-bit bus, just as in the original PC.

Y

YMODEM See **XMODEM**.

Z

Z80 The Z80, produced by Zilog, Inc., is an 8-bit microprocessor found in most machines that run the CP/M operating system. (See **microprocessor**.)

ZERO WAIT STATES See **wait state**.

ZIP A ZIP file is a file compressed with PKZIP, a program written by Phil Katz. PKZIP runs on the IBM PC and compatibles and is distributed as shareware. Like its predecessor ARC, PKZIP takes one or more files, compresses them, and stores them in a single file with a name ending in ".ZIP." This not only saves space but also makes it easy to keep a group of related files together. The contents of the .ZIP file can be unpacked by the program PKUNZIP.

PKZIP also creates "self-extracting" files. These are actually programs that, when run, will unpack themselves into sets of files. Like most executable programs, self-extracting ZIP files have names ending in ".EXE." See **ARC; data compression; StuffIt**.

ZMODEM See **XMODEM**.